The Story of the

GREEN & GOLD

Newton Heath 1878-1902

CHARBEL BOUJAOUDE

FOREWORD BY IAIN MCCARTNEY

First published in 2010

EMPIRE PUBLICATIONS
1 Newton Street, Manchester M1 1HW
© 2010 Charbel Boujaoude

ISBN 1901746 577 - 9781901746570

Cover images courtesy of Iain McCartney and Leslie Millman
Cover design: Ashley Shaw
Printed in Great Britain.

To the memory of my father
who gave me his love of football

CONTENTS

ACKNOWLEDGMENTS

Thanks to Garth Dykes and Tony Brown for doing half my job for me; to Justin Blundell and Richard Kurt who provided the inspiration; to Mark Wylie, Iain McCartney, Joseph Rouhana, and Mrs Greta Bottomley (your secret is safe with me); to Ashley Shaw for making my dream come true; and, most importantly, to my wife Mirna for her love and patience.

FOREWORD

For many, the history of Manchester United Football Club begins in the 1990's, while the halcyon days of Best and Law, the Babes and Matt Busby's first United trophy winning side can readily be recalled by others. But what of the early days of this world renowned institution, way before even the likes of Billy Meredith captivated the Old Trafford crowds?

The name of Newton Heath Football Club conjures up clouded images, of a mixture of moustachioed individuals, dusting themselves down after a hard day's graft at carriage and wagon works, before putting on their threadbare playing kit to take up the challenge against other like minded individuals.

Previously published histories of Manchester United skip over those early days of the late 1800's, giving a brief mention to the same handful of encounters and dwelling on the exploits of the same individuals.

But now, in The Story of the Green and Gold by Charbel Boujaoude, the fledgling football club of Newton Heath suddenly takes on a completely different perspective, as the story of those early days comes to life and the picture of how much of a challenge it was to survive, planting the roots of the global brand that the club has now become.

It is perhaps fitting that a book telling this story should be available at today, with the green and gold colours worn during those formative years well to the fore and being a significant feature of the Old Trafford match day scene.

At last the likes of the Doughty brothers, Donaldson, Errentz and my own relative John McCartney will get their moments under the spotlight, as their exploits and the history of Newton Heath unfolds in the forthcoming pages.

Iain McCartney
APRIL 2010.

1878-84

MADE IN MANCHESTER

MANCHESTER, 1878. The Carriage and Wagon Works department of the Lancashire and Yorkshire Railway received a special request. No demands were being made for a raise. Instead, a group of workers was asking permission to use a bare piece of land nearby to play football. The game was sweeping the region. New clubs were sprouting everywhere, especially since 1863 when 'soccer' had been handed its own set of rules to differentiate it from rugby. Things had certainly changed from the time in 1609 when an early version of the game was banned in the district of Manchester from all the broken windows caused by wayward shots. And, though football would still be performed in a primitive manner at places like Eastlands some time into the 21st century, the game was becoming diligently organised all over Lancashire.

In public schools, for instance, it was no longer sufficient to have a healthy mind, the body had to be healthy too, and football was consequently encouraged by the schoolmasters. In factories such as the Lancashire and Yorkshire Railway, a healthy mind was in no way a priority - men were hired primarily for their physique. Fit athletes, the company owners figured, made for stronger employees. A footy match also kept them away from the pub and all its demons on a Saturday afternoon and, more importantly, it distracted them from politics, strikes, and other such big business pet peeves.

"Football, eh?" the superintendent at the Carriage and Wagon Works may have thought upon reviewing the request, "not only could the lads play on that misused patch but the department's own Dining Room Committee itself would also handle all the irksome affairs." Just like that, Manchester United was formed.

This, of course, was not the original name. The club having spawned out of the Lancashire and Yorkshire Railway, and the depot being located in a district of the city called Newton Heath. Few brain cells were exhausted in naming the club Newton Heath LYR (Lancashire and Yorkshire Railway). Although this moniker would only be used for the next 24 years, in time its legacy would become the most famous football name in the world.

It all started in the northeast of Manchester. That is where Newton Heath is located, stretching from Miles Platting to Failsworth and overlooking Oldham. Its name, derived from old English, meant "new town on the heath", which shows what a blessing modern English has been. For centuries Newton Heath was a farming community. In the early part of the 19th century, it opted (or was more accurately co-opted) for the faster lifestyle of the Industrial Revolution. And when, in the 1840s, the railways began to spread out of Manchester (home of the world's first passenger railway station) the conversion was complete. Newton Heath was an industrialised, bustling area with cramped back-to-back houses. So much so that, as we shall see, there was hardly any room left for good, old-fashioned grass.

This was the prosaic environment into which Newton Heath (LYR) was born. Other clubs were hatching all over the place around this time to engage in this addictive sport. Football was a radically different beast back then, of course. Basic rules had been set and have lasted to this day, but so much else was different at that embryonic stage. These were the days when league football was yet to be invented. In fact, the only trophy around at the time was the FA Cup. Formations were totally unrecognizable from this 4-4-2 nonsense - initially there were no formations at all. Teams fielded one goalkeeper while the other ten outfield players marauded forward rugby-style, dribbling the ball until the other team gained possession. This approach lasted for ages until someone, possibly an Italian tourist, suggested one player stay behind to help his goalie out. Thus defensive systems were born. By the time Newton Heath came onto the scene, teams were down to using just the six forwards. In a short time, though, a 2-3-5 formation would be established and remain the norm for almost a century. It consisted of two full-backs (right and left), three half-backs (right, centre, and left), and a forward line made up of outside and inside rights, a centre forward, and inside and outside lefts.

The two-handed throw-in was still four years away from being, well, thrown-in. The first penalty would not be kicked until 1891. There were no nets attached to the goal yet; the concept of preventing the loss of balls still waiting to be proposed by a Mr. Brodie. There were no Scots - banned for being too good! - to prevent clubs from luring them south with financial inducements. This was (supposedly) an era before professionalism, players played football for the 'love of the game'. However, there existed at the time an 'under the counter' system of illegal payments operated by many clubs. Good players were paid cash and the authorities could never prove a thing. Eventually, the FA relented in 1885 when professionalism was legalised.

So, the first Newton Heath footballers played for the sake of sport and nothing else. They played for fun and they played hard. It was truly a man's game: you kicked, you got kicked, you got on with it. The tackle from behind, for example, was encouraged; while the professional foul, like the man who commits it, was still an amateur. And, of course, there were no substitutions allowed. If selected, you were stuck on the pitch for the whole game. If injured, you dared not leave lest your side dropped down to ten men and your self-respect to zero. Instead, you hobbled out on the wing. For an apt demonstration, see Ralph Milne's Old Trafford career.

THEATRE OF CLAY

NOT MUCH IS known about the first 'Heathens' that walked the earth (the obvious nickname the club soon acquired). 'The Coachbuilders' was another one, in reference to their day job, but that did not strike as much fear into opponents' souls. Neither did 'The Newtonians' that might have sounded like a team of scientists, which the players were certainly not. Either way, they remain a mysterious lot. Since no tabloids hung around on a daily basis relaying every wink and food fight, the players obviously would not have been recognised when they appeared in public. It is a wonder they even recognised one another, for when they gathered for their afternoon games, their faces were smeared with the sweat of a hard day's work. Straight from the yards and stations they came, wolfing down their butties like overexcited schoolboys to join in the kick-abouts.

No specific names have been traced from these early scrimmages. What is known for certain is that 1878 was the year of formation. A fixtures list for 1882-83, printed just four years later, says so. While the exact date is not noted, the fact that 1878 was not a leap year does narrow the range a bit. However, a niggling thought persists. Beggars cannot be choosers, obviously, but why on earth did the workers not pick a better field to play on? Owned by the church authorities of Manchester and rented by the railway company, North Road, Monsall, could qualify as a road, for it was as hard as clay. But that was only at one end. The other was an amalgamation of mud and whatever by-products were spewed from the works. Any curious passers-by who wished to look on endured the same fate as the players. Accommodation for spectators consisted of ankle-deep puddles and a rope that went around the four sides of the pitch to prevent the shorter ones from invading. And on top of that, the Heathens had to put up with the department's whining cricket-loving workers who complained that the turf was spoiled by summertime.

Changing rooms were notable for their non-existence. Obviously, at first there was no need for them since the Heathens played in their work clothes. Then the club had their first team strip made. It was a dashing green and gold halved shirt that represented the colours of the local rail wagons, and either black or white shorts to go with it. Shorts, actually, is a misleading description. As modelled by one of the players in a very early photo, these 'shorts' got to the knees, then kept going until they were tucked into the boots at the bottom, while the upper part looked like it could offer little discretion at times of great excitement. That apart, the shirt, with its cool lime and lemon combination, was so nifty the players wore it for 15 years. Even to this day it remains the kit most commonly associated with the club's formative era. Heath also went on to don red and white quartered jerseys with blue shorts. But as no two historians seem able to agree on the specific time this attire was used, it can be presumed this was probably the club's change kit at one time or another.

Either way, the introduction of a matching kit for the players brought to the fore the necessity for changing rooms. The solution was promptly found: the players could get kitted at the Three Crowns Inn, conveniently located half a mile away on Oldham Road! One advantage this arrangement provided was the elimination of a warm-up. By the time the players had jogged in sleet or snow to reach the pitch they were ready. Towards the end of Heath's tenancy at North Road, by which time this dreadful venue was incredibly hosting First Division football, the club had taken to changing at a hotel called Shears. It may not have been that much closer to the ground but it added variety to Heath's warm-up routine.

RISE OF THE HEATHENS

IT IS DOUBTFUL whether Newton Heath or Manchester United enjoyed such carefree matches as those way back in 1878 and 1879. The players were not too bothered with trophies, contracts, or the high expectations that would later pressure the club but that did not stop them from winning most of their early matches. When they were not busy kicking lumps out of each other, they kicked bigger lumps out of other department teams in the railway company. The biggest lumps of all were reserved for the sods from the Motor Power Division, Newton Heath Loco – the Heathens' first rivals. That was long before the likes of Manchester City, Liverpool, and Leeds decided to make bigger sods of themselves.

Satisfied with steamrollering their LYR opponents, Newton Heath then elected to test their mettle against teams from other stations such as Middleton, St. Helens, and Crewe. Several hard-fought victories later, the Heathens realized they were quite good. Obviously that initial class of 1878 was a decent batch, and this was crucial in elevating Newton Heath above the other pretenders on the tracks. Yet there were other factors that enabled the club to rise a bit higher and really kick-start their mission to eventually become all that Manchester United is about.

The Dining Room Committee, which looked after Heath's matters, was a canny group led by superintendent Mr. Frederick Attock, one of the company's finest civil engineers. He had taken charge at LYR in 1877 but he had ample experience and knowledge, which he used productively in building innovative coaches. Illness forced him to resign in 1895 before he passed away in 1902, just a few weeks after his footballing creation had morphed into Manchester United.

Attock was 36 years old when he assumed Heath's responsibilities and continuously sought ways of improving the team. There were no sunny beaches to offer as incentive and the North Road ground would not have been anybody's dream attraction bar the odd mud-wrestler but Attock had a trump card: a gig in the warehouse to go with a place in the team. What could be a better enticement for an amateur footballer than job security? An additional perk was the discounted use of the railway – the Victorian era equivalent of the sponsored company car! One talented player after another was seduced with these sweet nothings as Newton Heath grew stronger and stronger. It was a handy recruitment pick-up line that would continue to be used even after professionalism was 'legalised'.

With an ever-improving squad, it was only a matter of time before the Heathens attracted some media attention. Eventually, on November 20th, 1880, Newton Heath LYR entered history. And what an entrance it was – they lost 0-6 to Bolton Wanderers Reserves! That was all that the *Bolton Evening News* mentioned, plus the fact that the match took place at Bolton's Pike Lane. It could be safely assumed none of the goals came against the run of play. It may have been a shattering loss, but the exact score line would in time be avenged by Manchester United early in 1996. The next reported match was two weeks later, by which time Heath had worked on a defensive plan. They drew nil-nil at local side Manchester Arcadians. On January 22nd, it was time for Bolton's fearsome reserve side to make a return trip to North Road. Just to prove they were no one-hit wonders, Newton Heath again lost 0-6. But this was an historic occasion: Heath's first match report. No line-ups were mentioned, though Bolton scored once before half-time and saved the other five for the second half. It was 'a very pleasant and agreeable game', according to the *Bolton Daily Chronicle*.

On February 5th, the Heathens decided it was time to submit their first recorded goals. Avoiding any Bolton selections would definitely help, they reckoned. So Bootle Reserves and their suspect defence were summoned from Merseyside as Heath triumphed 2-0 at North Road, the groundbreaking scorers being Messrs Minchley and Cramphorn. Absolutely nothing else is known about Minchley. No games, no goals, no whereabouts. It is as if he sacrificed his identity in exchange for a goal in this match. No such moral quandaries afflicted John Cramphorn, a 22-year-old forward who hailed from Shalford. He had no lisp and it was not Salford, but Shalford, Essex. Along with his friend Arthur Webber, he had travelled up to Manchester to find work and to score Newton Heath's first ever recorded goal. The two found employment with the LYR as coachbuilders, appropriately enough, and resided in digs at 31 Ten Acres Lane, just around the corner from the ground. Though no evidence suggests that Webber was a Coachbuilder in the afternoons as well, his roommate's trail-blazing footsteps would be detected in the North Road mud for the next few years.

THE FIRST DERBY

As far as first impressions go, Newton Heath's introduction to the public eye was more Nemanja Vidic than Wayne Rooney. There were no debut hat-tricks but, as with the big Serbian defender, it would require several more impressions for Heath to show their true colours. Eventually they would go on to fulfil their destiny of greatness, but they could as easily have emulated the hundreds of clubs that were stifled in their infancy. A perfect illustration of the flimsiness of the line that separates the two paths Heath could have taken at this juncture came in a match on February 15th, 1881. North Road's invisible facilities were already creating problems. Hurst F.C. were able to travel through town faster than the Heathens could cross Oldham Road, causing a kick-off delay. This clearly incensed Hurst's captain, Ingham who impatiently picked up the ball immediately from kick-off, darted forward, and leathered home Hurst's first. The remaining 89 minutes and 52 seconds saw ample foreplay but no scoring. An edgy rivalry was born from this encounter that lasted the best part of the next decade. Eventually, the rivals took different paths, possibly as a study of their respective fortunes with the passage of time. They both go by the moniker 'United' today. One is the United we know and love. The other is Ashton United who are plying their trade in the Unibond Premier League at the time of writing.

However, some of Newton Heath's other 1881 opponents are still going strong today. Preston North End were freshly formed around that time and, in a few years, would become the inaugural champions of the Football League. But their tussle with Newton Heath was more notable for some good, old-fashioned hooliganism.

"It wasn't us", the Heath fans could claim, and they were justified. Instead, a group of Preston fans made a short stop at Wigan on the way to knock the consciousness out of a couple of railway officials. The North Road faithful generally behaved, though there were one or two instances down the years when their behaviour was questionable. Other erstwhile opponents were West Gorton St. Mark's of the St. Mark's Church. Does that ring a bell? Seeing as the religious connection was not getting them anywhere, they soon dropped the 'St. Mark's'. Then, after failing to lay claim to loyalty from the west, they decided to simply go by the name Gorton. That didn't work either. They tried Ardwick for a few years until stumbling on a more cosmopolitan-sounding name: Manchester City! Since then, they have been called a variety of colourful names by Reds...

November 12th, 1881, was the date of the first ever Manchester derby. Of course, it wasn't the only derby on the calendar as almost every other game was against one Mancunian neighbour or another. Yet this match's significance was highlighted by the presence of around 3,000 spectators – an extraordinary gate back then. The papers were intrigued enough to list the players, thus providing Newton Heath's earliest-known line-up, set up in a 2-2-6 formation:

E. Jones; A. Shaw, J. Morris; J. Rigby, C. Fulton; Myers, C. Latham, E. Thomas, J. Jones, J. Hopwood, and E. Edwards.

Two goals from Thomas and one from Jones gave the Heathens a 3-0 victory and set down the format for the frequently favoured derby outcome for eternity. West Gorton won the return fixture 2-1 later in the season but that was their only victory to crow about until 1889. In the same period, Heath handed them so many spankings they kept changing their name to spare themselves any embarrassment.

Unfortunately, hardly anything is known of Heath's first derby heroes. They were humble, working men who turned out for the team for fun, unaware of the future significance of their triumph. Brace ace Thomas was club captain for the 1881-82 season and for the next one too. Joseph Rigby, only 17 years of age, started out as a half-back but soon converted to left-back where he remained first choice until 1885. Although he was consigned to the reserves for the most part after that, he still made the odd first team appearance over the next few years. Fulton also specialised in stopping goals and was partial to doing so from half-back or as a goalkeeper! Mr. Versatility also proved to be Mr. Longevity, continuing his dual duty until Heath won their first trophy in 1886.

Although Heath's first scorer, John Cramphorn, did not face West Gorton, he popped up in other matches during the season. He was hogging the score sheet again in a 3-0 victory over Manchester Arcadians along with Rigby and nineteen-year-old John Hopwood. No other scorers were traced from that campaign but the pick of the games included a repeat result against the Arcadians, while a team called Haughton Green were rendered black and blue following a four-goal battering. Although a 0-4 loss to a Blackburn Olympic XI showed there was still a long way to go, the Newton Heath footballing engine was now steaming ahead at full speed.

INTO A COMPETITIVE WORLD

To THE DELIGHT and relief of football historians, a Newton Heath fixture list from 1882-83 exists to this day. No need for the futile trawling of a dozen newspaper microfilms in the hope of stumbling upon a drop of a match in a sea of words. The individual games are listed right there in the oldest surviving Heath document. And what a lovely manuscript it is, notable for a symmetrical roll of names that stares at you no matter which angle you eye it from! There is also a dignitary roll which shows that, even at that early

1882-83 FIXTURE LIST:
According to this document Heath were formed in 1878.

stage, Newton Heath was a well-structured club. Mr. Attock, as ever, presided with W. Lord and T. Gorst as his vice-chairmen. E. Thomas was skipper and Cramphorn second in command. The club committee was comprised of five other players: G. Smith, C. Chorlton, C. Latham, J. Rigby, and A. Shaw. And secretarial duties were handled by an E. Hole, if you would pardon my French, who was holed up at 493 Oldham Road.

The fixture list was packed with names that would not verge on the mighty no matter the era: Clitheroe, Bentfield, Astley Bridge, St. Helens. No champions of Luxembourg in there nor mysterious Eastern European dark horses, their exoticism stretched as far as the confines of Lancashire.

Manchester Arcadians were already assuming the role of Newton Heath's whipping boys as they suffered a 0-4 public humiliation in early November. A role reversal saw Heath submit 2-7 to Crewe Alexandra a fortnight later. An interesting dilemma arose the following week. In a North Road encounter against Bentfield, the newspaper reporter stated that Newton Heath scored "three goals to their opponents' one goal and two disputed goals". Except he didn't specify whether the disputed goals counted or not. The outcome, thus, is still open to debate with Heathen fans forever claiming a 3-1 victory whereas any Bentfield die-hards around can save face with a thrilling 3-3 draw.

An equally thrilling match might have occurred on January 6th in the return friendly with the Arcadians. The players lined up, the crowd assembled in anticipation, and the referee stood primed to officiate. Only he didn't have the balls to start the game. Not out of fear but because no one brought a ball! The players put their clothes back on and, along with the crowds, trudged home. This was another early lesson learnt by Newton Heath. Heath endured a record 0-8 defeat at Earlestown the following season (1883-84) and an even worse rout threatened

SAM BLACK:
Newton Heath's first prominent captain.

in a subsequent game. Hurst Brook Olympic raced into a 3-1 lead inside half an hour, their form so hot they even provided Heath's solitary goal in a careless moment. Something had to be done and the Heathens knew exactly what it was. A mighty lump sent the only available ball into the river. The referee had no option but to blow for time and a possible record loss was averted. Amusingly, this was not Heath's only 30-minute workout during the season. Arriving late for kick-off at Haughton Dale on Boxing Day, the Coachbuilders were faced with a rapidly-approaching sunset. A quick quarter hour per half contest was settled on which was enough time for Heath to squeeze out a one goal victory.

The Arcadians were twice thrashed 4-0 while Bootle received a 6-0 booting, but Newton Heath's most important match of 1883-84 took place on October 27th. That was the date of the club's first ever competitive fixture. The Lancashire FA had been formed around the same time as Heath, in 1878. The following year, the county introduced a senior cup competition. Previously indifferent to its developments, Newton Heath now decided to have a quick look and see what the Lancashire Cup was all about. As a welcoming gesture, the first round draw paired them with Blackburn Olympic. FA Cup holders Blackburn Olympic? Yes, in the flesh. There was only one major trophy in England at the time and Blackburn Olympic were its holders and now they were due at North Road to thrill the locals.

A wide-eyed Newton Heath lined up:

G. Smith; S. Black, J. Rigby; C. Fulton, G. Robinson, E. Howles; J. Morris, A. Shaw, C. Latham, J. Cramphorn, and E. Dixon.

Undaunted, the Olympic dispatched their reserve team to deal with those upstarts. The Heathens used that to their advantage and could have held the visitors to a 2-2 draw

LANCASHIRE SENIOR CUP:
It was for this trophy that Heath played their first ever competitive match – the less said about the 2-7 reverse at Blackburn the better.

had games lasted just 50 minutes. It was the final 40 minutes the Heathens had trouble negotiating as Olympic piled on the goals for a 7-2 demolition.

Nonetheless, the Blackburn officials were impressed with Heath's right-back Sam Black, conveniently turning a blind eye to the seven goals his defence had just shipped. An offer was made to sign Sam, who was considered one of the best full-backs around at the time, but luckily for Heath he turned it down. Born in Burton-on-Trent in February 1863, Sam was the eldest of five siblings. He had moved to Manchester to finish his apprenticeship as a joiner and builder, and he hooked up with the Heathens where he remained a full-time amateur. It is also claimed by various sources that Black was a founder member of Newton Heath. I find that hard to believe for he was only 15 years old in 1878 and would have been hard pressed to form facial hair let alone future football empires. He inherited the club captaincy from Thomas in 1883 and proved a great leader. By the time he returned home to play for Burton Wanderers in 1887, he had helped turn Heath into a power to be reckoned with.

Perhaps his proudest moment came on March 22nd, 1884, when, along with team-mates Blears, Fulton, and Moran, he earned Newton Heath's first representative recognition. All four were selected to play for a Manchester and District XI against an equivalent combination from Liverpool and District. It was a great honour for the club that so many of their players were considered good enough for the district. It may not have been an international occasion but even those can sometimes pale in significance when compared with a feisty Manc-Scouse skirmish. Black did such a decent job skippering the District selection he was invited to do so again in December 1895 for another such representative match – against a Hallamshire XI in his hometown of Burton. On this occasion, though, he was politely asked to come alone! Still there was a familiar face to Black on the pitch. Newton Heath's own official B. Ainsworth laid the principles of neutrality aside to referee the match himself. Nonetheless, this was another prestigious moment for the club that highlighted its rising status in these few short years.

1884-85

THE LOCALS

IT IS POSSIBLE to gauge Newton Heath's rise up the football ladder to date by the admission charge at the gate. Previously, entry into North Road cost a whopping 3d. For the new 1884-85 season, the ground was hosting sixpence football. The ragged collection of railway employees who used to gather for an evening kick about was now a well-run and respected club. Even the pressmen were getting excited with added coverage of most of Heath's matches. The *Manchester Courier* reporter was certainly impressed. After another huge win during the season, he stated that the Heathens were rapidly forcing their way to the top, their play characterised at times by some very fine passing. Perhaps, had he bothered checking as frequently in previous seasons, he would have noted their play and provided future generations with the lost chronicles of the club's earliest years.

Newton Heath's progress was not restricted to the field. Another measure of their standing was their inclusion in the newly formed British National Association (BNA), a body that sprung from Manchester to oppose the establishment led FA. Most of the Lancashire clubs were in it and even Scottish giants Celtic found it trendy enough to join. In a way, it was the precursor to G-14, the 21st century group that grew into 18 of Europe's fattest cats. The BNA also swelled, the original 36 quickly becoming 70. There was one big difference, though. The greedy G-14 mainly whined for someone else to pay their international stars. All the BNA wanted was to be allowed to pay its own players. Until now, to the virtuous, self-aggrandising members of the uptight FA, professionalism – as with double negatives – was a major no-no. Footballers ought to play for the love of the game, they preached from their stiff upper lips, and professionalism was outlawed. But the emergence of the BNA was to change all that. By the following summer the FA relented and player payment was legalised. Newton Heath, of course, were heavily involved, as the club always seems to be whenever the chance to challenge the authorities arose. Manchester United were always the leading culprits over the years, whether it was in creating the PFA, rebelling as 'Outcasts', pioneering European football, or co-founding the infamous G-14. This entire club tradition was initiated by the Heathens trying to live up to their nickname back in 1884.

For now, Newton Heath had to retain their amateur status. Or, at least, continue pretending. For the fact that some players received under-the-table brown envelopes was not a very well-kept secret. Most of the Lancashire clubs were doing it and the Heathens were no saints: they were also bribing players with warehouse gigs. Already we have seen the example of John Cramphorn, and, while Sam Black constantly adhered to strict amateur status as a matter of principle, he was originally lured to Newton Heath with the railway apprenticeship carrot.

Meanwhile, the latest enticed star probably grew carrots himself. James Gotheridge gave up a life as a farmer in Derby for a role in the Industrial Revolution. The 21-year-old ploughed up Newton Heath's wing for years. He was both a creator and a taker of goals in the Gordon Hill mode as Reds of a certain vintage can testify, or even Charlie Mitten for their fathers. He averaged close to a goal every two matches and appeared in five consecutive cup finals. By the time he left North Road five years later, the Heathens were playing organised league football and Gotheridge had played his part in getting them there.

However, not all of Heath's 1884-85 squad were imported. If Reds were overjoyed when several local lads were part of the double winners of 1995-96, their ancestors must have been more ecstatic when 111 seasons earlier almost the entire team was produced at home. Joseph Rigby was born and bred in Manchester, as was the teenage fringe player James Franklin. Another Mancunian was 22-year-old Edward Howles who lived around the corner at 426 Oldham Road. His older brother, Thomas, had also been a Heathen at one time. At 22 Salfordian William Siddons was also a regular, while the youthful Thomas Kay hailed from Chorlton. There would be several cases in the future of Manchester United attempting to build a pre-dominantly Mancunian squad but, in truth, 1884-85 would be the last time the team consisted entirely of players from the city. By the following summer professionalism had appeared to change the face of British football forever. The term 'Newton Heath' would be as misleading as a Jon Obi Mikel photo opportunity – over the next few seasons Heath would become a Who's Who of Welsh footballers while the following decade would reverberate with a heavy Tartan accent.

THE DAVIES QUOTA

ONE THOUGHT OCCUPIED Newton Heath's mind when 1884-85 kicked off: competitive football. That brief taste of the Lancashire Cup the previous year, albeit bitter, had them thirsting for more, and they were able to get a quencher with the first kick of September. The FA Cup had been going on for a dozen years but Heath were still debating whether they were ready to participate in it. There was also all that BNA business that made it awkward to socialise with the 'enemy' at the English FA. Perhaps the Heathens did not want to be seen cavorting with a tin pot twice their age. Eventually, at the risk of causing a decade-long public outcry at the devaluation of the cup, they opted to spare themselves the whole hullabaloo.

Instead, they tried their hand in the Lancashire Cup one more time with a North Road tie against Haydock Temperance. Four unanswered home goals saw Haydock split from the competition and Heath earn their first competitive victory. For that they had to be thankful to a lucky draw which did not pit them against Blackburn Olympic again.

Alas, Heath's cup run was rendered but a light jog a month later when Baxenden knocked them out in the second round. The 1-4 score line would be Heath's worst defeat all season. No blame could be attached to their only specialised goalkeeper, G. Smith, who had already put in the first of his bi-annual appearances a fortnight earlier and had now passed the gloves on to whoever was meek enough to volunteer. On this occasion, as with the majority of matches throughout the campaign, the versatile Fulton was the unlucky outfielder tasked with minding the sticks. Should he wish to skip a match or prefer to stretch his legs at half-back, William

Siddons would be willing to switch positions. A similar agreement existed between Moran and Rigby regarding the left-back and half-back slots and, though several other Heathens equally flitted around the field, the concept of total football should not be mistaken for that of total disarray. It was more a case of a means to an end as gaps in the line-up were randomly plugged. Captain Sam Black was one of the few who stuck to one position, never budging from right-back. Howles was mostly found at left-half while Thomas Kay eventually made the centre-half lark his own.

Six players competed for a place in the five-man front line. The key to permanent selection was outscoring the rest and James Gotheridge seemed the best at that. Always buzzing, always scoring, he proved to be the club's first proficient left winger. One surname that always appeared in Heath's attack was Davies. Whether it was preceded by the initials T, H, or E. T., Davies occupied the flank opposite to Gotheridge and for two years was almost as prolific. He was the Steve Coppell to Gotheridge's Gordon Hill – minus the scouse accent. 1884-85 was his best season as he played more than any of his team-mates and scored eight goals. A conundrum surrounded E. Davies and H. Davies' Mancunian stay. They both started their North Road careers at the same time in 1883; they both finished together in 1888; they were both forwards; and, between them, they wore Newton Heath's colours over sixty times. But never in the same game! Unless there were restrictions at the time on the number of footballers named Davies that could be fielded simultaneously, the most likely conclusion is that the two were the same player: Harry E. Davies. It just depended on the hack who reported on the match or on the documentation that was provided to the newspapers.

As for Blears and Beach, although their surnames were similar, they were for a fact two distinct individuals. Blears was Heath's first-choice centre-forward while Thomas Beach, a teenager with a sunny disposition, was usually camped at inside-left. Beach had a simple formula for success: 1. Loiter in the box. 2. Get on the end of crosses. 3. Tuck the ball in. Blears tried to copy this plan only he seldom got through to sdtep three. However, the club's most dangerous marksman was W.E. Jordan, whose scoring escapades exceeded even those of his namesake from a century later – the one known as 'Jaws', to be precise, and not the one of the fertile partnership with Dwight Yorke.

FIRST LOVE

NEWTON HEATH'S PLAYERS might seem to be names without faces. Heck, some are without details, backgrounds, or even first names. Yet this motley collection of mysterious origin formed a cracking selection that played its part in elevating Newton Heath to a higher level. That level was not a national one, per se, as the 1-4 defeat to Baxenden served to underline. But on the towns and boroughs front, the Heathens were turning into a fearsome force, and - the Baxenden loss apart - they went on a rampaging raid of the countryside that made the Vikings seem like door-to-door Ikea salesmen.

Heath had managed a couple of 2-1 victories before the Lancashire Cup exit but it was now that the bedlam began. Greenheys and Pendleton Olympic were both beaten 3-1 while the Heathens had more difficulty in pronouncing Oughtrington Park than in putting four goals past them. Jordan, with a goal in each of these games, had a smug grin on his face. But that was swiftly wiped off when Beach trumped him by scoring four goals in one go as Heywood surrendered 1-5. Manchester Reserves fell by the same score line. Dalton Hall limited the Heathens to four goals in mid-December, the players taking turns at scoring: T. Davies, Beach, Gotheridge, and Blears. Then a chap called Prow got on the score-sheet as Levenshulme were levelled 4-0. By Christmas, Newton Heath had played 11 matches and won ten. They had walloped 37 goals including four or more in each of their last five outings.

The unbeaten run extended into the New Year. It helped a bit that one or two of Oughtrington Park's players walked off with ten minutes to go of the return fixture. A Gotheridge double had already secured a 3-2 lead. A week later everybody walked off with a ten minutes to go – an early sunset cutting short the derby meeting with City, who were now in their Gorton phase. James Gotheridge and Jordan (2) were able to squeeze in enough goals before the lights went out for a 3-1 victory. But even this win paled in significance when compared to the result achieved the following week, January 24th: Newton Heath 12, Stretford 0. And, no, that is not a typing error for Stretford did indeed score nil. A dozen goals scored and two more chalked off for offside or something. Even the reporters, let alone the Stretford defenders, struggled to keep up with all of Heath's scorers. But that's hardly surprising as the Heathens themselves could have had a hard time keeping track while racking up the goals. Jordan grabbed at least three, while Blears and Lomax helped themselves to a brace apiece. It was the club's biggest recorded win so far but, refreshingly, the Heathens would be able to better it in the years to come.

Another week, another historic event. On January 31st, Newton Heath met their first love for the very first time: the Manchester Cup. Or, to give it its complete name, the Manchester and District Challenge Cup. This was a lovely trophy launched by the newly-formed Manchester FA to show that anything the county could do, so could the city. The FA Cup always seemed out of Heath's league while the Lancashire Cup had a tendency to embarrass them publicly. But the Manchester Cup was a trophy Heath could embrace. From the first rendezvous on a cold, winter day against Eccles, the Heathens realised they could not live without this fine piece of silverware. Hearsay has it that Sam Black bent down to place the ball for kick-off and that's when Cupid fired his arrow. So began a story of common affection that lasted throughout Heath's history.

The following eleven men sent to the field, tasked with sizing up this blind date, were: Fulton; Black, Moran; Rigby, Kay, Howles; T. Davies, Jordan, Blears, Lomax, and Gotheridge.

A great first impression earned a 3-2 victory over Eccles in Round One. Yet Newton Heath's first time was so good they decided to experience it again! Eccles whined so long and loud about the winning goal being offside that the Manchester FA, their ears ringing, ordered a replay. It did not matter. A fortnight later the teams met again, this time at a ground in Old Trafford of all places. Goals from T. Davies, Blears, and Gotheridge left no room for controversy or protestations. The Heathens were into the second round.

FINALISTS

GOALS GOALS GOALS! So advertised the newspapers as they

reported on Newton Heath's sweeping attacks. The style may still have been intrinsically 'kick and rush', but traces of fine passing were being detected in this pattern now. Our lovely neighbours Gorton were so impressed they decided to import half a dozen of those goals into their net on February 21st. Everybody was scoring: the half-back, the right-back, the left-back. The left-back in question was newcomer J. Mitchell who had made his Heath debut the previous week against Eccles. It was the first of over 200 appearances for the club in a long connection that would extend until 1891. Right-back or left-back slots, he filled them with equal loyalty and distinction for he could kick with either foot – though not simultaneously. His claim to fame was that he appeared in six Manchester Cup finals, winning four, which was more than any other Heathen. But if his home debut goal misled the club into believing they had acquired a futuristic attacking full-back then Mitchell ought to be sued for false advertisement. The next time he scored again, some two seasons later, would be to the utter surprise of all attending, whereas his third and final goal – in 1889 – was a complete fluke.

Progress and goal ratios were maintained in the Manchester Cup second round as Manchester (not City, nor United, just Manchester) were beaten 3-0. Then a 3-1 victory over Greenheys saw Heath doing their bit for the medical field as the gate receipts were added to the Manchester Hospital Fund. On March 21st another high-scoring win ensued, Heath defeated West Manchester: 5-2 - if you believe the *Manchester Courier* reporter who apparently snuck out a few minutes early; 5-3, if the *Manchester Examiner* journalist is to go by; or 5-4, if you listened to all those who stayed behind till the end to witness West Manchester's late rally.

However, there was more to the *Courier* reporter's early

THE MANCHESTER SENIOR CUP: *Newton Heath's first love.*

departure than first meets the eye. From the moment he left, with the Heathens leading 5-2, something went missing. It is as if, like Dr. Evil famously did to Austin Powers, he took with him Heath's mojo. After notching 81 goals in 23 matches, Heath allowed West Manchester two late strikes then fell flat at home to Earlstown 0-2. This was their first reverse since October, bringing to an end a 19-match unbeaten run. Tellingly, they also failed to score for only the second time all season. A week on Heath again fired blanks in a 0-1 loss to Blackburn Olympic Reserves and in the final friendly of the campaign, all they could muster was a goalless draw with Stretford. That's the same Stretford that were pummelled 12-0 a few weeks earlier. Now the firepower was gone and even the normally lethal Beach, after spraying wayward shots all afternoon, was left muttering something about the goalposts being lower at that end, or words to that effect.

The missing mojo was becoming a real problem now, what with the Manchester Cup semi-final up next. The Heathens had come a long way to blow it all at this stage. At half-time, despite Heath having finally broken their duck, Dalton Hall led 3-1 and looked certain to end victorious. However, Heath, just like the rejuvenated International Man of Mystery, were able to summon their passion before it was too late. T. Davies notched his second of the game and a goal from new recruit John Earp pulled Heath level at 3-3. But the biggest hero was Howles who used extra-time productively to complete a magical recovery and put the Heathens through.

On April 25th, 1885, the team that would later be called Manchester United appeared in their first ever final, the Manchester Cup final. Around 4,000 excited fans filed into the Whalley Range ground, home of Manchester Rugby Club, for the tie against Hurst F.C..

The following players were chosen to represent the club: Fulton; Black, Mitchell; Howles, Kay, Moran; T. Davies, Siddons, Earp, H. Davies, and Gotheridge.

However, despite the importance of the event, all that the final served to achieve was to champion the merits of the specialised goalkeeper. C. Fulton, as loyal and versatile as they come, was not the fill-in Heath needed to win this match. The scores were level at the interval, but the elements and ill-luck conspired against the Green-and-Golds. In the spirit of the event, a typically Mancunian downpour delayed the restart and bogged down Heath's momentum, while a nasty wind derailed their direct style. And, not to be outshone, Fulton stepped to the fore, the symbol of inexperience on his face. He did well to catch Ball's ball but, while a streetwise keeper would have quickly crumbled to the floor, he stood still and allowed Ball to charge him past the line. This was perfectly legal back then, of course, and that is how Hurst took the lead. But wait to see how they doubled it! Ingham lumped the ball goalwards; Fulton displayed his versatility by impersonating the fans in the stands: he stood by idly and watched assiduously as the ball snuck under the bar. There was no way back for Heath now, and Hurst were able to add a third shortly before full-time.

This may not have been how Newton Heath wished to experience the inaugural final, especially as the Hurst players went bouncing about in ecstatic celebration as if they had just beaten Manchester bloody United. However, in reality, just reaching this stage was a big achievement for a local works side who a mere seven years ago were begging the other departments for a kick about. And if it is any consolation, in seven years from now, Heath would have the last laugh. As they prepared to start their Football League odyssey, Hurst were folding! A cruel laugh, one could say. But that is still a long way into the future. There were immediate developments that would affect Heath that very summer.

1885-86

JUNIOR PROFESSIONALS

SHAMATEURISM! THAT WAS the name given to the under-the-table payments which football operated. The moniker was penned by the witty suits at the FA who considered it 'shameful' that even a single penny should be bandied about in football – unless it went into their coffers, perhaps? It did not matter that clubs sought to improve their teams with better players from around the land, or with one or two of those skilful Scottish 'professors' of the game who specialised in the dark secrets of passing the ball along the turf. Footballers should eternally remain amateurs, the authorities claimed, and should rigorously adhere to the idealistic virtues of pure sportsmanship.

However a lot of the clubs, led by a sizeable Lancashire contingent, were already recognizing the impact of business on football, and they formed their own coalition – the British National Association. It was a battle of tradition versus progress and, on July 20th, 1885, it reached its defining moment. For years the FA had tried to clamp down on widespread brown envelope payments and, in the process, save the trees and preserve the ecosystem perhaps. But now they were gradually realising the inevitability of professionalism. Hence, they concluded that if you could not stem it, integrate it. The clubs wanted professionals? Fine, they can have them. Let there be professionalism, but with a major condition: the abolition of the BNA. The FA would remain the supreme authority while the upstarts from the north would be wiped from the scrolls.

The bottom line was that this was the clubs' money to start with. They say you can't take it with you when you go, so you might as well splash it on the odd Scottish professor. And just how much could the boards spend? After all, most of the clubs were still in the dirt-poor stage of their development. Although there was no maximum wage yet, the scrooges at Derby County would see to that by 1893.

Back at North Road, the Heathens were clambering over each other to embrace the newly-legalised professionalism. Joiner, fitter, coachbuilder – they could all make a living now kicking a ball. But it was a sound idea to hold on to their day jobs until the first mega-million ad offer came along. Nonetheless, Newton Heath LYR was now a professional club and could feel smug for having taken another step toward the big time. Yet Heath's story was never that of a straightforward blissful ascent. The great times had to wait their turn while all the bad ones had had a go or two. In fact, almost every purposeful step forward seemed to be followed by two back. And, now, Heath standing tall actually exposed their midriff and made it an easier target for a mighty kick. The culprits? The Lancashire FA, to whom the Heathens had added their weight in the battle against amateurism. It seems that following the victory the county FA was now too big for its little people. Since the inception of the Lancashire Cup, any team registered with the county was welcome to participate. Year after year the number of entrants increased until the LFA decided it was no longer eager to handle the extra workload. It was then decreed that only the elite clubs would contest the glamorously-labelled Lancashire Senior Cup whereas the rest battled it out for the 'Junior' version. Ominously for Newton Heath, the LFA took one snobby look at their two embarrassing cup exits to date and immediately smacked a big, red 'J' on their application. One moment they were graduating into the big business of the real world, the next they were still being treated like children.

It was only appropriate then that they should now throw a strop. The authorities were treating them with contempt? They would similarly disregard the competition itself. When the first round draw paired them with lowly Lytham, Heath promptly sent the reserve team to lose 3-6 and not a tear was shed on North Road. In fact, for the next three years, Newton Heath's first eleven never bothered with the Junior Cup. Apparently, hardly did the seconds either, judging by the odd 1-7 or 0-9 mauling. It wasn't until 1889, by which time the Heathens were members of the esteemed Football Alliance, that the Lancashire FA would sheepishly ask them back and they would disdainfully accept.

LAST DAYS OF LOCALISM

FOR YEARS THEY waited for professionalism to come along and, when it finally did, Newton Heath resisted the urge to splash the cash. Well, they had to pay their existing players first before they could spend on any new ones. And Heath were not yet the type of club that could splurge £25m on the latest flavour-of-the-summer-tournament. If anything, the legalisation of professionalism was at first detrimental to Newton Heath's situation. Before, Mr. Attock could tempt potential targets over with the odd job at the railway station. But now that a budding hopeful could get paid transparently, the Heathens' advantage diminished. Apart from free transportation, why would he come to North Road? Heath might have been an emerging team but their journey to the big time was still at an early juncture. They were not even allowed to play in the Lancashire Senior Cup and it would require an administrative blooper over at Bolton Wanderers to kick-start Heath's de-localisation once and for all. That, though, would not come about until later on in the season.

In the meantime, the club had to get by using the players who made that long unbeaten run of 1884-85. A few more were added to avert the deflation of last season's climax. Sam Black was still leading the Heathens enthusiastically in sleet or snow. Unless a representative match came along, that is. Then he would leave his team behind, as happened on December 5th. This was back when club matches did not stop for international ones. A whole range of colourful expletives would have been invented by Sir Alex back then! Harry Davies, James Gotheridge, J. Mitchell, E. Moran, and William Siddons continued to form the side's backbone. Others, however, found themselves rejected by the body. Edward Howles, T. Beach, and Thomas Beach were mostly rendered but peeping Toms from the stands. Even W. Jordan, last year's resident goal poacher, was gone by late September.

In their place, new Heathens came along to contribute to the club's formative era. John Earp and A. Longton had actually joined at the tail end of last season and were now ready to assume a permanent first-team spot. Earp, at 21 years of age, could play anywhere across the front line. By the time he was 23, he could play anywhere in the half-back line. His progression continued to be inversely proportional to his age so by the age of 24 he was captaining the reserves. The opposite was true of Longton, who began in the middle and finished - though not prolifically - up front. It didn't matter to him where he was selected and, by the end of 1885-86, he had outplayed all his team-mates.

After J. Mitchell's successful start to his Monsall career, Newton Heath deduced that more Mitchells would obviously excel as well. His namesake, W., was subsequently recruited for the attack. However, his average impact over eight matches in 1885-86 curtailed at the root the board's plans for an all-Mitchell line-up. Also available for just the one season was J. Stanton, a half-back with an eye for goal. He brought experience from West Bromwich Albion and enjoyed an eventful year that culminated with a cup-winners' medal hanging around his neck. Jack Watkins's fate was almost identical. A forward with two eyes for scoring, he had a rewarding campaign before departing to Crewe Alexandra, only to return some time later for another stint at Monsall.

With all those players added, Newton Heath were ready for a unique event in their history: an August match! August 29th, to be exact, was the date North Road hosted a special ceremony to open the new term. The main attraction was a six-a-side tournament won by Crewe Alexandra. This was followed by a friendly game which Crewe again thought nothing of winning. The 1-3 reverse moved the Newton Heath board to decree: No more August games! Future generations duly obeyed. Nearly a quarter of a century elapsed before Manchester United participated in a replayed Charity Shield match on another sunny August day.

This heavy defeat saw another recurrence outlawed: the presence of Fulton in goal. He was asked to relinquish the gloves and move as far away as possible from goal, namely to the middle of the side stands. To that end, not one, not two, but three new goalkeepers were enlisted into the ABF (Anyone But Fulton) brigade. Beckett, Probert, and Seed would handle all matters between the sticks from this day on.

BOGEY NO MORE

ROBERT BECKETT MADE his Newton Heath debut in the second match of the season at Kearsley. Even though the 18-year-old Mancunian conceded two goals, he had a relieved look on his face. Unlike the Kearsley custodian, who sported that infamous Craig Forrest 'stick one past me' look honed over subsequent Old Trafford visits. The cause? Possibly the eleven goals the Heathens stuck past him! Alas, not a single scorer has been recorded from that massive victory. Reporters of the day had a bad habit of regarding high scoring matches as unworthy of detailed description. It's easy to imagine the hack adroitly jotting down one scorer after another in the early parts of the game. But as soon as the score reached six or seven, the report would be torn up and filed away in the nearest dustbin. Heaven only knows what sort of scoring records the Heathens amassed on that afternoon, especially considering that W. Jordan was making his penultimate appearance in green and gold.

With a big win comes an inflated head. A case in point was the railway hierarchy who reckoned Heath were now ready to test their mettle against stronger opposition. Blackburn Olympic and Bolton Wanderers accordingly dispatched their reserve teams to cut the North Road upstarts down to size; but not without a show of improvement by the home team. The Olympic, 7-2 winners last time around, found themselves engaged in a seven-goal thriller that they barely edged. As for Bolton's second string, twice 6-0 winners at the beginning of Heath's story, they were limited to a 3-0 success. If anything, the ensuing five years had proved that Heath's defence was now only half as bad. The Mancunians had a debutant, Seed, in goal; Black and Moran covered the flanks; Siddons, Stanton, and Longton were overwhelmed at half-back; while H. Davies, McGregor, T. Davies, Earp, and J. Mitchell underperformed up front. A 2-2 draw at Baxenden, Heath's Lancashire Cup conquerors of last year, further highlighted the improvement.

It is one thing having your mettle tested. The Heathens, however, were now longing for that winning feeling again. And the best way to recapture it was to stay away from the big boys' little boys and go back to picking on the little boys' big ones. This alternate plan worked to perfection. From the beginning of October until the end of January, Newton Heath did not lose a single game out of fifteen. As a matter of fact, they were unstoppable. If you caught them on a bad day, you'd do well to scrape a lucky draw. If you caught them on a good day, not only did you get walloped, but you had your features imprinted in the North Road mud too – at no extra charge. The only foolproof method to avoiding defeat was that devised by Darwen Casuals. Living up to their suffix, they simply failed to turn up for a scheduled Boxing Day fixture. Pendleton Olympic tried playing 10-a-side a week later and were hammered 5-0. Southport Central negotiated a 20-minute-per-half match on January 30th as the skies began to thunder, but it was Heath who struck four times. And Greenheys waited until Sam Black went to represent the Manchester District, only for Moran to assume coin-tossing duties and lead his men to a 4-1 drubbing.

The run included another Manchester Senior Cup Round One win over Eccles – no protestations to cause replayed ties this year – and a 5-nil demolition of Gorton Villa in the second round. When a defeat finally occurred, against Lower Hurst on February 6th, all it did was to activate Heath's turbo drive. They proceeded to hand Thornham the type of stuffing where only a thorough forensics expert could have pieced together the shredded match report. The 10-0 Manchester Cup triumph was a boon to lazy journalism as not a single scorer was chronicled for the ages.

A week on, an even more significant result was achieved, without the need for double figures. Heath's bogey side, Blackburn Olympic Reserves, were invited to North Road and eternally de-bogeyed, courtesy of a 3-1 victory. This so alarmed the Olympic management that they hastily arranged for their first team to kit up in all its might and exact revenge one month later. But the times were changing and the Newtonians maturing. The goals in that famous win were provided by Earp, H. Davies, and Watkins. Most of the club's forwards had maintained a decent scoring rate. The most prolific was Jack Watkins, who had come in to the team and more than adequately filled W. Jordan's boots, no doubt helped by matching shoe sizes. Out of the newcomers, Watkins had had the most telling impact so far with his consistent scoring of goals, along with W. Probert, who had secured a permanent gig stopping them at the other end.

JACK POWELL

WHEN IT COMES to impact signings, few have pounded the thud-o-meter as powerfully as the one Newton Heath made next. There is no denying Eric Cantona's catalytic effect in triggering Manchester United's 1990s period of dominance. Denis Law was similarly the last piece of the puzzle in that post-Munich renaissance. And, going further back, it was the capture of Billy Meredith and a clutch of his Manchester City team-mates that ushered in United's first era of success. But a long, long time before, in March 1886, one Jack Powell was signed and, while he could never compare with these aforementioned legends, his signature in itself propelled Newton Heath to a completely new dimension.

A caricature of Jack Powell, Heath's skipper in the late 1880s.

Jack Powell's story began on March 26th, 1860, the date he was born in a small town near Wrexham, Wales. Its name was Ffrwd but Jack played at the back. Being 6'2" came in handy when dealing with vertical threats. He also weighed in at a formidable 14 stone, which helped repel a lot of horizontal threats too. Surprisingly, his position was not at centre-half but at left-back, possibly so as not to obstruct the keeper's view. Needless to say, he was awesome in the air, with a powerful heading ability that greatly facilitated Newton Heath's Route One style.

Just how Jack got into football is a fantastic tale. In 1878, having supposedly never kicked a ball in his life, he travelled the short distance to Ruabon to watch a local team called Druids play. Loving what he saw, Jack decided to join them. Three matches later, he was selected to play for Wales! If reading this is tempting enough for you to put down this book and sign up as a superstar with the nearest Premier League outfit, you would be well advised to bear in mind that the last century has seen the odd improvement in a player's developmental process. Out of curiosity, this was Wales' third international match ever, and they proceeded to get creamed 0-9 by Scotland.

Nonetheless, Powell progressed into a skilful performer. With his help, Druids became the earliest superpower in Welsh football, reaching eight of the first nine Welsh Cup finals, the sole final they missed being on account of them not participating in the competition in the first place. Powell had earned three consecutive winners' medals from 1880 to 1882 when, in October 1883, he joined Bolton Wanderers. It is claimed that Powell was the first Welshman to ply his trade in England and this move was completed behind the FA's back, of course, considering their

Jack Powell (3rd left standing) poses with Druids, winners of the 1880 Welsh Cup

then repugnant stance on professionalism. This was a major coup for Bolton as Powell was already the holder of nine full caps at a time when you could trawl the whole world and come up with a maximum of three international games per year. It is a given that Sir Alex would still have complained. In his two and a half years at Bolton, Jack added only one more cap, but that was the only occasion during that period that the selectors picked an outfield player not attached to a Welsh club.

With such a CV, Jack Powell should never have played for Newton Heath. The Heathens, to put it gently, were mere nobodies from the northeast of Manchester. Powell took them out of there and put them on the map. For that, we have to be eternally grateful to Preston North End. Both Bolton and Preston were emerging as giants of the game in Lancashire and in two short years would become founding members of the Football League. This season,

MONDAY, MARCH 15th 1880

PROGRAMME

ENGLISH TEAM.

RIGHT.   GOAL.   LEFT.

J. SANDS
(Notts. Forest)

BACKS

E. LENTLEY   T. BRINDLE
(Notts. Forest)   (Darwen)

HALF-BACKS

J. HUNTER   F. HARGREAVES
(Sheffield)   (Blackburn Rovers)

FORWARDS.

T. MARSHALL   F.J. SPARKS   W.H. MOSFORTH
(Darwen)   (Clapham Rovers)   (Sheffield)

H.A. CURSHAM   C. MITCHELL   K. JOHNSON
(Sheffield)   (Upton Park)

UMPIRE: UMPIRE:
I. BASTARD, ESQ. UPTON PARK   LT. KENDICK, ESQ. DRUIDS

W. ROBERTS   J. PRICE   H. DAVIES
(Llangollen)   (Wrexham)   (Swansea)

J. ROBERTS   T. BODEN   W.E. OWEN
(Corwen)   (Wrexham)   (Ruthin)

W. WILLIAMS
(Druids)

FORWARDS.

S.C. EDWARDS   J. EDWARDS
(Wrexham)   (Druids)

J.D. MORGAN
(Derby School)

HALF-BACKS

J. POWELL
(Druids)

BACKS

R. HERBIOT
(Swansea)

RIGHT.   GOAL.   LEFT.

WELSH TEAM.

PROGRAMME

MONDAY, MARCH 15th 1880

Powell became an international around the same time Heath were born in 1878. This reproduction of Wales 1880 game against England at Wrexham shows him at right-back.

like playground bullies, the two locked horns in an acrimonious FA
Cup tie following which Preston were disqualified. Undeterred,
they came back childishly pointing fingers at Bolton's left-back,
Jack Powell. Apparently, he lived just outside the borders set by
the new professionalism rules. In a flash, an aghast FA banned this
transgressor from ever representing Wanderers again.

It was at this critical moment that the Newton Heath boardroom
pounced. A classy defender, who is a fitter by trade, is wandering
around looking for employment? Why, there is a place in the team
and a job vacancy at the works right now. The railway company
had again exercised its pulling power as Jack Powell found a
convenient new home. There is no doubt, though, that this was
a symbiotic arrangement. Newton Heath had just acquired their
first international player and a well-known one at that. Suddenly,
their profile undertook a shiny, new makeover and they became
an attractive destination for the hordes of new professionals out
looking for work. This was particularly well-timed to coincide with
a mass exodus from Wales. Powell's pulling power gave Heath an
edge over the swarm of the other little clubs in the area. In a few
months, North Road would contain more Welsh internationals
than Rhosllannerchrugog has syllables. As for Powell himself, he
would soon inherit Sam Black's armband and captain Heath until
early in the next decade, collecting a further five caps along the
way.

MANCHESTER'S SENIOR CLUB

BLACKBURN OLYMPIC RESERVES had been rendered second rate.
Bolton Wanderers had been stripped of their lauded left-back.
One more giant (of that time) was needed to make it a trio of
spring scalpings by Newton Heath. West Bromwich Albion, fresh
from appearing in the FA Cup final, were invited to pander to
Heath's ego boosting next. However, they thought better of it and
sent their unsuspecting second team instead. Approximately 2,000
spectators gathered to see the FA Cup finalists in the flesh. What
they saw was lips pouting, arms folding and feet stamping after
the referee, Mr. Edwards, disallowed an Albion goal. In fact, they
refused to resume play until Mr. Edwards had had his marching
orders and been replaced by a Baggie-friendly prototype. Albion

still lost 0-1.

The **Manchester Examiner** was very proud of its local victors the next day, noting how the Heathens had played 34 games so far this season and won 23 of them. They were certainly advancing with the years. A couple of seasons back there had only been a handful of names on the fixture list but now they had matches to burn. One of these was a critical tussle on March 13th in the Manchester Cup semi-final. In one corner stood the hungry, love-struck Heathens from Monsall; in the other, their conquerors from the last time around, the holders, the succinctly-named … Hurst. Yes, the same Hurst who not only cantered to a 3-0 triumph over Heath in the 1885 final, but had also strutted around as top dogs in the two clubs' interlinked histories so far. Taming them would represent a rite of passage for Newton Heath in the quest to rule Mancunia. In scientific terms, it is called surpassing the rate-limiting step. In Salford-speak, it was akin to United finally rolling Juventus over in Turin on the way to the 1999 Champions League final. On this occasion, Heath too found themselves in the final – and the second in a row to boot – with a momentous 3-1 victory. Goal scoring winger Gotheridge and leading marksman Watkins both netted, as did the man in the midst of a purple patch, John Earp.

As many as six thousand fans witnessed this tie. Newton Heath were already garnering a cult following and another six thousand, or possibly the same ones to a man, followed on to the final on April 3rd. The venue again was at neutral Whalley Range, just to the northwest of Chorlton Road. And, considering this was the Manchester Cup final, the opponents were, aptly enough, Manchester F.C.. Jack Powell was unavailable for the Heathens as the competition's rules had not yet been updated to account for paid professionals. Hence, the line-up was made up of the following penniless paupers: Probert; Black, Mitchell; Stanton, Moran, Fulton; Watkins, Longton, Earp, H. Davies, and Gotheridge.

Barely three minutes in, Newton Heath took the lead with the type of educational incident that brought the referee, Mr. Marshall, up to speed on the latest expletives going around. Harry Davies was camped in an offside position when he gained possession and shot toward the Manchester goal. The ball was then allegedly fisted in by Jack Watkins, who would have been even more offside then. Mr. Marshall, however, awarded the goal to Davies after rejecting

Manchester's 'offside' complaints then later claiming not to have heard any 'hands' calls regarding Watkins' Maradona-esque touch. Surely this makes him unique in the long history of the refereeing fraternity in being both blind and deaf. It was definitely a lucky break for Heath, but sometimes you need that in your hunt for glory, especially considering the Fulton-induced misfortune of the previous year's final.

Manchester tried to retaliate: Thistlethwaite went on a dribble almost as long as his name, whereas inside-right T. Rowlands so impressed the Heath management they gave him a trial a month later … in goal! The fact that trial lasted one match gives an indication of its degree of success. Meanwhile, Manchester's custodian, Southworth, was not on trial here yet still demonstrated some of his qualities. One such example was his indecision at collecting a loose ball, to the benefit of Sam Black who gleefully put Heath two up. Thereafter, even though much time remained, the men from Monsall willingly retreated and sat on their lead. They then parked the railway carriage yet still allowed the opposition another goal, Farrington scoring for Manchester with a solo effort. Still, Heath's tactics worked and the whistle soon sounded to signal Newton Heath's first ever trophy.

With time, so many trophies, all of them more prestigious, would be brought home by this club and its ancestor. Yet this very first one, The Manchester Senior Cup, needs to be cherished as a symbol of the club's rapid rise, without which Heath might never have morphed into Manchester United. Just a few years before, the Heathens had been jockeying with the likes of Newton Heath Loco for bragging rights in the LYR corridors. Now, even as early as 1886, the Coachbuilders had attained the status of top team in Manchester. The fans, now nearing 8,000 on average, were thrilled, and they escorted the players to the main stand. The Newton Heath Brass Band was even more excited, blaring "See the Conquering Hero Comes" as Sam Black hoisted the trophy. In that moment, a club tradition was born.

By the end of the season, Newton Heath had struck one hundred times. Only half that tally has been traced. Luckily for Jack Watkins, he had more goals scribbled down for history than any of his team-mates. Earp and, of course, Gotheridge also troubled the reporters on a frequent basis. Watkins' exploits, however, did not ensure his presence at North Road the following season. He departed to Crewe Alexandra but returned briefly in 1888. Time was up also for the club's longest servant, Fulton. He left Monsall in the summer of 1886 but his trailblazing efforts – and goalkeeping clangers – would not be forgotten for years. Not so many memories were left behind by other Heathens on the go. Siddons, Moran, and Stanton would no longer offer any significant contributions to our story. But fear not for their places would soon be filled by one or two legendary heroes.

1886-87

THE BARGING BROTHERS

A BIG FUSS has been made in recent times about the proliferation of foreigners in the English game. They smother the growth of home-grown talent, it is claimed, and peeve the Little Englanders no end. And it is easy to spot who is at fault: Jean-Marc Bosman for allowing them to move anytime they wanted, and the European Union for telling them they could go anywhere they wished. However, you can blame neither Bosman nor the EU for the first foreigner to invade English football a long, long time ago: the Welshman! Only a few months had elapsed but, in the close season of 1886, the Powell effect had already kicked in. Newton Heath's management went looking for any Welshman who could shoot straight and came back with Tom Burke and a trio from Jack Powell's old Druids club, Joseph Davies and the brothers Jack and Roger Doughty.

THE DOUGHTYS:
Jack 'Crasher' (with the cap) and Roger his younger brother, also a master of the same trade.

Ah, the Doughtys! A cheekier pair of sibling verve this club has never seen. One would have been a handful yet it is a shame there weren't three. For they came to North Road and created a legend that can still thrill to this day. Jack was four years Roger's elder but you would have thought they were conjoined twins from the way they played. As they hared forward chasing the ball, one of them would shove the opponents' defender to the side allowing the other a clear run on goal. Both were experts at shoulder-charging but Jack was the master. "Crasher of the first order" was his depiction in those days when such violent acts were considered compulsory on-field manners. He possibly pioneered the first needle-free tattoo as this pastime covered the skin on his upper arms with all sorts of artistic bruises. It is believed that Roger should have been born first until Jack shoulder-barged him and all the other sperms out of the way.

Crashing aside, there were many other qualities in Jack's armoury such as his speed and his loyalty to team-mates. Or, at least, to his brother, as this surreal tale from the past illustrates. There was a big Newton Heath fan who happened to be a successful local tailor. One day, in a eureka moment, he stumbled upon an innovative marketing gimmick: a free overcoat to whoever scored for Heath in an upcoming match. In those days, of course, such an item of clothing was a luxury few could afford, and that made this ad quite the incentive. But as a tactical plan, it was revolutionary in its chaos-creating capability. When the game kicked off, forwards, midfielders, and defenders alike tore up field in search of a goal, a free coat the overriding motivation. Yet amid the mayhem one Jack Doughty emerged to clinch the all-important jackpot strike. A coat was all his... or so it seemed. But then he went on to grab another goal and demanded he should receive another coat – for his brother! So much commotion ensued that the embarrassed Heath management begged the tailor to rescind his offer. The poor fellow received all the exposure and got to keep his coats.

Jack's most outstanding feature, however, was his scoring touch. He piled goal upon goal until he became the first Heathen to reach a century. Roger was almost as prolific, especially at the start of his North Road stay for he later did most of his barging at half-back. They scored a hatful in cup finals. Among Jack's other feats, he netted what stands today as Manchester United's first competitive goal (in the FA Cup), and his name was also on the score-sheet in their inaugural Football Alliance fixture. Even the Doughtys' early days at Druids were legendary. It was a random occurrence they started their careers there considering they were born in England. In Staffordshire, to be precise – Jack in 1864, Roger in 1868. Their father was Irish and their mother was Welsh, and it was according to her request that the family moved to Wales.

Jack and Roger grew up at 33 Crane Street in the small town of Ruabon in the hub of the mining country. It was subsequently understandable then that the Doughty kids went down the pits: Jack as a coalminer and the young Roger as a horse driver. There was a famous ad in the 1990s featuring Ryan Giggs. It mockingly depicted how, had he not purchased a particular brand of football boots, he would have wound up as a roadside tulip seller. Well, the early Welsh Wonders, Jack and Roger, proved you could combine football with the average 60-hour week of hard labour.

The club that made it happen initially was Druids, Wales' first crack side. The Doughtys joined when Jack Powell was still there. Soon they established regular first-team spots and by 1886 had won two consecutive Welsh Cup medals. Jack, in fact, had just scored in the final in April when Newton Heath came sniffing for talent. He was quickly snapped up, with Roger to follow. Druids were clearly miffed and complained to the FA about their best players being poached. And they were right too, for soon their era of dominance would come to an end. But the Doughtys couldn't possibly refuse Newton Heath's professional terms: £1.50 a week and a job at the LYR. According to my trusty calculator, that is equivalent to what the modern six-figure-a-week footballer makes in roughly nine seconds! But these were just Jack's wages. Roger was not considered as big a star and his pay was just £1. It was money well spent, however, as the brothers carried their trophy-winning habits with them to North Road. Jack, for instance, appeared in cup finals in eight consecutive years from 1883 to 1890, be it in the Welsh Cup or the Manchester one. He was on the winning side in five of them and showed his big game temperament with a seven-goal return.

The Doughty's

WREXHAM 1882 – WELSH CUP WINNERS
Among them is the man with the biggest moustache in Wales, Tom Burke, seated right next to the trophy itself.

international exploits also brought so much prestige to Newton Heath the club could distribute it wholesale. Jack represented Wales on eight occasions, seven of them as a Heathen, which made him the club's most capped player. Roger earned two caps, the first of which, in 1888, made the Doughtys the first Newton Heath siblings to be jointly capped. It was a great occasion for Wales too. Four goals from Jack and two from debutant Roger propelled the principality to an 11-0 demolition of Ireland that stands as a record to this day. On that famous afternoon, Wales finished the game with just eight players after three of them left early to catch a train! Jack actually netted in all three home internationals in 1888 to set a Welsh record, while his six goals made him the country's all-time leading marksman until 1895. They were so proud of him they awarded him the first actual cap to be handed out by the Welsh FA. It would have looked nice with an overcoat!

The Doughtys' Newton Heath influence further transcended Jack and Roger. Their only sister, Ellen, married Heathen Bob McFarlane. If she was anything like her brothers, you could wonder what hurt the poor chap's shoulders more: a night in bed or training the morning after?

With a bit more cool and a ton less drool I would have been able to talk about newcomers other than Jack Doughty. My favourite Heathen he may be but he could not have earned such an exalted honour without the significant help of the pair of half-backs the Newton Heath hierarchy stationed behind him. Both Joe Davies and Tom Burke proved to be excellent acquisitions to North Road. Like the Doughtys, Davies came over from Druids where he had been a Welsh Cup winner in each of the last two seasons. Incredibly, he was one of five brothers who turned out for Druids. However, lest they be labelled an overachieving family, only four of them were good enough to represent their country. Joe was one of the internationals though he did not become one until he arrived in Manchester. In the next four years he would play over 160 matches for Heath where he was almost always ever-present at centre-half. Of the few games he missed, five were due to national call-ups. He would later add another two caps in a spell with Wolverhampton Wanderers in the Football League.

Tom Burke had already played five times for Wales in the four seasons before coming to Monsall. He would win three more caps as a Heathen while establishing himself as a rugged half-back who could make onions cry. He was a much-travelled footballer and everywhere he went, his moustache got there first. A photo of Wrexham's 1883 Welsh Cup-winning team shows him with enough sub-nasal rug to warm the entire half-back line. Burke appeared for several teams in the Wrexham area but he was registered with Liverpool Cambrians when Newton Heath found a dual use for his skills. In addition to his footballing skills, he would serve the depot as a painter.

A NEW HEATH

THE NEWTON HEATH Dining Room Committee had executed quite an impressive quartet of signings for the new season. And it needed to – as a riposte to the cruel dissing it received in the summer. Applying to be re-admitted to the senior section of the Lancashire Cup, Heath were rejected by the pompous county association, "until they show proof of their ability" being the precisely worded slap in the face. It can only be hoped the LFA did not dispatch someone to take notes on said ability on the opening day of the season. Heath travelled to Northwich Victoria and contrived to lose 0-5. That could conveniently be dismissed as an experimental match since five of Heath's players that day never honoured the first team with their presence again.

The Welsh lads would begin to filter through during the next few matches which, as can only be expected, produced a mixed set of results. By October 2nd, however, a mouth-watering foretasting of their true potential was served. A huge crowd gathered at North Road for a re-match of last season's Manchester Cup final: Heath, the holders, against Manchester F.C., the team still debating that handball goal. Jack Doughty, Joe Davies, and Tom Burke were all in the line-up while Roger, who was a few years younger, was still awaiting to be unleashed in a couple of months. Beckett had triumphed in the goalkeepers' battle to cement a place at the expense of Probert. The latter was restricted to a couple of matches all season, one of which was that opening day debacle at Northwich Victoria. Despite the 0-5 hammering Probert had kept a clean sheet, no doubt helped by being selected at inside-right! For this tussle with Manchester, however, neither goalie was available, prompting Jack

Powell to mind the posts. Mitchell filled in at right-back whereas Sam Black, in one of his last appearances for the Coachbuilders, continued on the left. Howles, Joe Davies, and Burke formed a new-look half-back line. And Earp, Longton, Doughty, Harry Davies, and Gotheridge played up front. In the event, as many as six of these men got their names on the score-sheet as Manchester were rendered speechless with an 8-1 pummelling: Doughty (2), Gotheridge (2), J. Davies, H. Davies, Burke, and Longton. It was a comprehensive demolition of supposedly the second best team in the city, and it had the North Road faithful salivating over the new Heath and no doubt drooling over one Jack Doughty.

STROP IN THE CUP

There are those who claim October 30th, 1886, to be the start of Manchester United's history. The statistical history, to be exact, and that is according to one or two fact-obsessed anoraks. These cold, calculating chaps believe that, since this was the date Newton Heath played their first ever FA Cup tie, everything that went before is irrelevant, even if it may have been the most romantic, innocent, and carefree era in the club's story. In truth, any one thing is as important as you make it, and there may come a day in the distant future when even the FA Cup is treated with the same indifference shown by current historians to the Lancashire or Manchester Cup competitions.

Either way, it was about time the Heathens tried their hand at the old competition. To hell with the Lancashire Cup and its feudal segregation. Here was a trophy where no ability was required to participate and so began a new romance that in time would see the club become its most frequent suitor, as well as creating a plethora of indelible memories that will forever be enshrined in United lore. It remains a competition that has never let the club down. Even in its darkest days Heath, and later United, would always be up for the cup.

There were as many as 126 teams in the FA Cup first round draw and Newton Heath looked forward to the possibility of meeting any new, unfamiliar name that the vast British Empire had to offer. Instead, they got drawn away at Fleetwood Rangers of, yes, Lancashire. The Heathens dusted off the rarely-worn change strip of red-and-white jerseys and blue shorts, and off they went on the relatively short stroll down to the seaside.

The following eleven men were picked for the first eternally competitive match: Beckett; Powell, Mitchell; Burke, J. Davies, Howles; Earp, Longton, J. Doughty, H. Davies, and Gotheridge.

Some historians wrongly list L. Davies as having played instead of Harry. That subsequently makes them cold and miscalculating, for no such individual appeared elsewhere for the Heathens, while this very line-up remained unchanged the following weekend.

With a couple of thousand watchers in the stands, only one man was fit enough to handle the responsibility of scoring Manchester United's earliest competitive goal: step forward Mr. Jack Doughty. He duly obliged then added another one for good measure. Fleetwood, however, exhibiting no understanding of the game's significance to United's history, equalised on each occasion. This created a dilemma at full-time. The referee, Mr. Norris, ordered the players to continue with extra-time. Heath were under the impression that a replay was now in effect and sent acting captain Jack Powell over to argue their point. Mr. Norris was insistent. Hoping for a bumper gate at North Road and eager to catch the next train back home, Powell could not agree with the referee's decree. The man in black had no option but to relay the matter to the FA.

Now the authorities were only too happy to hold Newton Heath's fortunes in the palm of their hands. There is an old Eastern European proverb which says that the sword does not chop off the head that bows. It may have originated as words of wisdom for Manchester United's frequent clashes with authority. The predeccessors, of course, were no different, what with the BNA business and all. History has seen a variety of ways employed to stop this club from winning the FA Cup: dodgy decisions, such as in 1989 or 2008; the fabrication of a mandatory tournament halfway around the globe as a diversion; or the blatant goalie crocking that was trendy in the pre-substitute days of the late Fifties. Back in 1886, the means was as straightforward as a guillotine: the FA simply disqualified Heath for not playing extra-time in the original tie. Just like that, the unbeaten Heathens were kicked out of the old tin pot. If this is what you get for having a go at long last, then Heath's next self-imposed period of exile was going to have to last long. It would take another three years for the boiling blood to cool sufficiently for a second stab.

At least one good thing came out of Newton Heath's FA Cup night out. Their participation, albeit brief, raised their profile and public awareness. Competitive league football had yet to be spawned and, until now, clubs faced each other in mostly pointless friendlies. Only the cup competitions had any purpose, with the FA Cup being the most prestigious. Win it and you're the toast of the universe. Just partake in it and you're guaranteed a gulp. From this game on, the media coverage intensified and the unreported Heathen goal scorer became a rarity. What also helped was the thrilling encounter a week later when the subjugation of old adversaries Blackburn Olympic was completed once and for all. The 4-2 victory had probably as much to do with Olympic's decline as with the rise of Newton Heath. The real surprise then wasn't in the score line but in full-back Mitchell giving the North Road masses a pleasant shock with a goal so rare you could trace all the missing Heath scorers and still struggle to spot his name. Think Paul Parker in an FA Cup tie at Reading in 1996 for an apt parallel.

THE SCOTTISH SPY

SOON IT WAS time to bid farewell to one of Newton Heath's greatest servants. Sam Black played his last game for the club on November 20th against Rawtenstall. Some people in the crowd were sobbing; at least the family of the late W. Lord. Heath's long-serving financial secretary had passed away earlier in the month and this 30-minute a half outing was played in his memory. Neither team scored but the spectators raised sufficient proceeds for his loved ones. So, Manchester United's first prominent captain moved back to his hometown of Burton to finish his playing career with Wanderers. His pioneering efforts would not be forgotten by the Newton Heath regulars. Later he became a referee and even then he still brought joy to the Heathen fans, particularly when he once chalked off an Arsenal goal because the ball, no doubt frustrated at being endlessly passed around, spontaneously burst to make it impossible for the opposition goalie to catch.

Part of the legacy Black left behind was the captain's armband. This was permanently seized by Jack Powell, the directors apparently heartened by his negotiating tactics in the cup exit at Fleetwood Rangers! Well, he did have the club's interests at heart, which is the least we expect from our captains and, in truth, nobody was more qualified than Jack to lead the new Heath. He had been everywhere, done it all, and got the cap to prove it; and he had lived in Lancashire the optimal time for his modified brogue to be comprehensible by both the locals and the new Welsh invaders.

The team was changing - Edward Howles and A. Longton also accompanied Black out of the North Road door - destination Ten Acres. So much so that Heath's line-up for the December 4th friendly at Manchester F.C. contained only three of the players who faced the same opponents in the Manchester Cup final the previous April: Mitchell, Earp, and Harry Davies. The outcome was the same though. Newton Heath used a 3-2 score-line to simultaneously vanquish revenge-seeking Manchester as well as their reserves back at Monsall. New players were replacing old ones. Roger Doughty finally made his debut a week on against old chums Hurst in front of 7,000 fans. He did enough pushing, shoving, and shoulder-charging that his brother was free to slot three goals. Jack's first hat-trick for the club secured a 5-0 drubbing that tilted the Hurst rivalry in Heath's favour for good.

The Heathens must have wished they had saved a goal or two for the harsh winter ahead. In six matches they were able to score just once. Or twice, if you count the one by Robert Beckett. Heath's custodian was gradually proving he possessed two left hands, and he used one of them to turn the ball into his own goal for the

IRELAND v WALES 1887
*Jack Doughty reclines before the
Belfast international on March 12th.*

only strike of the match against Notts Rangers. But there were legitimate excuses for the drought. On December 18th, only ten brave Heathens were present to face Bury's full force as well as rain, frost, and snow. When some spectators started building an ark, the referee finally saw sense and stopped the match shortly after half-time. On Christmas Day, Sam Black brought his new team, Burton Wanderers, over but forgot to gift-wrap any goals. And only two first-team regulars appeared in the line-up that lost 0-2 at Crewe on New Year's Day. At last the Heath forwards provided a couple of goals against Stanley of Liverpool while Jack Powell provided the comic relief. His 'over-my-dead-body' approach to holding off his Scouse opponent earned the loudest cheer from the crowd.

It might have seemed like Heath were launching an educational incentive in February with the introduction of Reed and Wright. However, the staunch illiterates among the North Road faithful had no reason for concern. J. Wright was employed intermittently for now and only deemed compulsory in the Manchester Cup. Reed, meanwhile, turned out to be false advertisement. Sure, he made his debut at Macclesfield and scored in a 4-1 victory, but a few eagle-eyed fans who then travelled to the subsequent friendly at Hurst noticed something suspicious about the new inside-forward listed as Tait: he looked identical to Reed! It eventually transpired this was indeed the same new signing, William Tait, who was originally given a trial under the pseudonym of Reed. "Wully" - as he preferred to be called in a successful attempt to create even more confusion – was a 23-year-old forward who hailed from Glasgow. Great Scot! Could Newton Heath be blatantly attempting to introduce sophisticated passing into their play? It would be more credible if Tait were a Tartan spy sent to Monsall to repel the Welsh invasion. At least that would explain the double identity as well as his claim that he randomly arrived in town unaware of Newton Heath LYR's existence. In reality, the Heathens had acquired a talented footballer with experience at Glasgow Parkside, Glasgow Pilgrims, and Third Lanark RV. Wully would grace North Road for the next three years barring a short stint when he made Football League history...

The Welsh contingent had no reason to fret just yet – it would take until the early 1890s for the Scots to cross Hadrians Wall in sufficient numbers. This was still the Age of the Welsh and, in fact, the day Tait's cover was blown, Jack Powell and Tom Burke were away creating history of their own. As Wales faced England in London, Powell and Burke took advantage to become Newton Heath's first international players.

A ROUT A ROUND

Caps and cups, Newton Heath now had it all. Jack Doughty was the next Heathen to double up as a Dragon – alone against Ireland and alongside Powell and Burke when Scotland came to Wrexham. It was another accolade in a season where he topped the scoring charts alongside Gotheridge with 15 recorded goals. Meanwhile, as Manchester Cup holders, the Heathens again made their way through the rounds taking not so much the scenic route as the routing scene. In the first round, Hooley Hill visited Monsall and got routed 7-0. And this happened without the cup-tied Wully Tait as well as Powell, who was still deemed too professional for this competition. Their absence was nothing that a large-scale positional reshuffle couldn't solve. The club committee yanked out a piece of paper and started scheming. Joe Davies will relocate from centre-half to right-back. His vacant slot would be filled by one of three players promoted from the reserve team T. Whatmough (who would hardly feature at any other time). At outside-right would be J. Wright with the promise that he would get a permanent place next year. And Harry Bates would take Tait's place. Contrary to Wright, Bates would play regularly this season then leave. With John Earp having added versatility to his modest repertoire and converted to right-half, it put the 'mental' in experimental line-up. Somehow it worked, even the newcomers Bates and Whatmough scoring against Hooley Hill.

The second round went even better. In fact, the outcome and the date of February 19th, 1887 should be sporadically sprayed in graffiti on the walls around Eastlands, as well as casually brought up in conversation with anyone from the blue third of Manchester. For on that day Newton Heath faced City – answering to the catcalls of 'Gorton' at the time – and gave them a thrashing so complete it made the Kanchelskis-inspired 5-0 drubbing of 1994 seem like a hard fought draw. The result? 11-1! There is no need to list the line-up. Just a mention of the goal scorers nearly covers that: Gotheridge, J. Davies (2), H. Davies (2), Whatmough, Bates, J. Doughty, Wright, Burke, and an own goal. At least we know that a chap named Drinkwater played for Gorton since he was able to sneak one goal back just as the referee was about to blow for time.

Signs the team was in decline appeared in the next round when Heath were only able to knock eight goals past Gorton Villa. But don't mention any of that to Jack Doughty who was quite satisfied with his hat-trick, nor to Gotheridge with his brace. After 26 goals had yielded three fine wins, Heath's semi-final victory was semi-fine. Ten Acres, boosted by ex-Heathens Howles and Longton, were a tough proposition, while the cup holders were missing the injured Jack Doughty. Yet Ten Acres could not take advantage of a Doughty-free situation because the younger version, Roger, stepped in to make a name for himself. Before 7,000 spectators at a neutral Hurst, he grabbed his first goal for the club - and the only one in this game – to send Heath to the final.

For the third year in a row, Newton Heath appeared at Whalley Range to contest the Manchester Cup final and they did so on the back of ten undefeated cup matches. April 23rd was the date, with 4,000 at the gate. The line-up was the same as the one fielded in most of the earlier rounds: Beckett; J. Davies, Mitchell; Earp, Whatmough, Burke; Wright, Bates, J. Doughty, H. Davies, and Gotheridge.

It was left to West Manchester to provide the diversity in terms of opposition. They were lucky to have made it this far having been ejected from the competition in an early round before being allowed back in. That was of no concern to Newton Heath who immediately stormed into action. West's keeper Beardshaw had already made two good saves by the eighth minute when Gotheridge put the cup holders ahead. They were still celebrating when a surprise shot by Tomlinson levelled the scores. Heath instantly tore forward and pounded Beardshaw in the West Manchester goal but he was having the game of his life, blocking shots by Harry Davies and Jack Doughty, and even withstanding one of the Crasher's trademark charges. Gotheridge should have easily completed his hat-trick. First he pounced on a parried save but he blazed his shot so high it may have been responsible for the hole in the ozone layer. Then, as Bates' cross rolled invitingly along a gaping goal, Gotheridge slid in but came short by one shoe size. As a sign of their dominance, Heath had tallied ten corners before West Manchester forced one.

In the second half, Heath again dominated despite playing against the incline, the wind, the sun, and God's favoured goalie. Beardshaw's Heathen-proof goal seemed divinely shielded. Gradually, West Manchester began to get into the game and, with nine minutes to go, their inside-forward Bolton smashed home a shot Beckett was fortunate to evade. It was enough to win the game and wrest the Cup from Heath's grasp. Beardshaw, if no one else, deserved his gold medal. As for the Heathens, after missing so many chances, they missed out on their silver medals too having left before the presentation.

In truth, Newton Heath's season had tailed off flatly even before the final. The only way to brighten the place up was to invite a couple of high profile teams for some prestigious end-of-season friendly fun. They did not come much larger than Bolton Wanderers and Blackburn Rovers, the Lancashire giants trotting out at North Road for the first time. Crowd estimates for the Wanderers game range from 8,000 to 9,000, and the Heath players must have spent the entire match trying to get an exact count because Bolton were left free to plunder five unanswered goals. It went better when Blackburn came to town in the last match of 1886-87. No matter which wing the Rovers attacked they ran into a Powell, for captain Jack was partnered at full-back by his brother Albert, guesting from Druids. The younger sibling had recently missed out on becoming an international when he had to withdraw at the last minute. At the other end, Blackburn's defence performed resolutely but, with no anti-Scot mechanism in place, they were susceptible to William Tait's raids. Wully duly tucked in the game's solitary goal. It was a fitting finale to the campaign. They may have lost their posh seat atop Manchester football, but the Heathens showed that, on their day, they could now give anybody in the land a game.

1887-88

A WALK REMEMBERED

ASSOCIATION FOOTBALL WAS still meandering about in search of an identity. The idea of an organised competitive league was one genial brain spark away and Newton Heath, steady though their growth may have been, had yet to paint the world gold and green. However, as the 1887-88 season got underway, it was apparent a quite decent team was being moulded in the North Road mud. The management had obviously cottoned on to a trick or two from years of splish-splashing. From never having bought into the over hyped benefits of line-up stability, they now developed a fear of the tinker: ten players would each appear in 35 matches or more out of a possible 45 throughout the campaign. Then they amped that up with a high-scoring goal option: the forward line would not net exactly five goals in any game but they would exceed it on nine occasions! The end result was one fine side. They may have spent nearly a decade heading in the right direction but, finally now, the Heathens had truly arrived.

Pat O'Donnell strolls into the picture at this time, quite literally as he'd walked all the way to north Manchester from Glasgow hoping to play for the team and blag a gig at the LYR depot. This fellow should be held up as the yardstick by which anyone aspiring to join Manchester United should be measured. In the process, O'Donnell became the first known Irishman to play for the club. After eight matches – and two goals – the versatile O'Donnell was politely asked to walk on to Oldham.

Or might he have mistaken North Road for Wales so he turned back? Heath's ground was certainly buzzing with Welsh accents at the start of this campaign, more so than the last one. Heath had noted the Doughtys' initial impact and decided brotherly partnerships were the way forward. Having already depleted

Druids' sibling reserves while simultaneously ending their era of dominance, the Heath committee turned its attentions on Wales' new superpower. Chirk had just won the Welsh Cup fielding as many as three separate sets of brothers. The pick of the pairs were the Owens, half-back Jack and inside-forward Bill, the latter having notched a brace in the cup final. Unlike Irishman O'Donnell, the Owens kept their day job back in Chirk, working down the pits and catching the train to Manchester every Saturday. This made for quite an impressive congregation of Welshmen in Monsall during September weekends. But then the principality called asking for one or two of its players back. Bill Owen was reluctantly allowed to return, and he rejoined Chirk where he again bagged a couple of goals as the cup was retained in 1888. Bill would then make his second annual September visit to North Road for three historic matches before leaving for good. That was a shame, as Bill would go on to amass 18 caps in a long international career from 1883 to 1895, including a significant spell as captain. He would also collect Welsh Cups for fun, his haul reaching six after seeing service at Druids and Wrexham.

The younger Owen was no small consolation, mind, albeit in size. 5'6" was all God gave him, but he stocked it heavily enough to

POOR CHIRK
As soon as they won the Welsh Cup for the first time in 1887
they found themselves prey to Manchester's scheming scouts -
Brothers Jack (middle row 1st left) and Bill Owen (front row,
2nd left) were soon whisked off to North Road while Di Jones
(standing, 2nd left) would also become a Heathen later on.

become a force at left-half. He was 22-years-old when he came to Monsall, and he went on to wear - and wear off - Heath's colours in over 200 matches in the next five years, eventually earning a full cap for his troubles. His specialities included long throws and pain infliction. Indeed, any throw-in in the opposition half was considered to be Owen territory.

But perhaps the most inspired signing of the new term was a plain old Englishman with the uncomplicated name of Tom Hay. The arrival of the Staveley-born 29-year-old meant that Newton Heath had at long last recruited a decent shot stopper after years of winging it. Here was a man who was head and shoulders below any goalkeeper before or since; literally, for he was 5'7½" and specialized in low saves. But don't let his height intimidate you – it certainly didn't the opposition forwards who kicked him around so often he boasted a varied assortment of breaks and fractures. Hay was brave and good, actually, if winning representative honours for the district was the criterion to go by. He had enjoyed a year in the limelight a few seasons before when he was on Bolton's books. That spell ended disgracefully one Christmas week. Hay reported for duty sporting a brewer-induced cerebral stupor and proceeded to deliver a masterpiece in clutching at thin air. He topped it off by letting in the softest of goals when he spectacularly dived the opposite way. His explanation was that he had seen three balls heading towards him and, unfortunately, he dived for one of the two illusions! The Bolton officials had not heard that one before and instantly packed him off. Such eccentricity, though, was considered a prerequisite for a job at North Road. Hay was the perfect match for the Heathens, if only because that meant the end of Robert Beckett's days in goal. The unlucky Mancunian would have no further role to play in Newton Heath's tale and would accompany J. Blears and Harry Bates out of Monsall, forever, to be lost in history.

THIS TEAM WILL SORT YOU OUT

Three Englishmen, one Scot, an Irishman, and six Welshmen lined up for Newton Heath against Accrington on the opening day of the season. De-localization was already in full swing and this, remember, was in 1887. The only Mancunians present had to pay to get in and watch from the stands. Jack Owen scored on his debut as Accrington were beaten 2-1 while Pat O'Donnell struck two weeks later to help stuff Earlstown 7-0. But the real scoring sensation was young Roger Doughty, starting in the first team as his brother struggled for fitness. Like a new teenager who just discovered the joys at his disposal, Roger was scoring in every outing, and sometimes twice in one day. A jealous Wully Tait satisfied himself with a hat-trick in that demolition of Earlstown before making more modest contributions of a goal per game as Heath achieved a couple of massive results. In the space of five days in late September, Newton Heath exacted sweet revenge on two of last season's rivals and, in the process, took the opportunity to demonstrate what an improved team they had become. First, West Manchester and their Manchester Cup-winning pedigree were sequentially introduced to each North Road puddle before being dispatched with half a dozen homemade goals as a memento of their visit. Then Bolton Wanderers, 5-0 winners at Monsall the previous campaign, were defeated 2-1 at their own place despite Newton Heath having not won away from home in the preceding seven months.

It was a clear statement of intent from the Heathens: 'mess with us and we'll sort you out'. And they now had the team that could back up bluster. The winner at Bolton was provided by Jack Doughty, finally back to fitness to complete the first-team line-up. Now Heath possessed the first settled team in their history. Almost always present in goal was Tom Hay, the management obviously postulating this was the best way to keep him out of the pub. At full-back, Powell and Mitchell were forging a useful partnership that allied resolve to rhyming surnames. Tom Burke, Joe Davies, and Jack Owen turned the midfield into an Inquisition tribute zone. And this from a half-back line purely made in Wales. Tom, the man whose moustache had a moustache, was a full international already and Joe was set to emulate him in a few months. While it took another four years for Jack to do likewise, he settled in the meantime on being portrayed as a stylish footballer, based on his fashionably-late tackles. Outside-left Gotheridge was a model too, of consistency at least, if not looks - the goal scoring winger was now into his fourth year of prolific service. Wully Tait was proving to be even hotter on the opposite flank, boasting an average that guaranteed a two-goal return every three outings. The surprise breakthrough player of the campaign was J. Wright — last year's Manchester Cup fill-in. He searched all around the front line for a permanent spot and found inside-right most accommodating.

The most potent part of the attack, however, was the Doughty double act. Has the club ever known a more free-scoring sibling setup? Certainly not in the last thirty years whose sole candidates are G. and P. Neville! A better comparison would be the lethal partnership of 'soul brothers' Yorke and Cole. Yes, the Doughtys were that good. By the sixteenth match of the season they had contributed 25 goals despite missing a combined eight appearances. Their best moment came on November 5th against Ten Acres. By the second minute of the match they had both scored! Roger went on to tally three goals in a 9-0 swatting job. Jack's hat-trick arrived two weeks later when Heath failed to replicate the Ten Acres score line and had to settle on just eight goals. The Doughtys were certainly putting the pride in the green-and-gold shirt.

Of those 16 matches, a dozen were won and two drawn. Such success, however, was bound to invite a certain degree of murk to go with the North Road mud. There is no shadow without light, and Newton Heath's burst into the limelight had attracted that most shadowy of characters: the politician! When Lancashire neighbours Burnley paid their visit to Monsall at the end of October, local MP Sir James Fergusson decided he wanted to associate himself with the grand occasion. Newton Heath were only too happy, what with the added gloss and the 8,000 rubberneckers coughing up cash into the coffers. As for the actual game against the highly-regarded Clarets, the Heathens gave as much as they got. Which was nothing really as the match finished goalless.

HOME MUDDY HOME

EIGHT THOUSAND SPECTATORS must have made for quite a sight, especially considering the North Road ground had no stands. That wooden innovation would remain a futuristic impossibility at Monsall for another four years. You could rely on the fans, however, to create their own visibility-facilitating slope. As the front row occupants sank ankle-deep into the mud, those behind stood tall on the slightly drier back turf to peek over. Kids, meanwhile, would crawl under the perimeter cable to gain a point-blank view of the action. That is where the groundsmen, brothers Charlie and Ned Massey, came in handy. Anything the Doughtys did in the goalmouth, the landscaping siblings replicated all around the pitch boundaries as they shoved the encroachers behind the wire. At least this gave the Masseys some work. With the paucity of grass, there wasn't much else for them to do, I would imagine, except perhaps maintain the pitch puddles at a hydraulic equilibrium.

If you assumed that was bad enough, spare a thought for the players. Not only did the poor sods have to compete in that quagmire, but, to get there in the first place, they also had to walk half a mile from the clubhouse at Shears Hotel where the dressing rooms were located. It would be interesting to know whether this recurring inconvenience was the reason Irishman Pat O'Donnell did not hang around too long. Yet despite all these complications, Newton Heath loved playing at North Road. Their dream was for every match to be held at Monsall and, for a two-month period from mid-December, they got to act out their fantasy. After losing 0-1 at Astley Bridge, Heath played nine consecutive home games. Even the Manchester Senior Cup draw was a willing partner and of those nine fixtures only one was lost while seven were won. The first visitors were Leek who (ahem) leaked three goals. Jack Doughty netted the first and was heavily involved in the third, scored by Tait while Leek's keeper received Jack's 'special attention'. That was a refined way of saying he was bulldozed into a flat humanoid form and had to be resuscitated. On New Year's Eve, London Casuals were beaten 2-1 with a signature Newton Heath winner – the orchestrated penalty area mêlée. This is when a brutish pack of Heathens converge on the goalmouth and bundle ball and bystanders past the line in a whirlwind of blurred furore.

Two days into the New Year, Heath's winner was again controversial, supplied this time by ex-captain Sam Black. He may have been representing Burton Wanderers, of course, but, for the sake of the good old days, he headed the ball into his own goal. Or was it over the bar, as Black fervently insisted? Being the honest gentleman that he was, Black's word should have stood. But the referee was hearing none of it and, this being a time before goal nets, ruled it a goal and helped Heath win 2-1.

On January 14th, Newton Heath required just a 70-minute

run-out to gain revenge on Astley Bridge with a 3-0 bashing. Although the Doughtys supplied all the goals, it was Tom Hay who collected the midget of the match award with an assortment of blinding saves. How on earth could Hay have been so good? This, remember, was a man who would have had to look up to Paul Scholes! I can visualize him aping up and down the goal in that fragmented way of old newsreels, stopping anything hurled in his direction. Or perhaps it was a reflection of the inadequacies of contemporary opposition forwards. Otherwise we would have to proclaim Hay as (inch-for-inch) the greatest keeper in history.

Soon the Manchester Cup came around and it was time for Manchester City's great grandfathers, Gorton, to start bricking it with flashbacks of last year's 11-1 nightmare. Luckily, the draw spared them on this occasion. Not as fortunate were Gorton Villa who had also been administered a spanking of their own in 1887. Quivering, they made their way to North Road one backward step at a time. When they got to the ground, they were welcomed by the sight of Jack Doughty repetitively banging his shoulders against the wall in preparation for the tie. That was it. To hell with the Cup - Newton Heath could have the forfeit! A friendly match was all they could handle. Heath still beat them 8-1.

Wully Tait bagged a hat-trick in that rout and then he added two more goals when Bell's Temperance lost 4-2 a fortnight later. Gotheridge notched the other two goals. Jack Doughty's name was also on the score sheet that afternoon, but he was 25 miles away

WALES, v ENGLAND, CREWE FEB 2ND, 1888
Wales were full of Heathens when they met England on February 2nd, 1888: Joe Davies (top, 3rd right), Jack Powell (top, 2nd right), Bill Owen (front, 1st right), and Jack Doughty (front, 2nd right).

in Crewe representing Wales against England. Jack Powell and Joe Davies showed they were genuine mates by keeping him company.

MIND GAMES

ON FEBRUARY 11TH, 1888, Newton Heath ventured away from Monsall at long last. Doughty, Powell, and Davies had returned from Crewe with exotic tales of green grass, rolling balls, and gentle falls. The Heathens were enchanted. Off they set to Crewe taking with them 300 enthusiastic fans. Grass was not the major attraction, of course, as there was always extra interest in matches against teams from rival railway outposts. The two sets of fans must have enjoyed some extended banter for there were no goal distractions during the game. Not as much interest was shown the following weekend. In fact, Heath did not even pack enough players for the trip to Oswaldtwistle Rovers, arriving there with just ten men. Perhaps the absent Gotheridge had a premonition that this was going to be the sort of day that comes every once in a while when no matter how hard you try, you can do no right. In the circumstances, the short-handed Heath fell 0-6, which was good enough to register their worst shellacking since December 1883. Tom Hay had a miserable afternoon, the glowing praise of the previous pages apparently going to his head. However, he still remained the club's main custodian, for in a land of Roches, he was a Stepney. His understudy, mind, was not a bad stopgap; at least according to his games to goals against ratio. James Pedley was a Mancunian who joined Heath in 1886 at 25 years of age. For four years he soldiered on in the reserves while remaining ready to block first team shots when called upon. His final figures were an impressive 15 matches played and only 12 goals conceded.

The rut continued for two more weeks culminating in a 1-2 home defeat against Blackburn Olympic. The management was miffed at having to play without four starters as Powell, Davies, and the Doughtys were away representing Wales. The Newton Heath-lite selection thought they had done enough to earn a 1-1 draw until Olympic snatched a late winner. Mr. Attock and his committee may have calmed down sooner or later but chose later after the Welsh boys came back bragging about record wins. Wales had pummelled Ireland 11-0 with Roger Doughty scoring twice and Jack getting four! His last goal even came after three of his team-mates had run off to catch an early train back to their respective clubs. This was the missing spark to fire Mr. Attock's ire, and he kick-started the 'us-against-them' approach a full century before Sir Alex Ferguson's mind games began with that infamous 'choking on their own vomit' Anfield rant. The outburst had its desired effect: Heath's match was cancelled the following weekend as Wales took part in their final British Championship international against Scotland. It was a good job too as five Heathens with Welsh blood were called up: Powell, Davies, Burke, and the Doughty brothers. But wait! Two other members of the principality's selection, George Owen and Di Jones, would transfer to Monsall within the next few months. With seven current or future Heathens in the line-up, you could almost claim this as a Newton Heath fixture. Yet you shouldn't – Heath were no international team and they certainly had nothing to do with a 5-1 Scotland victory!

Bearing in mind the Welsh team's composition, there was a fifty-fifty chance their goal was obtained by a Newton Heath player. And so it was as Jack Doughty (who else?) scored his sixth goal of this year's Home Championship to finish as top scorer. This was actually a magnificent achievement by Jack. In the entire history of the British Championship, which went on for 100 years, his tally of six goals in one season was only surpassed twice, and

WALES V IRELAND, WREXHAM, MARCH 3RD, 1888.
*The Welsh team that trounced Ireland 11-0 included 5 current or future Heathens:
Joe Davies (back, 2nd left), Jack Powell (back 2nd right), Di Jones (back 1st right), Jack Doughty (front, centre), and Roger Doughty (front, 2nd right).*

only just. On both occasions it took a legendary striker to reach seven goals: Hughie Gallagher for Scotland in 1927 and Jimmy Greaves for England in 1961.

At least the end of the international matches settled the club v country issue for the time being. The Heathens could now focus on cups rather than caps, what with the Manchester Cup second round coming up next. Hooley Hill should be complimented on their bravery. They had been battered 7-0 in the corresponding tie last season but, unlike Gorton Villa, they did not scratch upon returning to the crime scene. Their reward was a pat on the back for courage and another 7-0 beating. An envious Rawtenstall arrived at North Road the following week begging for the same treatment Hooley Hill had been afforded. Heath gladly obliged with a replica 7-0 win. Joe Davies, Jack Doughty, and brother Roger netted a brace each while Wright was stuck with the odd one. His own moment, however, would come on April 7th when he grabbed Heath's only goal at mighty Burnley. It was the first time the club had scored away from home since December 10th. But there was bad news: Burnley scored seven! No wonder the Heathens preferred to play in muddy Monsall. The moral of the story was that you couldn't go around putting seven goals past everyone because eventually someone will do the same to you. Newton Heath had had a taste of their own medicine and it was so bitter it put them off tasting any more defeats for six months.

FRANKENSTEIN

It would not be spring in Victorian Manchester without Newton Heath powering their way to their customary place in the city's Senior Cup final. Hurst were defeated in the semis with a goal apiece from the Barging Brothers. This would turn out to be Heath's last ever meeting with their old rivals. The separation was by mutual consent. Hurst were happy with a life in the slums whereas Heath sought to experience a new world. Incidentally, in the very same week and just a few miles away, a whole new world was being created behind Heath's back. Directors from a dozen different clubs met at the Royal Hotel in Piccadilly, Manchester, to announce the formation of the Football League. It had all started with an Aston Villa suit named William McGregor. He'd had enough of the friendly nature of soccer and craved a cut-throat league where bigger gates made for fatter wallets. Five giants of the game went to the initial meeting in March: Villa, Blackburn, Bolton, W.B.A., and Preston. After adding up the available weekends of the season then subtracting sufficient dates for the FA and County Cups, they concluded there was enough room left for a 12-club league. Now they had to find the parts for their Frankenstein.

How do you determine the best clubs to put in a league when no such previous league existed by which to gauge them? Apart from reviewing recent cup performances, the selection process was so random it might possibly have been conducted using the eeny-meeny-miny-moe method. Accrington won the Lancashire Cup in 1888, so they were invited. A team was needed from Nottingham, so old Notts County was preferred to the still-amateur Forest. Likewise, Stoke City were picked to represent the Potteries.

But what about the club in whose backyard the ultimate meeting took place? If Manchester was deemed big enough to convene in, surely its leading team should be worthy of consideration. The heavy loss at Burnley aside, Newton Heath's recent record against these fancy outfits included victories against Accrington and Bolton as well as an earlier draw with the Clarets. The Mancunians had improved steadily in their ten years of existence. They now boasted some prominent names in the game like Jack Powell and, of course, Jack Doughty who revelled in the limelight, especially considering he spent his whole week underground in a mine somewhere. The Football League, however, were not too dazzled with Heath's minimal FA and Lancashire Cup involvement, and they sheepishly sneaked out of town while avoiding eye contact. It couldn't have possibly been Heath's age – Derby County had only been around for four years and had yet to go anywhere in the FA Cup. And, with some due respect: Stoke? About the only thing going for them was that they were an old club, yet they would be over a century old before they won their first and only major trophy: the League Cup! But Heath were not the biggest club given the cold shoulder. The likes of Sheffield Wednesday and Darwen were also frozen out. And play a sad, little violin for Sunderland who discovered the harsh truth of the estate agent's maxim 'location, location, location'. The League deemed excursions to Wearside too pricey for their taste.

Newton Heath did not sulk, though, at being overlooked. Privately, they were perhaps hurt while, deep down, they might have known they were not yet of the required standard. Nonetheless, their immediate reaction was to go out and make sure they would never again be passed over when it came to historic footballing creations. Bolton were confined to a 3-3 draw whereas Derby Midland were trounced 6-1 just for sounding like Derby County. Then, in May, three of those crack 'original members' were invited to parade their silky skills at Monsall. Preston were lucky to muster a draw in front of the Heathens' first five-figure crowd (at least the gates at North Road were Football League-sized); Wolverhampton and Aston Villa, meanwhile, were both rolled over. Those three guests, coincidentally, would occupy the top three spots at the end of the first Football League season. The winner against Aston Villa came from Poland, not the country but rather an inside-right with the first initial 'F'. Born in Dundee, he had recently arrived from Burnley while fellow Scot Wully Tait travelled in the opposite direction. Poland would soon return to Turf Moor and score in Burnley's opening League match. For symmetry's sake, Wully would subsequently rejoin the Green-and-Golds.

While his short spell away proved fruitful, Wully Tait missed out on playing in the Manchester Cup final. Newton Heath appeared in their fourth annual final when they faced Denton at Whalley Range on April 28th. The stands were packed with around 8,000 spectators but there was still room for little Tom Hay. Heath's goalie was prohibited from appearing in this competition by the small print of the complicated rules that governed professionalism. Pedley was selected in his place but the Heathens need not have worried. Peter Schmeichel once controversially stated that Manchester United's defence was so good in the early Nineties that they could have won with a dustbin in goal. Similarly, the 1888 Manchester Cup final was so one-sided Pedley's name was not mentioned in the match report except in the line-up. Denton did score a goal but it was a complete fluke. Brumley lumped the ball up-field and the wind carried it all the way into the Heath goal, much to the amusement of everybody present. Barring, that is, the embarrassed Pedley who probably wished the ground would swallow him up at that very moment.

The rest of Heath's line-up was mostly first-choice. The

defenders and midfielders would each make over 40 appearances in the season: Powell, Mitchell, Burke, J. Davies, and J. Owen. The only change in attack was John Earp, who was back in flavour after Tait's departure. He was joined up front by Wright, the Doughtys, and Gotheridge. It was a selection too hot for Denton to handle as Heath achieved a record Manchester Cup final score of 7-1. All seven goals were made in Wales. Tom Burke opened the scoring as late as the 40th minute and Joe Davies also netted once. Jack Doughty illuminated the final with a second-half hat-trick to help bring his season's total to 26 goals. Roger, on the other hand, split his brace on either side of the interval on his way to an overall tally of 29 goals. Between them, the Doughtys managed 55 strikes – an astonishing figure that goes a long way towards endorsing violence on the football field. And it could possibly be more since six goals remain untraced to date.

Heath had certainly made scoring simple this season, rattling in a tidy total of 115. The Doughtys were not the only prolific ones. When they were preoccupied barging opposition defenders, the likes of Tait and Gotheridge took advantage to score 15 and 13 goals respectively. Even Wright and Davies claimed eight each. Newton Heath were the top club in Manchester again, and Powell and his men let everyone know with a rowdy bus tour across the city, cup in tow. The plucky team from the railway tracks was packed with internationals now, the Heathens collecting more caps than any other club in the world that year. And if all that could not get them into the haughty Football League, it at least allowed them access into the next best thing, as we shall see in a very short while.

1888–89

THE FOOTBALL COMBINATION

"Like any uncharted territory,
I must seem greatly intriguing,
But you, you're not allowed,
You're uninvited,
An unfortunate slight".

So SANG ALANIS Morissette in her single **Uninvited**. While the Football League didn't commission Ms. Morissette, this message of exclusion would have been an accurate measure of the feelings of Heath supporters in the summer of 1888. As unjustly treated as the Heathens may have felt at being 'uninvited', this was no time for mourning. Instead, it would be more fitting to put away the sackcloth and ashes, bring out the confetti, and light the birthday candles. Newton Heath were ten years old! Yes, the seed that sprang from a railway depot in 1878 was now a fully-grown club – except, perhaps, for Tom Hay. While the past decade had seemed like a really long time to the class of 1888, few could have imagined that the story would still be continuing more than a century later. It is a measure of Heath's progress that they felt so hard done by when the League overlooked them, and embarking on a period of soul-searching would have been totally justifiable. But Heath had barely started searching when they found what they were looking for. It was the ideal calling.

Have you been ignored by an elitist league? Feeling disappointed and betrayed? Are you longing to be included in such a chummy coalition? To you, I present: the Football Combination! It is a replica of the Football League, purposely formed to cater for the best of the rest. This may have been Crewe Alexandra director JG Hall's sales pitch. He had observed what William McGregor and his pals had done and realized he could do the same. One of the

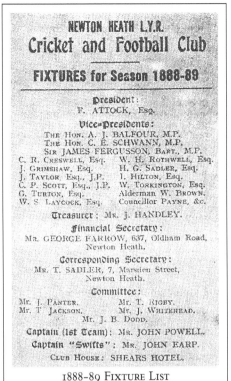

NEWTON HEATH L.Y.R.
Cricket and Football Club
FIXTURES for Season 1888-89

president:
F. ATTOCK, Esq.

Vice=presidents:
THE HON. A. J. BALFOUR, M.P.
THE HON. C. E. SCHWANN, M.P.
SIR JAMES FERGUSSON, BART., M.P.
C. R. CRESWELL, Esq.   W. H. ROTHWELL, Esq.
J. GRIMSHAW, Esq.   H. G. SADLER, Esq.
J. TAYLOR, Esq., J.P.   I. HILTON, Esq.
C. P. SCOTT, Esq., J.P.   W. TORKINGTON, Esq.
G. TURTON, Esq.   Alderman W. BROWN.
W. S LAYCOCK, Esq.   Councillor PAYNE, &c.

Treasurer: MR. J. HANDLEY.

Financial Secretary:
MR. GEORGE FARROW, 637, Oldham Road,
Newton Heath.

Corresponding Secretary:
MR. T. SADLER, 7, Marsden Street,
Newton Heath.

Committee:
Mr. J. PANTER.   Mr. T. RIGBY.
Mr. T JACKSON.   Mr. J. WHITEHEAD.
Mr. J. B. DODD.

Captain (1st Team): MR. JOHN POWELL.
Captain "Swifts": MR. JOHN EARP.
Club House: SHEARS HOTEL.

1888-89 FIXTURE LIST
The cover page showing the club's dignitaries.

first names he contacted was Newton Heath; good lad, Hall. And so, just 10 days after the Original Twelve had launched the Football League at Manchester's Royal Hotel, the Duplicate Eleven met at the Royal Hotel, Crewe, on April 27th to announce their own Football Combination.

It was almost perfect. In addition to Heath and Crewe, there were the likes of Blackburn Olympic, Burslem Port Vale, and Small Heath Alliance (now Birmingham City). All they needed was to add one more member and they would have had themselves a competition to rival the Football League. Mr. Hall, however, was a very nice man, God rest his soul. When Birmingham St. George's, Derby Junction, and Halliwell got wind of this new league, they wanted in. Mr. Hall politely accepted. Then other clubs came knocking too and, by the time Mr. Hall had summoned enough self-esteem to say 'no', the number had swelled to 20! Now, in these days of the Premier League, such a figure is considered the norm. Yet way back then when no previous template existed to help manage such a competition, a bloated league was as ill-conceived as a zebra named Spot. The Combination had goofed before a ball had been hoofed. But when they attempted to sort this out, they only blundered further.

A Birmingham St. George's suit, Mr. H. Mitchell, was elected president. Here was a man who could write a thesis on incompetence then finish it off by dotting the t's and crossing the i's. No meeting of the twenty clubs was deemed necessary. Since home-and-away matches against everybody else were impractical, teams were encouraged to devise their own fixture lists. The actual number of said fixtures was purely optional, as long as it reached or exceeded eight. And only one contemporary league table was ever issued for the benefit of the keen few remotely mesmerized by the title race.

As we shall see, the Football Combination was not destined for a long journey. But there was one thing that can never be taken away from it. On September 1st, 1888, its first week of action saw Blackburn Olympic and Darwen draw 1-1, Long Eaton Rangers win 3-1 at Grimsby Town, and Burslem Port Vale defeat Birmingham St. George's 2-1. The Football League's first set of matches took place on September 8th making the Football Combination the oldest league in the world. The Football League may have been formed before and is the oldest league in existence today, but the Combination was the earliest to have a ball kicked in anguish. And, although Newton Heath were busy elsewhere on that opening afternoon, they were destined to play a very prominent part in it.

FRIENDLY FIRE

The Combination had elevated Newton Heath to the status they felt they deserved and now their attention turned to finding the optimal combination of Heathens to compete in it. Equipped with the added pull that being Manchester Cup holders brings, Heath contacted Grimsby Town seeking to sign Macbeth and Dave Riddoch. Both players declined. But the committee had no fear, not as long as Wales was near. When all else failed, the Heathens had to just swing by the principality and pick up an international or two.

A new left-back was needed. J. Mitchell, the incumbent of the last three and a half years, had joined Wully Tait and F. Poland in an exodus to the Promised Land of the Football League. Mitchell went to Bolton Wanderers and a historic role in the inaugural weekend of league football, while the other two ended up in Burnley. As ever, Mitchell's replacement was cherry-picked from Chirk's fertile fields, twenty-one-year-old David 'Di' Jones was

Chirk's captain, no less, and already an international player. He hailed from Trefonen and started out with Oswestry before moving to Chirk where he had won the Welsh Cup in the previous two seasons. Di was a refined full-back – diving in was not for him preferring to time his tackles. Unfortunately for Heath, Jones did not stay long at Monsall, choosing to dive-in when Bolton came calling. He would spend a decade there, mostly as captain, before returning to Manchester for a worthy stint with City. A winner of 14 caps, Jones gave his life to football… literally. He gashed his knee in a close season friendly in 1902. A few days later, the wound turned septic and 'Di' died.

On the contrary, Bill Owen lived a very long life. Yet, of his 85 years on earth, only two months were allocated to Monsall. He had signed for Newton Heath last September, of course, only to return to Chirk for the remainder of the season. This summer, he stopped by to check on his young brother Jack, and he was able to squeeze in three games before completing a return trip home.

Almost all of Heath's new signings for 1888-89 seemed to fall into the short-term category. Inside-forward Walton's spell at North Road was so brief nothing is known about him except that he appeared in four Combination fixtures, scored two goals, and moved on, possibly into the Football League. E. Kirkham was another temp at inside-forward. In three months with the club, he played ten matches and almost scored in every one of them: almost on his debut, almost in the next match, almost in the one after, etc… The only new face to last until the end of the campaign was that of J. Gale, and that is only because the striker had come in for a trial at the end of the previous season and seen what he was in for.

Before starting their Combination programme, Heath played two friendly matches against high-profile opposition. For Bolton and Blackburn, these were their last respective games before embarking on their Football League odyssey. It was also one final opportunity to get shown up by the men from Monsall. Or should that be Cymru? There was something palpably peculiar about Heath's line-up for these two games. The goalkeeper was English and so were two of the forwards. But that was it. All other eight players were imported from Wales: Burke, Davies, J. Doughty, R. Doughty, Jones, B. Owen, J. Owen, and Powell. You could be forgiven for mistaking the line-up for Cardiff's phone directory. A club record seven of these men were full internationals whereas the odd one out, Jack Owen, would later earn himself a cap.

The friendly against Bolton had other topics of interest. It was the first day of September. The sunshine sprayed the Manchester skies; traces of grass were detectable on the North Road pitch; and Tom Hay was sweating ale from every pore. The Heath keeper and his right-back, Jack Powell, had their work cut out trying to keep their old club at bay. Coincidentally, and this was no misprint in the programme, Bolton's own goalie and right full-back were ex-Heathens. As mentioned J. Mitchell had moved to Bolton in search of the big time only to find out it all started back at North Road. Behind him between the sticks stood Charlie Harrison, a Heathen by birth, who had made one previous appearance for his hometown outfit. The opponents on that occasion in April 1887? Bolton, of course. Moreover in the peculiarity department, the Wanderers' skipper, Roberts, was also a Welshman. It can be assumed the Newton Heath directors had no idea, though, otherwise they would have signed him. Curiously, it was left to an everyday Englishman, Gotheridge, to score the only goal of the match. The 'Prance of Wales', Jack Doughty himself, was otherwise engaged in reacquainting Harrison with Heath's techniques. Without a valid motive, except perhaps for old times' sake, he ran up to Bolton's keeper and socked him one. That may have been Jack's default setting, but the referee nonetheless cautioned him for his exertions.

Blackburn Rovers were also defeated a week later by two goals to one, thanks to a Jack Owen double. This meant that in their last four matches, encompassing the end of the previous season and the beginning of this, Newton Heath had beaten Wolves, Aston Villa, Bolton, and Blackburn. All four would finish in the top five spots when the first Football League campaign concluded, right behind champions Preston. It was the most telling confirmation that Newton Heath had perhaps been admitted into the wrong league.

Newton Heath's first Football Combination game took place on September 15th, 1888, against Walsall Town Swifts, but you would not have known that from the match report. With no fixture list released confusion set in. It was hard for journalists to tell whether a particular dual was in the Combination, a friendly, or a game of tiddlywinks. Consequently, Heath's opening match as well as the third tussle against Gainsborough Trinity are often listed as friendlies. It wasn't until late November that a considerate reporter gave a detailed breakdown of Heath's statistics. Only then did it emerge that the club were as much as eight matches into their Combination programme.

And they were doing quite well too. Walsall were beaten 2-1 in front of 3,000 fans at North Road. Heath's historic line-up was: Hay; Powell, J. Owen; Burke, Davies, R. Doughty; B. Owen, Walton, J. Doughty, Gale, and Gotheridge. Gale notched both goals.

The following weekend, Jack Doughty finally scored his first goal of the season, and his second, and his third. The accommodating Darwen defence thus negated their attack's good work to tilt a seven-goal thriller Heath's way. Playing away at Gainsborough did not faze Jack. He grabbed two goals in a 5-1 win. The Heathens did allow for a couple of draws at Derby Midland and Burslem Port Vale, but poor Leek had to pay for that. Heath won 4-1 at North Road and 5-0 at Leek's patch where another Jack hat-trick took his tally to nine goals in six Combination fixtures. His legend was spreading.

A couple of familiar faces had re-appeared in Newton Heath's line-up by now. In his match report of the opening day tussle with Bolton, the reporter had remarked that Heath had obtained a better player in Di Jones than they had in J. Mitchell. Apparently the eagle-eyed Wanderers directors had noted that observation and hatched a cunning plan to make an 'even' exchange with their Heathen counterparts. Jones headed west and, in early October, Mitchell appeared over the horizon, but he did not brag too much about his Football League exploits. After his two matches saw Wanderers ship 10 goals, he realized the Football League was not the competition for him. In his second and final match, he was in direct opposition to his old Heathen team-mate Wully Tait, now of Burnley. Conspiracy or not, Tait was allowed all the freedom he needed to tuck in three goals. This bestowed upon Tait the honour of being the scorer of the first ever hat-trick in the Football League, or in any current league in the world for that matter. Mitchell no doubt received a thankful pat on the back for his permissive role. Despite bagging five goals in his short spell at Turf Moor, Tait would soon be off. By mid-October, he was back at Monsall just

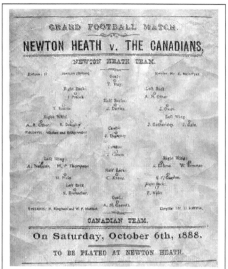

PROGRAMME V CANADIANS.
Newton Heath's longest surviving programme.
It commemorates the day in October 1888
when a Canadian touring team became
Manchester United's first foreign opposition.

like Mitchell.

CANADIANS IN MANCHESTER

MITCHELL MADE IT back in time for an historic Newton Heath match. Just in time – his name wasn't even printed on the programme. The reason I know that is because to this very day it remains Heath's (and Manchester United's) earliest surviving programme. It marks a special occasion too: Heath's first international opposition. A team of Canadian footballers were touring Britain and now stopped at Monsall. It was not until 1951 that Old Trafford hosted its first foreign visitors – unless you count the German bombs of a decade earlier – but North Road welcomed them as early as October 6th, 1888. And they were a crack side too, composed of the best players from all over Canada. They were wealthy men, four of whom went on to become doctors, here to face the fitters and boilermakers of Newton Heath.

The match could have provided Heath's earliest team photograph but it hasn't survived the intervening century. And to think that kick-off was delayed by 20 minutes, with the Canadians idling about, as the Heathen posers figured out their best angles! The 7,000 fans who packed North Road at threepence a head did not show such disrespect to the guests though. They enthusiastically applauded the Canadians onto the field and the early Red masses were already showing their appreciation of the vistor's good football which the Heathens struggled to match. This was, after all, an ever-changing line-up. The left-back slot alone was seeing its fifth different occupant in five games. After Di Jones' departure, mediocrities such as Benfield and Watson had been tried in one Combination match apiece, before Mitchell's return. There was another blank spot in the programme and that was filled by Bridgewater for his solitary 90 minutes of fame. The full line-up was: Hay; Powell, Mitchell; Burke, Davies, J. Owen; Bridgewater, R. Doughty, J. Doughty, Gale, and Gotheridge. The Canadian XI capitalised on the Heathens' inconsistency to triumph 2-0 and hand them their first defeat in six months. On top of taking away their host's 14-match unbeaten run, the Canadians also walked away with a cool half of the £100 gate receipts.

INVINCIBLE

DOMESTICALLY, Newton Heath were still untouchable, no doubt aided by not having to take on any more huge countries. Interest was intensifying in their quest for the Football Combination title. However, a new problem appeared on November 17th when the first Combination commitment was broken. Also-rans Halliwell concluded they were financially better off playing a friendly match than showing up at Birmingham St. George's. The Combination committee had warned that clubs could be penalized for breaking fixtures but, without 'sticks and stones', Halliwell weren't too bothered. Newton Heath had a friendly of their own that day, against West Manchester, but no one told Jack Doughty. The hostile host nabbed a hat-trick to steer his side to a 5-0 victory. A week later, Halliwell were scheduled for a Combination game at North Road. When kick-off time came and they had not yet arrived, there were concerns for the existence of the Combination. Eventually, the visitors turned up over half an hour late to the cheers of North Road's patient crowd, but there was only time left for a 35-minute-per-half match with no break. Goals from Roger Doughty and Wully Tait gave Heath a 2-0 victory though we have to take the players' word for that: the last quarter hour was played out in total darkness! The supporters, as in so many other cases since, were blindly following.

The media were now more excited than a compass near the North Pole. Heath were leaders of the Combination race. When they defeated Bootle on the first day of December, the press declared the Heathens 'Champions of the Combination'. It was, of course, a premature coronation. Since teams were required to play a minimum of eight matches, observers assumed the Combination was drawing to a close. Besides, there had never been a league competition before, so no one was familiar with how a championship was won. The 20 clubs had each contested a varying number of fixtures and there were still more left. The only thing that was certain was that Newton Heath boasted the best record so far. They had won seven of their nine matches and drawn the other two. They were developing into a top outfit, one of the best association teams, the media reckoned. Their record against Football League sides was quite decent. 1888-89 was the season of Preston's 'Invincibles', but that description was rendered erroneous when they visited North Road in February. In fact, had Heath been League members in that inaugural campaign, they probably would have comfortably finished in mid-table, they were that good. Of course, Heath would eventually join the elite in 1892. By that time, however, the gap would have widened between the 'Originals' and the newcomers, and a much-changed Heath would struggle to survive.

The 1888-89 vintage were a tasty batch though. To start with, the players were useful and the team was jam-packed with characters. Jack Powell's dominant aura came complete with the crowd-pleasing ability to bollock his team-mates at full volume. Tom Burke was one of those creatures who were always right. Tom Hay played like a man possessed ... by all types of spirits. And then, of course, there was the fearsome Jack Doughty, the goal ghoul. In the return Combination fixture with Bootle, the opposition temporarily left the field complaining about Jack's overzealous vigour. Indeed, being shoulder-barged by Jack when visiting Newton Heath was the second worst thing that could possibly happen to you – aside from being tied down to the nearby railway track before an LYR train.

When the Doughtys got a goal each to help beat West Manchester 2-1 in the Manchester Senior Cup on December 15th, Heath were unbeaten in their last 13 competitive matches. The previous competitive defeat was a year and a half before against the same opponents in the same tournament's final. That actually was their one and only loss in 24 competitive fixtures (Manchester

Cup, FA Cup, and Combination) dating back to April 1885.

Heath's next Combination commitment was three weeks away. Time would surely pass by faster if they could arrange friendlies whenever possible: Christmas Eve, Christmas Day, Boxing Day, New Year's Eve, and New Year's Day, not to forget weekends too. There were all sorts of games. Third Lanark Rifle Volunteers became Monsall's first visitors from Scotland, with Hearts one day too late. Darwen Old Wanderers lived up to their name. It took them so long to limp to North Road there was barely time left for 45 minutes of football and a solitary Jack Doughty hat-trick. Results varied from the 13-1 thrashing of Davenham, when the reporters lost track of the scorers, to a 1-6 loss at Wolves in the third match inside 48 hours. But the most glamorous encounter took place on December 29th when the famous amateur team, Corinthians, stopped by. The match pitted five Welsh internationals against as many England representatives, including the full-backs with the timely initials, brothers AM and PM Walters. The Corinthians – football's answer to the Globetrotters – cruised to a 4-0 triumph. That wasn't too bad, actually. When they returned in 1905, they handed Manchester United their worst defeat to this day.

UNOFFICIAL CHAMPIONS…

ON JANUARY 5TH, 1889, Preston North End battered Notts County 4-1 to become the first champions of England. They still had three matches left to play but their season-long unbeaten run meant they could no longer be caught. Up until that morning, Newton Heath had replicated Preston's invincibility over in the Football Combination. By the afternoon, the symmetry ceased. Playing eight friendlies in 12 days sure beats training, though it also breeds spraining. Heath arrived at Darwen for a Combination fixture with only eight fit men, which is never a good portent of invincibility. Powell and Gotheridge were missing, and so was Jack Doughty, whose omission was equivalent to taking the warhead out of the nuclear missile. The club staff trawled through the reserve team and rustled up one Major and an Ashworth. Heath were still a man short. The only viable solution was to borrow someone from the crowd! Anyone. League experience was optional, and he didn't even have to be Welsh. Eventually, a very fortunate nobody named Eccles was randomly picked to turn out for the team that would later be called Manchester United. He proved to be a lucky charm… for Darwen. They won 6-0.

Fresh blood was needed. In an unprecedented step, Heath turned to Wales for players… Surnamed Owen, plying his trade with Chirk, and Welsh-capped, the new inside-left met all the specifications that Heath looked for in a potential signing. George Owen was not related to Jack and Bill. He did belong, though, to another pair of Owen siblings who wore Chirk's colours around the same time. His brother, Harry, was the only one of the Owen quartet who hadn't tried his luck in Monsall. Their father had passed away while they were still young and Harry – four years George's senior – always preferred to stay behind to care for their mother and even younger brother. Similarly, George was a Chirk man through and through. No matter where they sold him, he always found his way back home. By the time he retired in 1896, he had been through more spells at Chirk than the town's resident wizard.

George had already represented Wales twice, and he would play a couple more times this season. When he finally grabbed a hat-trick against Ireland in 1893, they never picked him again! He also had a habit of getting his name on the score sheet in Welsh Cup finals, doing so in three of the four finals he appeared in.

George was anxious to make an instant impact at Newton Heath. He scored on his debut – a friendly defeat at Sheffield Wednesday – and also in a Combination fixture against Burslem Port Vale, when Heath finally fielded a full set of first-teamers. The days of crowd loanees were over. Hay, Powell, Mitchell, Burke, Davies, J. Owen, Tait, R. Doughty, J. Doughty, G. Owen, and Gale secured a 3-0 victory. Bootle and Derby Midland were swept aside next as Heath consolidated their favourable Combination record. But things were not going alright in the competition in general.

Back in January, Blackburn Olympic decided they had had enough of the professional world altogether and reverted to amateur status. Moreover, they simply stopped participating in any Combination matches. Other clubs caught the lazy bug and started skipping odd commitments. With the increase in broken fixtures came a decrease in attendances. By April 5th, the committee had given up and the Football Combination was disbanded. Any funds left were donated to a charity in Derby.

Newton Heath's last Combination match had taken place on March 30th when they surprisingly lost 0-1 at home to South Shore, bringing to an end a run of sixteen consecutive, competitive home wins stretching back to 1883. Word was not apparently passed on to one newspaper writer who covered the return fixture a fortnight later. He earnestly reported on a 2-2 draw unaware the game had been upgraded to a friendly. When the dust had finally settled and the maid had come to clean up, it transpired that Newton Heath had the best record of the 20 sides. They had collected 22 points from 14 matches. Although Notts Rangers had one more point, they had played two extra games. Newton Heath were thus crowned unofficial 'Football Combination Champions' based on a superior point percentage. This method had to be used since the funny-looking final table showed teams had completed a varying number of games. Blackburn Olympic stopped at five whereas Burslem apparently stamped 'Combination' on all their outings and ended with 25.

The Football Combination was ultimately deemed a failure, and historians have tended to overlook it altogether in their accounts. Yet it did serve a significant purpose, apart from drawing a certain degree of prestige Heath's way. The clubs involved had acquired a taste for competition, learned from the experience, and would soon bounce back with a vastly improved and consequential version. Also, following Manchester United 2009 Premiership triumph, it could be claimed that the club has reached the magical number of 19 league titles rather than the 18 that is conventionally recorded...

AND CUP WINNERS

ONE TROPHY WAS out of the way but there was one more to go. The Manchester Senior Cup already resided in Newton Heath's trophy cabinet, and that is where they intended to keep it. The second round draw brought the newly-named Ardwick to North Road but the Heathens instantly recognised them. They had visited Monsall two years earlier under the guise of Gorton when they were walloped 11-1. They had obviously improved in the interim for they only lost 1-4 on this occasion. Manchester City's old-timers were still Heath's whipping boys. The semi-final opponents, on the other hand, left the Heathens in awe. Here they were in their shiny green-and-gold attire parading six Welshmen only to discover the opposition's entire selection came from Wales! So many men had left the principality to reside in the city that they were able to form their own team: Manchester Welsh. It took goals from two of their compatriots – Jacks Owen and Doughty – to secure a 2-1 victory for Heath.

All of which meant that for the fifth year running, Newton Heath were in the Manchester Cup final. On April 27th, they travelled the well-known road to Whalley Range where a crowd of 4,000 awaited. The line-up was as follows: Pedley; Powell, Mitchell; Burke, Davies, J. Owen; Tait, R. Doughty, J. Doughty, Gale, and Gotheridge.

The challengers this year were Hooley Hill who again looked familiar. They had actually faced Heath in this competition in the past two seasons and lost 0-7 both times. But now they were finalists, proudly representing the city, standing shoulder to shoulder with the cup holders themselves. Newton Heath again beat them 7-0! Final or not, that is what Heath always did against Hill, so thought Jack Doughty as he banged a hat-trick to go with the one he got in last year's final. Back then, the Heathens had defeated Denton 7-1, so now they had set a record score for the final. Gale played his part with two goals, including one straight from the kick-off, while Gotheridge and Roger Doughty chipped in with one each. For their part, Hooley Hill did threaten, heading just over on one occasion, whereas Heath's keeper, Pedley, was at least twice called upon to make saves. Tom Hay was ineligible as always as Newton Heath secured the double.

Indeed, the Heathens had proven themselves the best in all competitions in which they participated in 1888-89. They would probably have gone for the Merseyside Cup as well had they been permitted to. They did, in fact, pit their skills against Merseyside's only team, Everton, during that month, only to lose 1-3. That loss, however, can be attributed to Jack Doughty, Joe Davies, and George Owen being over at the Racecourse Ground, Wrexham, where they pitted their particular skills against Scotland in Welsh colours. The principality's next match coincided with the Manchester Cup final and was consequently skipped by Doughty and Davies as they put the finishing touches on Hooley Hill's hiding. George Owen, although cup-tied, still could not have the afternoon off as he was busy getting capped in Ireland.

Apart from collecting trophies, Newton Heath also figured out a way of defeating Preston's 'Invincibles'. It was a simple plan, really: stop when you're ahead! In a friendly on February 23rd, the Heathens led 1-0 through a Jack Doughty goal. With seven minutes still to go, the 8,000 fans packed inside North Road could not contain their excitement any longer. They kept encroaching onto the field forcing the referee to blow early. A re-match took place in May when Jack again scored only for Preston to grab a goal of their own. The 1-1 draw suited both teams – Preston could boast they were untouchable over 90 minutes whereas Heath showed they could hold their own against the best club side in the world.

Another noteworthy encounter took place on February 26th and it was for a good cause: to raise money for the families of victims of an explosion at Hyde Colliery, a nearby mine where 23 people had died. A measure of Heath's status was that the only selection deemed suitable enough to face them was a representative side drawn from various teams in Manchester, such as Ardwick, Denton, and Hyde. A club record 12,000 fans crammed into Belle Vue stadium to watch Newton Heath triumph 3-2 and to provide £140 for the disaster fund. The huge attendance, however, was also attracted by another novelty value: Heath's first floodlit match! If you could call "Wells lights" floodlights, that is. These were 10-feet tall electric lamps and 20 of them were positioned around the ground. They were so effective only parts of the field remained totally dark.

This match might also contain one other futuristic innovation. Newton Heath had a reserve player named J. Davenport on their books around this time. The match report describes him in action late on, yet his name was not mentioned in the starting line-up. Unless he was added just before kick-off, Davenport might well be Manchester United's earliest recorded substitute. Although substitutions were not widespread back then, they did at times take place. As a matter of fact, in the Home international against Scotland that season, Wales replaced their injured keeper during the first half. It may very possibly have occurred in the Belle Vue darkness as well.

There were other players who flitted into Newton Heath's first team in the latter part of the season. Alf Farman turned out in three matches and scored a goal each time; Willie Stewart appeared in the last four games, scoring once against Ardwick; and T. Craig donned the green-and-gold top on a couple of occasions. By next season, all three would become established players at North Road, and at least two – Farman and Stewart – would evolve into Newton Heath legends. For now, though, an existing legend was hogging the limelight: mighty Jack of the Doughty clan. Two days after his Senior Cup final exploits, he nabbed three goals as Manchester Welsh were trounced 5-0. In case you have lost track, this was his sixth hat-trick of the campaign. By the end, his tally had risen to an astonishing 42 goals, perhaps more, as six scorers were never traced. No one else came close, although Heath's grand total of 125 goals meant the other four members of the front line – Roger Doughty, Tait, Gotheridge, and Gale – also reached double figures. A very stable outfit had laid the foundations for a successful campaign. As the near future would show, Newton Heath would soon be moving further up in the world, but never again with the joy and panache of 1888-89.

1889-90

THE FOOTBALL ALLIANCE

How do you move on after you have won the Double? Ok, so the Double in question consisted of one competition that had since become defunct and another that was but a city-wide knockout cup. Yet these were the only trophies Newton Heath were able to compete in. Had they been eligible for anything else in that period of time, the pumped-up Heathens would have fervently gunned for it. The Football League, the FA Cup, the Lancashire Cup, the Boat Race – Newton Heath wanted it all. From the moment the club was born they had continuously strived for the top, it has always been Manchester United's philosophy, whether it involved establishing professional footballers' rights, breaking through the insular wall into European competition, or dragging an impossible Treble from the realms of fantasy into the real world. It was in this spirit that their predecessors approached the 1889-90 season determined that, one way or another, they would be part of a competitive league.

The previous year, the Heathens had allowed themselves to be ignored when the Football League was looking for members. This time, however, Heath opted to initiate the first move. The League committee had agreed that the four bottom sides would have to apply to be re-elected for the following season, whether they liked it or not. Burnley, Derby County, Notts County, and Stoke now had some sweet-talking to do, especially Stoke, who had finished bottom making them most susceptible. This seemed to be Heath's chance following their dual success. But the Mancunians were not the only suitors. By the time the likes of Sheffield Wednesday, Sunderland, and Grimsby Town had woken up to the opportunity, there were a total of 13 teams applying for one of the four coveted spots. The admittance process was both straightforward – each of the Football League's 12 clubs voted for the four teams they liked - and received backhanders from. Conveniently the teams applying for re-election could vote for themselves should they wish to. There was little surprise then that the 'Fraudulent Four' were able to garner enough votes to keep their precious places. Stoke, in fact, received 10 votes as the other League clubs showed their appreciation of City's never-say-try attitude.

Newton Heath only secured one vote. In all honesty, though, they never stood a chance. Even if the re-applying clubs could not have voted for themselves and had picked Newton Heath instead, the men from Monsall would still have been one nomination short. Royally miffed, on the contrary, were Sheffield Wednesday. The general impression had been that they were bed fellows with the Football League and that they would most probably get in. Apparently, however, Wednesday's side of the bed had lately remained made. Owls' president, John Holmes, vowed revenge. He summoned all the clubs whose heart had been broken to a meeting at the Douglas Hotel in Manchester. The main item on the agenda: re-launching the Football Combination! Yes, that damp squid from last season was back on. But wait! The lessons had been learned and things would be done right the second time around. Only twelve clubs would be allowed to join and, as in the Football League, they would play each other on a home-and-away basis for a total of 22 weeks that would determine the championship.

It was a replica of the League for it too would include two teams from Birmingham (Small Heath Alliance and Birmingham St. George's), one from Liverpool (Bootle), and one from Nottingham (Forest). What was better was that this league would stretch further north and encompass Sunderland and their bitter rivals Sunderland Albion. And best of all, as far as our story is concerned, was the inclusion of a team from Manchester: the cup holders themselves, Newton Heath.

To throw last year's indifferent fans off the trail, the new product was marketed under a new name: the Football Alliance (no relation to Small Heath). Sunderland soon declined to participate in this competition, their place going to Long Eaton Rangers. Newton Heath did not care one bit. They were handed an arranged fixtures list with names like Darwen, Crewe, and Walsall Town Swifts printed on it. If that was not glittery enough, associations were trampling over each other trying to readmit the Heathens: the FA Cup? Heath were back in; the Lancashire Cup? Heath were back in there too. The Boat Race, however, remained but a pipe dream.

NEWISH FACES

THIS WAS AN era when 'The Arsenal' still referred to a military equipment storehouse, Manchester City were trying to settle upon an adequate name to go by and Chelsea were still over a quarter of a century away from inheriting their first pound let alone rouble. As for Liverpool, let's just say that the world was a more beautiful place... Over in Monsall, meanwhile, Newton Heath were already preparing for the brave new world of the Football Alliance and they were quite proud of their achievement too. In a little over ten years, they had progressed from depot kick-abouts to a genuinely competitive league, as the Alliance surely was. This was no fizz-free Combination. Different leagues were popping up like zits all over the face of British football around this time. Judging by the calibre of some of the Alliance's founding members, however, you could easily tell this was the next best thing after the Football League. Sheffield Wednesday were one of the top teams around whereas the likes of Nottingham Forest and Darwen were almost as old as organised association football itself.

Newton Heath were chuffed to bits to be among such exalted company. For that the club had to be thankful not just for the players on the field, but also for the diligent committee behind the scenes. Before we move on, it is worth acquainting ourselves with the members of Heath's committee, as a tribute to their achievements in the Manchester United's nascent first decade.

Mr. Fred Attock was the president as ever, but most club matters were decided by Messrs JB Dodd, J. Whitehead, T. Jackson, J. Panter, and T. Rigby. Mr. Sadler sorted the junk mail while penny-pinching was the responsibility of Mr. George Farrow. Their efforts had helped get Heath into the Football Alliance, but now more work was required to keep the club in it. The committee skimmed through the squad list and concluded that if these players were good enough to manage the best record in the Football Combination they should do just fine in the Alliance. The solitary new face signed for the upcoming season was a direct replacement for the departing J. Gale. As far as historians are concerned, Gale completely disappeared , but Heath, incredibly, were able to replace him with the one footballer more mysterious than him. Edgar Wilson was his name and inside-left was the summation of his fact file. For someone who would soon play a historic part in Newton Heath's season, it is perplexing that absolutely nothing else is known.

To be fair, several players had been introduced to the ways of North Road at the back end of 1888-89 in the hope of being blooded in the new campaign. One was Alf Farman, a Brummie born in Kings Norton back in the summer of '69. He had previously turned out for Birmingham Excelsior, Aston Villa, and, briefly, Bolton Wanderers. But at Monsall he found his true home. For the next six years, he performed legendary feats on the right wing. He dribbled solely for the entertainment of the North Road faithful. .As for his shot, Alf could really kick far, man... In another life he might have been a missile launcher. In this one it could be argued penalty kicks were invented for him, as will become apparent over the years. And on top of that he was of a free-scoring disposition. His goal tally would nearly approach three figures. Another new chap who made his Heath debut in April was Craig. Only 'T' has ever been traced of his first name but it is probable his middle initial was 'V' for Versatility. Over the next two seasons he would appear in all five forward positions as well as both right and left-half.

However, the only player brought in during the previous campaign who was deemed ready to start this one was the Scot Willie Stewart, possibly the man with the best coiffured moustache in Manchester United's history. He was just 17 years old when he joined the Heathens yet he already had time to squeeze in stints with Dundee Our Boys and Warwick County. Willie began his North Road career as an inside-right with a decent goal return but he went on to make a name for himself as a centre-half. There he excelled for years and was so good at reading the game before anyone else it made you wonder whether he was some kind of psychic. It would not be until the end of April 1895 when Willie kicked his last Newton Heath ball.

Ironically, Stewart's inclusion in Heath's current starting line-up only became possible following the conversion of Roger Doughty to right half-back. The Heathens figured this way the shoulder-barging would be spread evenly up front and at the back. This move worked out well for everyone concerned. Roger retained a first-team slot, Wales maintained a stronghold on the half-back line, and previous incumbent Tom Burke got to experience the leisurely atmosphere of reserve team football. The rest of the line-up remained the same. Tait, Gotheridge, and Jack Doughty completed the attack, Jack Owen and Davies the half-back line. Goalie Tom Hay continued his one-man crusade against opposition forwards, the drink demon, and the force of gravity. And Powell and Mitchell preserved the steady efficiency at full-back. Mitchell, incidentally, had an eventful afternoon in a friendly against Witton on September 14th when he scored his first goal in three years. He had lumped the ball forward from the halfway line and was as surprised as everyone else to see it go all the way in. His gigantic effort, however, did not turn him into a global sex icon nor did he end up dating a Spice Girl, though he was offered a cinnamon stick after the match.

SCAPEGOATS

NEWTON HEATH KICKED off their Football Alliance programme on September 21st. The competition had begun two weeks earlier but Heath were not in a hurry. They were too busy racking up friendlies instead of league points. But now the opening fixture was upon them and 3,000 fans turned out to greet Sunderland Albion to North Road. Heath afforded them top respect by fielding the first-choice welcoming committee: Hay; Mitchell, Powell; R. Doughty, Davies, J. Owen; Tait, Stewart, J. Doughty, Wilson and Gotheridge.

First on the agenda was an onslaught on the visitors' goal. Albion keeper, Angus, was peppered with shots until eventually he cracked - Jack Doughty finding Edgar Wilson for the newcomer to fire in the club's historic first Alliance goal. The Wearsiders were immediately up the other end and a melee ensued. Tom Hay blocked two quick efforts before the ball, and possibly the tiny prostrate keeper, were unceremoniously bundled into the goal. This beastly incident brought out the beauty in Heath's play. The five forwards initiated an intricate passing move – think Ronaldo, Rooney, and Tevez circa 2008 – that culminated in Stewart restoring Heath's

SUNDERLAND ALBION, 1889.
Newton Heath's first Football Alliance opponents were Sunderland Albion on the 21st of September 1889. This photo of Albion was taken a week before they lost 1-4 to Heath. In the back row, 3rd from right, is Bob McFarlane who would later move to Newton Heath and wed Jack and Roger Doughty's sister, Ellen.

lead. Both newcomers had scored on their competitive debut, Stewart doing so at a mere 17 years of age. Yet Heath were not done passing: Tait to Jack Doughty, and he made it 3-1 by half-time. This remained the score until minutes before full-time when Heath launched a counter-attack and Wilson slotted his second. He could have had a hat-trick had the referee not insisted an earlier effort was saved before it crossed the line. But a 4-1 victory over a highly-rated Albion was not too shabby a start. This Alliance lark seemed quite easy.

Two full days later, the Heathens were brought back down to earth when the 4-1 score line was reversed at Bootle. This was no Combination! By the end of September, following a 2-2 draw at Crewe, Heath found themselves in seventh place out of twelve. Leading the table, surreally, were Walsall Town Swifts with five points. Undeterred, the Heathens took some time off to engage in a couple of friendlies including one game which, if it doesn't qualify as a derby then no other will: Newton Heath LYR versus Newton Heath Central. The team amassed eight goals in these two matches, three of which were own goals, but this was the calm before the storm. A rainstorm, to be precise, away at Alliance leaders Walsall. It poured throughout the match and only 600 spectators attended, though these might possibly have been Walsall's entire fan base. Heath were used to playing in wet conditions yet they did not have much luck that day. They ended up losing 0-4, a result that was compounded by James Gotheridge getting in trouble with the referee.

Things only got worse the following week when Heath were crucified 1-5 at Birmingham St. George's. They had dropped to tenth, and yet another setback was up next. On November 2nd, Newton Heath made their first appearance in the Lancashire Senior Cup since 1884. They had been waiting for so long to have a crack at it only for the out-of-form Heathens to find that it had arrived at the wrong time. Despite taking the lead at Haliwell through Willie Stewart, the men from Monsall went down 1-2. Any 'Quadruple' aspirations were choked before the term could be introduced into football-speak.

Although the Lancashire Cup adventure had lasted one game more than in the previous five years, it was time for some changes. The FA took the lead. James Gotheridge's unspecified misbehaviour in the defeat at Walsall had been deemed unacceptable, and he was handed a three-month suspension by the FA. Ashamed, Newton Heath opted to move him out. It did not matter that Gotheridge was the club's longest-serving player having made his debut back in 1884. That was long enough, the directors thought, and they sold him to West Manchester. Then they turned across to the other wing where Walter Tait frequently loitered. He only seemed to turn it on in the big games, they convinced themselves, and he too was packed off to West Manchester. In a flash, two of the club's most prolific scorers had gone: Gotheridge with over 60 goals in 150 appearances, Tait with around 35 in 85. Incidentally, they never got the chance to play together for West Manchester. By the time Gotheridge's ban finished, Tait was serving his own time at Ardwick. Gotheridge would never let such indignity taint his CV, preferring to eventually call it a day (after a stint with Stockport in 1891-2) become a cop in Loughborough.

At least one player was glad to see them go: George Owen. The Welsh international was now able to regain a place in the front line. He slotted in at inside-left pushing Edgar Wilson out to Gotheridge's old position on the left wing. Tait's right-flank vacancy, meanwhile, was filled by the lad blazing a trail of goals in the reserves: the Birmingham Bullet, Alf Farman. In he came to claim that spot as his permanent home for the next five years by which time he himself would have become Heath's longest servant.

A FAMOUS CUP TIE

POOR LITTLE LONG Eaton Rangers. They were the unlucky visitors to North Road the day Alf Farman made his Alliance debut. Having been held back in the reserve team for months, he was raring to explode down the wing. Try to remember Steve Coppell's debut against Cardiff in 1975. If you can't, think instead of Ronaldo's introduction against Bolton in 2003. Now top these performances off with a goal. That was Farman's debut. He was involved in most of the attacks, much to the benefit of Jack Doughty whose brace helped yield a 3-0 victory. These two hit it off instantly - a deadly finisher and a deadly supplier who can finish. Within two weeks they had plundered a combined seven friendly goals as Sheffield United were trounced 7-1 and the Football League's Stoke City 6-2.

This put Newton Heath in the right form as a triple header against the Alliance's top three teams came up. Sure, the Heathens trailed the leaders by five points, but they had played fewer games than almost everybody else. A few good results now and they would be right back in the race for the Alliance title. First up was a trip to Sheffield Wednesday, which was never going to be an easy fixture. The Owls had piled in 17 goals in their three home matches so far, and they seemed to be the fittest team in the league. The best Heath could achieve was leading at half-time before settling for a 1-3 defeat. Then leaders Bootle came to Monsall and wished they hadn't. Heath thrashed them 3-0 to knock them off the top, allowing Wednesday to take their place, a position they kept for the rest of the campaign. Jack Doughty scored for the fourth successive Alliance outing, Farman got a goal, as did Stewart, but only at the expense of a serious injury. Heath's youngster was sidelined for the next two months.

The next guests scheduled for North Road were Walsall Town Swifts, who arrived in Manchester to find the ground a mud bath. When Newton Heath had visited them in October, the conditions were just as terrible, but the Swifts did not mind as they clobbered their guests 4-0. Now that the muddy shoe was on the other foot they suddenly became aquaphobic. On and on they nagged until the game was downgraded to friendly status, the 3-0 drubbing obviously contributing to their inconvenience. The Heathens obtained the victory but not the points that come with it.

The next Alliance fixture was at Darwen on December 28th. To prepare for it, the Heathens played friendlies on the 25th, 26th, and 27th! A worn-out Heath consequently lost 1-4 to bottom-of-the-table Darwen prompting the club committee to wisely conclude that four outings in as many days was not ideal preparation. At the turn of the year, North Road welcomed Scottish guests just like last season. Were Hogmany parties that dull in Scotland?

January 18th, 1890 saw the FA Cup Round One come around. Newton Heath had not partaken in this competition since 1886 following a 'misunderstanding' and a refusal to play extra-time following a 2-2 draw at Fleetwood Rangers. The FA's subsequent disqualification and Heath's refusal to have anything to do with the Cup meant the club missed out for three years. Now, however, Heath believed it was time to forgive and forget. They were, after all, an Alliance team as well as champions of the Combination, albeit, whisper it softly, unofficially. Not only did the FA welcome them back, but they were also ushered directly into the first round proper. Only Football League clubs were guaranteed such posh treatment, plus a lucky few chosen ones. Even the likes of Crewe, Darwen, and Small Heath had been made to work their way through the qualifying rounds. So it seemed that the authorities and the club had fully kissed and made up.

When the first round draw was made, Heath were drawn away at the 'Invincibles' of Preston North End. The champions and double winners had sauntered through their first season without losing a single competetive game. This season, they were three points clear and again set to claim the title. Preston were also the defending Cup-holders having won the 1889 FA Cup when none of their opponents had the

PRESTON, 1888-89

Invincibles schminvincibles, for 5 minutes at least! Preston North End, 'Double' winners the previous season, fell behind to Newton Heath early in an FA Cup tie in January 1890. They did reply with 6 goals, though.

temerity to so much as score a goal against them. It is feasible the Heathens privately wished their self-imposed FA Cup stand-off had dragged on for one more year.

Nonetheless, the following eleven Heathens took to the field: Hay; Harrison, Powell; R. Doughty, Davies, J. Owen; Farman, Craig, J. Doughty, G. Owen, and Wilson. This line-up included five capped players, but the Preston selection had six, while the remaining five were overqualified for international recognition; at least, according to Scotland, who refused to select anyone plying his trade south of the border.

Over 7,000 spectators filled the Deepdale stands and sighed with relief a minute in when, after a quick-fire passing move by the Heathen forwards, Wilson missed a sitter. What a start that would have been! Nonetheless, after five minutes, following another incisive Heath attack, Craig tried a daisy-cutter from outside the area: the ball arrowed into the goal. The Alliance's eleventh-placed Newton Heath had taken the lead at the home of the Football League leaders! Invincibles shminvincibles! As usually happens, however, the goal served as a wake-up call for Preston, as the Deepdale outfit immediately switched to Invincible mode – just ten minutes later, they led 2-1. Craig again came close for Heath, but the home side quickly added two more goals. In the second half, the Heathens seemed content to sit back on their 1-4 deficit while Preston opted to entertain and struck twice more. The final score was a 1-6 spanking for Newton Heath. Name on the Cup? Not for another couple of decades.

ALLIANCE DALLIANCE

A COUPLE OF unfamiliar names were appearing in Newton Heath's team around this time. The Heathens had brought Bolton Wanderers' utility player, Charlie Harrison, back to his neck of the woods. The 27-year-old had played both for and against Heath as a goalkeeper but he generally turned out wherever he was asked too. Heath now had two such total footballers on their books as they already boasted George Felton's services. For three years now he has been displaying his flexibility in every position imaginable, possibly even inventing one or two by serendipity at the odd times he was caught in no man's land yet he always found himself back in the reserves, much to the dismay of the reserve team.

The first team, meanwhile, seemed to be in a lull. In contrast to their rapid exit from the FA Cup, they could not get anywhere in the Football Alliance. Their first Alliance fixture of 1890 ought to have been against Grimsby Town, and the Heathens did race to a 4-1 victory. Grimsby, however, had gone over the Wimpy Walsall Way-out manual devised by Town Swifts a fortnight earlier. Rain falling from the Manchester sky? Check. North Road living up to its quagmire-state reputation? Check. Visitors turned over by their Alliance hosts? Check. Grimsby had all the prerequisites needed to protest to the authorities. Without much hesitation, the result was voided just like the Walsall match and Heath were again robbed of their points (as this story goes on, don't be alarmed if you instinctively develop a rising hatred of Walsall).

The next Alliance obligation resulted in a 0-2 defeat at Sunderland Albion on January 25th but, of course, that match was not voided. Before the upcoming return encounter with Grimsby Town, Heath played a friendly against those lovely folks in Ardwick. For a friendly, it was a bruising derby in which Heath obtained a three-goal victory in exchange for a three-man injury. Tom Hay, Roger Doughty and Jack Owen joined Willie Stewart on the casualties list leaving a depleted Heath to crash 0-7 at Grimsby. The only consolation was that this did not equal, let alone break, the club's record loss, which remained a 0-8 hiding against Earlstown back in 1883. Although it seems irritating that the club frequently crammed meaningless friendlies between important fixtures, the Alliance was not yet the be-all-and-end-all of their existence. Local derbies were still the surest way of swelling the coffers, and the Ardwick game attracted around 10,000 fans at threepence a head. There was also the small matter of local bragging rights even if a third of Heath's squad did their bragging in the treatment room.

ROGER DOUGHTY

So, an optimal mixture of null

matches, ill-preparation, and tough away trips meant Newton Heath had not collected a single Alliance point in over two months. This new competition was panning out a little differently to its forerunner. To start with, Heath were mired at the bottom of the table with just seven points from eleven matches, with only Long Eaton Rangers considerate enough to keep them company. The likes of Sunderland Albion and Crewe had at least 10 points more than Heath, and even they were left trailing by Sheffield Wednesday, who led with 23 points. To be fair, the Heathens had played an average of four matches fewer than the rest meaning that, technically, they could still win the Alliance title, though technique-ly they couldn't. There was another problem: Jack Doughty seemed to score in all the wrong matches! He had netted 21 goals so far but only six of them came in the league where his desire to rough up the big boys burnt stronger.

The scoring solution, once Heath cared to look, was on the treatment table. Willie Stewart, after a two-month layoff, was now ready to return. In his first game back he grabbed a brace as Heath won 3-1 at Nottingham Forest on February 15th. Results were still inconsistent but a hard-earned 1-1 draw at Small Heath moved the Heathens off the bottom. Up next was one of the most important matches of the season – yes, the bottom-of-the-table clash with Long Eaton Rangers! Heath won the 4-pointer 3-1 with a goal from Farman and two from Wilson. Now Heath had seven matches left to play, all of which were at home, thanks mainly to the frequently voided fixtures. Seven wins would do nicely, but the Heathens had less than 30 days in which to complete them. The task seemed arduous enough for the North Road mud to withstand, let alone the players.

SUCCESS AND FAILURE

Newton Heath's attempt to rack up seven competitive home wins might have been more successful had they distributed their goals more evenly among the remaining fixtures rather than dumping them all in one place. The dollop fell on an unsuspecting Small Heath Alliance who visited North Road on April 7th and were handed a 9-1 mugging. Roger and Jack Doughty scored one and two goals respectively, the only occasion in Manchester United's history when brothers have netted in the same league game. The Doughtys, however, were upstaged that Monday afternoon by young Willie Stewart. With no siblings alongside him, Willie alone shouldered the responsibility of providing three goals, thus recording Heath's first Alliance hat-trick.

Three other victories in the remaining matches helped Newton Heath make a late surge up the table to finish eighth. They would have finished higher had the voided 4-1 demolition of Grimsby stood. As it turned out, the Shrimpers' evil plan worked out to perfection. In the replayed match – like you just knew it – the 4-1 win became a 0-1 defeat that cost Heath sixth and a crack at joint fourth. The Heathens lost their last match against Sheffield Wednesday but, although the Owls were the Alliance champions, they were not insurmountable. They had no real incentive to win that ultimate encounter. However, while this was their first outing in two weeks, all the postponements meant that Heath were forced to complete five matches in the same timeframe.

So eighth it was but, to be fair, this was a strong league. Sheffield Wednesday, in addition to winning the Football Alliance, made it all the way to the FA Cup final where they lost to the Football League's Blackburn Rovers. The Alliance runners-up, Bootle, got as far as the quarter-finals. Therefore, the Alliance teams' hopes were high when the time came for election to the Football League. Newton Heath, as ever, wanted in, and they submitted their application along with several other sides.

The League, however, pettiness its motto, did its best to crush the Alliance's aspirations. The bottom four League clubs were supposed to apply for re-election but as eighth-placed Aston Villa and ninth-placed Bolton Wanderers had finished on the same number of points, both were conveniently exempt from re-election. Then the League committee skipped past the voting process altogether and decided to keep Burnley and Notts County. Only bottom club Stoke were ushered out, but the League ignored all the Alliance applications and plumped for Sunderland AFC instead. The Wearsiders had promised to chip in when travelling expenses to the northeast were discussed. If Newton Heath's application was a waste of time, spare a thought for Sheffield Wednesday. They almost won the Double only to find themselves on the outside looking in. This was a big blow for the Owls who would consequently lose their momentum for a couple of years. If anything, the Alliance would be tougher next season after bottom club Long Eaton Rangers dropped out and were replaced by Stoke City of Football League fame.

Regardless of which league Heath were in; there was always one competition they made time for... It starts with Manchester and ends with Cup. Yes, the beloved Senior Cup was back around again. This was its sixth year and, for the sixth time, Heath were contesting the final. The Heathens weren't even bothering with the early rounds anymore. They had a brief look-in at the semi-final stage and did the business with a 4-1 defeat of Denton. Then, on May 3rd, they made their customary appearance in the final where they always met a new challenger, this year's victims-to-be being Royton. One other thing had changed this season – the venue. The final was moved from Whalley Range to Brook's Bar, which, despite the label, was West Manchester's ground and is only about a mile away from Old Trafford.

The 4,000 in attendance must have thought they had wandered out of a bar when they saw Jack Powell standing between the sticks. The Heath skipper was just returning from injury but was considered only fit for a standing role. Charlie Harrison took Jack's place at full-back where his partner, Mitchell, was appearing in his sixth Manchester Cup final. The rest of the line-up saw R. Doughty, Davies, and J. Owen at half-back and Farman, Craig, J. Doughty, G. Owen, and Wilson up front.

It was no surprise when Craig gave Newton Heath the lead, but Royton, capitalizing on Powell's goalkeeping naivety, equalised and scored another soon after! Royton's claim to fame, in addition to fielding a forward named Grewcock, was that they were leading against the two-time defending Cup-holders. Their claim was soon resolved, however, when George Owen levelled the scores. The second half belonged to Newton Heath, who alternated between corner kicks, disallowed goals, and good ones. Eventually, after two strikes from Craig and one from Farman, Heath triumphed 5-2 to win the Cup for the third year running. The Heathens were still the kings of Manchester.

Surprisingly, Jack Doughty did not score in this year's Manchester Cup final, leaving the customary hat-trick for Craig. He did, however, finish as top scorer again with a tally of 26 goals.

Also, on March 15th, he achieved the impossible feat of being in both Wrexham and Birmingham at the same time – if you believe the newspapers! The local ones claim he led Heath's line in the Alliance fixture at Small Heath; the national ones insist he turned out for Wales alongside Joe Davies to take on England in Wrexham. It is most probable his brother Roger covered for him with Heath while he was adding to his cap collection, but try convincing the local papers.

For all his goals, Jack was not Heath's leading marksman in the Alliance. Only nine of his strikes came in the league and Willie Stewart notched one more to finish on ten (15 overall). But there were enough goals – 115 in total – for several players to reach double figures: Farman got 17, Craig 12, Wilson 12, and George Owen 10. Even opposition players were lining up to attain double digits too - seven of Heath's overall tally were own goals.

By the end of the season, the club committee decided to break Heath's first prominent team up! This fervent batch had enjoyed a few momentous years, plundering away the goals and lifting Heath to a new level but they had failed to earn a place in the Football League. Perhaps a fresh batch would give Heath the extra oomph, the committee reasoned, and they embarked on a space-creating mission. All three goalies had to go. Tom Hay had been the number one Number One for three years, playing around 120 matches. But at 32 years of age, Heath realized he wasn't getting any taller. Also, Hay wanted to experience Football League action, and that was his destination. Only he picked the wrong club: in 70 games for Accrington he shipped around 200 goals!

James Pedley had done a splendid job being Hay's deputy. His ratio of 12 goals conceded in 15 Heath matches almost stands comparison with that of Peter Schmeichel. Evidence of loud-mouthed barkings, however, is not conclusive from contemporary reports. Pedley and Charlie Harrison never appeared for Heath again.

Tom Burke was off too. Being demoted to the reserve team would irk some, and it was bound to irk Burke, especially after gracing the first team 120 times. The Welshman had represented Wrexham, Wrexham Grosvenor and Wrexham Olympic before joining Heath. Upon his departure he was able to find yet another team in Wrexham to sample – Wrexham Victoria. Burke would eventually return to settle in Manchester until his death at fifty.

Perhaps the most unexpected departure was that of another Welshman: Joe Davies. Around 160 times he had worn Heath's colours, but now he wanted to try on a Football League kit. Joe moved to Wolverhampton Wanderers and spent four seasons there before returning to his previous team, Druids. When he ultimately retired, Joe found the best profession to mirror his football career – a butcher.

A third Welshman followed Burke and Davies out. George Owen realised he still had to go through umpteen spells at Chirk, but first he gave West Manchester a try. Even after retirement he still ached to be on a football field, so he became a referee. Finally, the player who arrived mysteriously in Monsall departed just as mysteriously. Edgar Wilson enjoyed a good season with Newton Heath, making around forty appearances and scoring the club's first Football Alliance goal. Now, however, he disappeared over the horizon without so much as a forwarding address for the sake of future Newton Heath storytellers.

1890-91

THE REPLACEMENTS

IT TOOK THE release of the 1890-91 fixtures to ease the mind of the most pessimistic among the North Road faithful. Interspersed in between the usual mass of friendly matches was the Football Alliance programme. That is what the fretful fans were looking for. By this time last season, the Football Combination had bitten the dust. The Alliance, to the contrary, was here to stay. If anything had changed, it was the general composition of the Newton Heath squad, the club committee having used the summer break to schedule a few cosmetic changes. It was a big gamble. In the past three years, the team had plundered 360 goals, won the Combination title, and had the Manchester Cup earmarked as Newton Heath property. Their reward from the suits was to be treated to a complete makeover.

Perhaps the committee decided the solution for the irritating club v country row was to sell all the internationals! To that end, they initiated the de-Welshing process. George Owen, Joe Davies, and Tom Burke had all departed during the close season. And, of the Welshmen left, Jacks Powell and Doughty would have a dwindling role to play in the 1890-91 campaign due to age and ache respectively. Captain Powell was the new Tom Burke – relegated to the reserve team and politely advised to keep his day job at the depot. To be fair to Powell, at 30, his body was too old to deliver – and receive – the type of football demanded of a Newton Heath full-back. Jack Doughty, meanwhile, was only 26, but his physical style was now hurting him as much as it did his poor opponents.

Regardless, there was a new trend in transfers taking effect in England. The authorities had relaxed the rules barring the purchase of Scottish footballers. Everyone had observed Preston North End's kilt-kitted stalwarts stride away with nearly every trophy available and were now advocating Tartan imports. Agents went trawling the country, advising English teams to 'snap up the Scottish players while they were still hot'. The Heathens would not be coerced into this 'jock rush', preferring instead to wait until all the good ones were taken. What they were looking for - and could now afford after selling so many players - was Football League experience. With that in mind, Newton Heath spent a few bob on a two-Bob purchase: Bob Milarvie and Bob Ramsay. Both had played their part as Stoke City finished bottom in the inaugural League season. Milarvie was a Scot who hailed from Pollockshaws, just south of Glasgow. A skilful left winger by trade, he was a goalscoring one by nature, if 4 goals in 15 matches for Stoke in '88-89 and 5 in 14 for Derby County in '89-90 are the stats to go by. His compensation now for dropping to the Alliance was inheriting Edgar Wilson's smelly shirt out wide.

Unlike Milarvie, Bob Ramsay had stayed behind at Stoke for one more season to make sure they got relegated. He was their league top scorer in 1889-90 with an impressive tally of four goals! Impressive for a centre-half, that is; which might also explain the gaping hole in defence that led to Stoke's demotion. It was now hoped that Ramsay could replicate his efforts in the Joe Davies role.

Two more players were acquired for the forward line. One was George Evans, who had enjoyed a decent season at WBA, signing off with two goals against Everton. The Heath committee was so proud of this capture he was made captain in place of the rarely-selected Jack Powell. The other arrival was inside-left William Sharpe who was not as sharp as it said on the label. Somehow, though, he would find a way of inscribing his name into Manchester United's history in 1890-91. Heath still needed a new goalkeeper to fill the tiny space vacated by Tom Hay. The man they signed was JF Slater, of unknown origin. Unlike his predecessor, Slater was of normal height, so, to stand out in an hirsute era, he was always impeccably clean-shaven and wore a trademark flat cap.

Finally, the committee addressed the left-back vacancy. The Heathens headed to Scotland and obtained one of those much talked-about pass masters for their own. But W. McMillan's experiences left a violent first impression, the sensation of studs raking down his ankle during his second game was enough for the braveheart who soon whimpered back from whence he came, never to be seen in these parts again. The Heathens had no alternative but to buy a plain Englishman instead, John Clements of Notts County, with a smidgen of Football League know-how. Here was a man who could uphold Heath's values of physical exuberance. At a rough estimate, about fifty percent of the times his name was mentioned in match reports were for committing fouls, the other fifty being when the line-up was listed. Clements' moustache alone could halt an opponent in his tracks if used properly as a lasso. With a quirk of fate, Heath had got solid left-back cover for the next four years.

A POSE ON PAUSE

THE BEGINNING OF September was a time for handshakes and introductions at North Road. Slater: keeper. The full-backs Mitchell and McMillan said their 'hellos'. "Ramsay, Bob Ramsay" was the answer when half-backs Roger Doughty and Jack Owen sought to meet the man in the middle. And there were even more newcomers as Jack Doughty scanned the fellow forwards – Milarvie, Sharpe, Evans. Only Farman's face seemed vaguely familiar. The eleven men had been summoned for the team photo. "This one will last the ages, lads". With time it would emerge as the earliest known group photograph of Manchester United, the one against which all future squad images should be measured. Somehow the club directors had gotten wind of this historic shoot and they all showed up forcing the players to squeeze into the centre. In front sits the actual Manchester Cup, surrounded by players the majority of whom did not shed one drop of sweat in winning it. The enormity of the occasion must have got to the players – not a single smile could be seen on their faces. Snap! And MU Pictures was born.

This photogenic lot made a flashy start to the campaign. Burslem Port Vale were trounced 5-1 in a pre-season friendly when, of the newcomers, Milarvie got a brace and Evans a single strike. Milarvie made an identical encore 24 hours later as Hyde were beaten 2-1, but George Evans saved his next goal for his Alliance bow against Darwen on September 6th. Jack Doughty, Alf Farman, and Jack Owen also scored to give Heath a 4-2 opening day victory. As is always the case, though, the good times could not last forever.

NEWTON HEATH, 1890.
*This is Newton Heath's earliest known team photo, taken at the start of the
1890-91 campaign. It had more suits than footballers but they have been
left out for your convenience. The players, from left to right, are:
J. Mitchell, J. Slater, and W. McMillan (back row); Roger Doughty, Bob
Ramsay, and Jack Owen (middle row); and Alf Farman, Jack Doughty,
George Evans, Bob Milarvie, and William Sharpe (front row). And all the
way in the front is the Manchester Senior Cup, won in 1890.*

They didn't even last a week. When the Heathens visited Grimsby
Town they were missing Jack Doughty, now showing the first
signs of mortality. Then W. McMillan scarpered leaving behind
nothing but the top portion of his face that appears in the team
photo. The resulting 1-3 loss initiated a sticky run.

Heath were now experiencing some growing pains. Perhaps
they concluded that, no matter how they performed in 1890-91,
their hopes of admittance into the closed shop of the Football
League would be scuppered in any case. It could alternatively
be that so many new players were tossed into the line-up that it
would take a while for them to gel. Otherwise, there seems to

be few excuses for the pair of abject results that took place in the latter part of November. On the 22nd at Nottingham, the Heath defenders collaborated with the Forest forwards to create a unique score line in Manchester United's history: 2-8, providing the one and only instance that Heath/United have conceeded eight goals in a competitive match. Although they showed some improvement a week later, losing by only 1-5 to Sunderland Albion at North Road, this was the worst competitive home loss for seven years. It was a bad time to be a Heathen… unless you enjoyed being mired in ninth place, with just seven points from ten matches. Already the Alliance title appeared to be beyond them, for Nottingham Forest were ten points better off, closely shadowed by Stoke and Sunderland Albion. Heath, meanwhile, seemed to still be stuck at the handshakes stage.

Yet not all batterings went one way. The highlight of Heath's league programme had been the 'Battle of the Railwaymen' against Crewe Alexandra on November 1st when Heath triumphed 6-3. They actually led 6-1 at the interval then took their foot off the gas or, in terms both teams would understand, stopped shovling coal into the furnace. Heath also found the time for a friendly 4-3 win at the Football League's Burnley and a 4-1 whipping of Manchester City's grandpas Ardwick.

Another friendly on December 6th, 1890, saw South Shore beaten 3-1 in Jack Powell's final appearance for Heath. He had at last abdicated his full-back slot to John Clements after almost 170 matches at Monsall. Jack's place as a Newton Heath legend is guaranteed. Since arriving in 1886, he had led the club from the wilderness, through the Football Combination, until they proudly became also-rans in the second highest league in the country. This is a bit unfair as he was a fine professional and had experience long before it became widely accessible. His 15 Welsh caps reflected glowingly on the club and his bark would still echo around North Road as he was staying behind, not fit for footy but as a fitter at the nearby works.

THE DAY THEY PLAYED TWICE

ALLIANCE NUISANCES ASIDE, Newton Heath were experiencing better fortune in the FA Cup, then again as they were still to

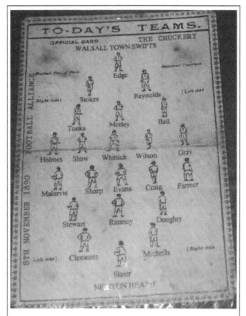

WALSALL TS PROGRAMME, 1890.

A programme of Newton Heath's Football Alliance match at Walsall Town Swifts on November 8th, 1890. Only 5 of the Heathens' names are printed wrong, including that of William Sharpe, who scored Heath's goal in a 1-2 defeat.

record their first win in that competition, things couldn't really get much worse. If you care to remember, they had had a great chance in 1886 when the Gods that govern cup draws handed them a trip to Fleetwood Rangers. The Heathens, however, were eliminated after refusing to play extra-time. This so upset the fickle Gods they next sent Heath to mighty Preston where they got whupped. The outcome was that, in 1890-91, Newton Heath had to start out in the qualifying rounds. There they were drawn away to Higher Walton, the inaugural champions of the Lancashire League, who begged Heath to move the tie to North Road so the good people of Manchester could come out in their droves (who said that switching ties is a modern phenomenon?). The only glitch in this plan was that they overestimated how many good people in Manchester actually wanted to see this team. As it turned out, just 3,000 fans cared to make the trip to Monsall.

The hosts-turned-guests put up a decent fight Heath's new goalkeeper Slater heroically keeping the 'home' side in it until the last ten minutes when Alf Farman finally lowered Higher Walton's colours. A second goal from George Evans confirmed Newton Heath's historic first FA Cup win.

Heath were then pitted away, this time at Bootle on October 25th. Only a fortnight earlier, the Heathens had played an Alliance fixture there and received a 0-5 mauling. A full-back crisis had forced them to field E. Sadler at right-back where he gave such a convincing deer-in-the-headlights impersonation he was released into the wilderness immediately after the match. On the same day as the cup-tie, Bootle had an arranged Alliance outing at Grimsby Town. Rescheduling, however, was not for them. In a move foretelling of the current regard with which the FA Cup is held, Bootle decided to fulfil their Alliance commitment and dispense their reserves to contest the cup tie. Here was an outstanding chance for Heath to extend their cup run. But the club committee was having none of that. If Bootle could field their stiffs then so could Heath. The first team not assigned any Alliance obligations on the same day? We'll engage them in all the glamour that a friendly at Darwen can provide.

The friendly was actually a good opportunity to try out a couple of possible candidates for the problematic full-back positions. Gallagher, a Scot, and Crosby, of unknown heritage, were trialled in the troublesome positions. The rest of the squad was composed of the regular first-teamers: Slater in goal, R. Doughty, Ramsay, and Stewart in the middle, and Farman, J. Doughty, Evans, Sharpe, and Milarvie in attack. The FA Cup team, meanwhile, resembled a typical Sir Alex era League Cup selection. There were few first-team players: Powell was making his last competitive Heath appearance while Mitchell and Owen provided further experience. T. Craig was given a run-out having lost his place to the attacking newcomers. Also selected was George Felton, the eternal reserve, who flitted in and out of the starting line-up for seven long years.

The remaining six players were all making their competitive debuts. William Gyves was in goal, a Mancunian by birth who had to wait till he was 23 years old to represent Newton Heath and would go on to make one more appearance in a friendly. The same statistics applied to Rattigan at left-half. Outside-right T. O'Shaughnessey's long name matched his long career with the reserves which lasted till 1894. He would get one more break with the first team, both figuratively and literally, thanks to a nasty injury in 1892. Left winger J. Donnelly and centre-forward W. Turner were never granted a second opportunity after this match. In contrast, 23-year-old Herbert Dale enjoyed a long association with the game. The Stoke-born inside-forward had to retire first, though, before embarking on a career as a Football League referee.

The full FA Cup line-up, then, was: Gyves; Powell, Mitchell; Owen, Felton, Rattigan; O'Shaughnessey, Dale, Turner, Craig, and Donnelly. They put up a good fight at Bootle, the stiffs, before succumbing 0-1. Over at North Road in the trial match, a 1-6 defeat to Darwen rendered the trial an error. Interestingly, 3,000 fans had seen the match at Monsall and just as many at Bootle. It seems Newton Heath had split the crowd evenly just like they had their players. George Evans, incidentally, could alone hold his head high. Of the 22 Heathens in action that afternoon, he was the only one to score a goal.

VIOLETS IN THE MIST

After all their struggles, December proved to be 'Revival of Newton Heath' month. Starting with a 3-1 friendly victory over South Shore, the Heathens enjoyed a seven-match unbeaten – and mostly triumphant – run. They even won a couple of Alliance games to climb up to seventh. All that Willie Stewart wanted for Christmas was to score five goals. He got his wish when North Road hosted Irish visitors Belfast Distillery and Newton Heath served up a special 8-4 thrashing to commemorate the occasion.

By this time, two major alterations had been made to the line-up. Firstly, John Clements had been signed from Notts County to finally solve the full-back dilemma. And secondly, George Evans had been randomly held to blame for every misfortune to blight the club since formation and shunted to the reserve team. This brought a reprieve to T. Craig who had lurked in the shadows since Evans' arrival. Clements partnered Mitchell in front of the ever-present Slater. Roger Doughty, Bob Ramsay, and Jack Owen gained a stronghold in the half-back line. The attacking unit, meanwhile, took and maintained the following shape for the rest of the season: Farman, Stewart, Craig, Sharpe, and Milarvie. Craig justified his promotion back to the starting line-up with a New Year's Day hat-trick in another friendly goal-fest, this time Cambridge Trinity were trounced 6-1.

Bad news was around the corner however. On January 2nd, a friendly derby at Ardwick was abandoned as a pea-souper engulfed Manchester. The thick fog itself was no big deal, except that Walsall Town Swifts were scheduled for an Alliance fixture at

North Road the next day, and these sods were known to complain about the elements if Jack Powell's missus stepped outside to water her violets. Sure enough, Walsall succeeded in nagging their way into a second annual cancellation. A 30-minute-per-half match was contested instead for the sake of the fans that had turned up because, apparently, unlike the players, they could see through fog. Heath won 5-2 with two goals from Stewart and one from Sharpe while the other two scorers were lost in the mist.

The Heathens now faced their most important challenge of the season: Stoke City at North Road. The Potters held a two-point lead at the top of the table, closely followed by Nottingham Forest and Sunderland Albion. Although, Heath had just 11 points, or half their guests' tally, they had four games in hand, - victory now would keep them in with a feasible chance of the Alliance title. Only 3,000 fans were optimistic enough to believe this hokum however. The forward line froze too, failing to score at home for the only time that season. Stoke emerged with a 1-0 victory and Heath's brief title tilt was over before it had begun and there were still nine matches to go.

The Heathens put that disappointment behind them by losing 1-6 at Birmingham St George's before allowing Walsall to leave North Road with a 3-3 draw before snatching their first away league win of the campaign by beating Sheffield Wednesday 2-1 with goals from Sharpe and Stewart. A smashing result – if it had still been 1889-90 but the Owls were still gutted at being overlooked for a league place and their form a year on left them stranded at the bottom. Meanwhile the Heathens were struggling to make an impact. This was not the glory the original Coachbuilders had in mind when they first decided to dabble in Association Football. The brochure had foretold of knighted gaffers and kings with upturned collars. Now they would settle for a fit Jack Doughty for their main problem brightly shone in the 'goals for' column: 31 strikes in 16 league fixtures as compared to 51 in just as many non-Alliance outings.

Four of those 51 goals had to be scored at Witton on February 7th, 1891 to surpass the three the hosts obtained of their own. If that was the only way for Newton Heath to register their first Lancashire Cup victory since September 1884 then so be it. Heath could now taste the previously forbidden fruits of the second round, namely a daunting away tie at the champions of England, no less. This called for the men from Monsall to raise their game and improve their aim. It worked to the extent that it inconvenienced Preston into having to stay behind for extra-time. Eventually the Heathens lost 1-3 with Alf Farman shaking the North End net. Incidentally, it was now accurate to use this term for only recently that invention had been implemented and the goals were now clothed. Word on the grapevine was that goal-line technology was up next for discussion…

A win at Crewe and a home draw with Sheffield Wednesday on February 21st was as good as it got for Newton Heath that season, although at least this meant they had avoided defeat in their last four Alliances matches, their best run in the competition so far. What's more, with 17 points already, Heath had risen to the dizzy heights of fifth. Nonetheless, they did not concern themselves with developments at the very top – Stoke were already out of reach. What they did worry about, however, was the bothersome nosebleed that being fifth brought about. The remedy was simple: blow your last four matches and tumble down the table to a more sedate ninth. This was even worse than last season! Stoke, with almost double Heath's points total, marched on to the title, though Sunderland Albion could have snatched it had they not made a mess of two of their last three games.

MANCHESTER REIGN FALLS

IT WAS THAT time again when flowers bloom and Alliance clubs flaunt themselves in front of the Football League selectors in the hope of getting picked for next season. And this time, there was an added incentive: the Football League was getting bigger and – supposedly – better, for the 12 clubs had decided to inflate to 14. This meant that there were now six places up for grabs. Despite finishing ninth, Newton Heath put in their annual bid, founded on audacity and not much else. The Football League voters got a good chuckle out of that and proceeded to pick anyone but Heath, Manchester's finest didn't muster a single vote! The four league clubs applying for re-election got their wish while Stoke became the first club to cross from the Alliance into the League. The real surprise, however, was that the final berth went to Darwen. They had finished as low as sixth in the Alliance but boasted friends in places as high as general secretary of the Football League JJ Bentley. An old Darwenian at heart, Bentley convinced the clubs to pick the Lancashire side rather than travel to places further afield. It was the sort of daylight corruption Arsenal would later resort to in order to claim their current top flight place. This so upset runners-up Sunderland Albion they opted to quit the Alliance and folded within a year.

Newton Heath, on the other hand, had no reason to get so worked up. The season had been one to forget. The committee's plan to discard its successful team and build another had failed miserably. It was like the rock band which, come the end of the concert, smashes its guitars on stage only to discover it can't afford replacements of the same quality. The campaign deteriorated by the month. In March and April, Newton Heath played 15 games and lost nine of them. But therein lays the consolation. If Heath could cram all their defeats into the 1890-91 season and write it off, there might yet be the promise of a brighter future.

A creaky backdoor seemed to be Newton Heath's main problem, while Jack Doughty's prolific spree was greatly missed up front. Five Heathens may have reached double figures in goals but the leading overall scorer, Willie Stewart, only notched 18. Wingers Farman and Milarvie were next with 16 apiece, while Sharpe got 14 and Ramsay 11. Quite impressive... until you realize the bulk of those goals came in friendly matches. In competitive football, six goals were all you needed to be Heath's top scorer, the same total, incidentally, managed by one G. Best in a single game some 80 years later. Bob Ramsay and William Sharpe found themselves with that total and sheepishly celebrated.

The wildest celebrations, however, were reserved for the Heathen fans upon hearing the club was booting out the whole sorry lot! Most of last summer's arrivals were shipped back out. George Evans - gone. Bob Milarvie was sold to Ardwick where he would become the first man to play league football for both Manchester clubs. Bob Ramsay was eventually offloaded to West Manchester who didn't want him either. On he moved to Northwich Victoria and Burslem Port Vale. T. Craig had arrived before the previous summer but he too was released. And William Sharpe may have been retained for a few more months but only until a gullible club came in for him.

But, as ever, it would not be the end of a season without Newton Heath's participation in the Manchester Cup final. For seven years now this competition had been contested, and for the seventh time Heath were present in the ultimate round. The trophy itself had been collecting cobwebs on their mantelpiece for the last three years. On April 18th, 1891, the green-and-gold shirts reappeared on the Brook's Bar grass lining up as: Slater; Felton, Clements; R. Doughty, Ramsay, Owen; Farman, Stewart, Craig, Sharpe, and Milarvie. One name missing was that of J. Mitchell, the man who had appeared in all six previous finals. But this match came one month too late for the record-setting full-back. On March 14th, he played his last match for the Heathens before retirement. His name has been traced in just over 200 Heath matches since 1885, though he probably appeared in another 25 unreported line-ups as well. His brief spell with Bolton Wanderers in 1888 made him the first footballer with Football League experience to represent Manchester United.

Mitchell's vacancy at right-back had lately been filled by J. Denman, who had been signed from South Bank for the benefit of the reserve side. In the final, however, the spot went to the more experienced George Felton, which was a bad omen, as far as the North Road faithful were concerned: whenever Felton had been called upon for an FA Cup or Alliance assignment, the Heathens had lost!

Incredibly, yet another new name awaited Newton Heath in the final – Ardwick. This meant that, seven years into the Manchester Cup, Heath remained the only side to have reached multiple finals. Ardwick were finally showing up on the radar now. Like Heath, they had just applied – and failed – to get into the Football League, although they had secured an Alliance spot for next season. This was going to be the most exciting final yet, and a competition record 10,000 fans gathered to see it. Barely seven minutes in, Weir fired a ferocious shot from distance that smacked the crossbar then cannoned in. Ardwick were ahead. The Heathens retaliated with shots that skipped Ardwick's bar altogether. In typical fashion, a John Clements foul saw both sets of players lectured by the referee. As time passed, the Heathens pressed hard. Their previous defeat in this competition was way back in 1887, but Ardwick were holding their own. Chance after chance was missed as Heath's forwards kept getting their kickers in a twist. Eventually, Ardwick, resorting to clearances of the 'Anywhere Will Do' variety, held on to win by that early goal.

Newton Heath's long Manchester Cup reign had finally ended. This was an obvious disappointment, but 1890-91 was a season to be written off. In a few months, a new campaign would kick off to find the men from Monsall stronger than ever. The Ardwick players would regret the day they dared to upset the mighty Heathens.

1891–92

THE FIRST RED DEVIL

A VERY LONG time ago, early in Manchester United's history, there had been a legendary hero at North Road by the name of John Doughty, or Jack to you and me. He was a crasher, a bruiser, a terror of the fields. He was the man who shoulder-barged Heath's enemies out of the way so the club could stride ahead towards its glorious destiny. Jack was a red devil before the term entered football folklore. In the last fifty years, perhaps the only United player who remotely compares to him is Joe 'Jaws' Jordan, and even he had to pull his front teeth out to scare opponents. Jack didn't need to. He simply lifted his sleeves all the way up to expose his battle-smeared shoulders. They were instantly recognizable, for they were imprinted on almost every Lancashire and Midlands club's centre-half's face.

If there was one thing Jack loved even more than pitch violence, it was scoring goals. 116 have been officially recorded but Jack scored at a rate faster than historians could keep track. One year he notched 42, or more. They were all for a great cause: to make Newton Heath 'Kings of Manchester'; to earn them the Football Combination title; and, ultimately, to consolidate them as an established Football Alliance outfit.

For all his deeds we will forever love Jack Doughty. Like all Heathens, he will always live in our hearts and in our thoughts. Well, have you ever heard anyone say a bad word about Jack? There is no one around who could do that, for Jack's era is long gone. To get a better idea of the timeframe involved, if you think World War II is ancient history, Jack's time was fifty years before that.

By the autumn of 1891, that era was coming to an end. Doughty was only 27, but his body was 72. A weekly diet of baiting, bumping, and shoulder-barging can do that to you. In the previous campaign, Jack had made intermittent appearances. In the upcoming one, he would put in four more stints before calling quits on first-class football. He had sacrificed his well-being and dashing looks for the good of Newton Heath.

A replacement was now needed of equal or greater value. It was obvious in the previous campaign that, when Doughty was absent, the Heathens were toothless. Thus, it was necessary before 1891-92 started to obtain new dentures. The club committee set out searching high and low. Wales didn't have any left. England proved fruitless too. Finally, the directors had to travel all the way up to Scotland to find their man, who went by the name of Robert Donaldson, or Bob to you and me.

Bob hailed from Coatbridge near Airdrie where, apparently, they made them rather strong. Bob was only 5'8" tall, but he weighed 12st 8lb, and none of it was fat. It wasn't muscle either, but rock – solid, hard rock. He may have been an apprentice moulder in his teenage years, but on the football field he was into demolition. His style of play was simple: he generally preyed inside the penalty area, and, whenever the ball was sent over, he made a beeline for it, squashing any earthling in his way. Ask the goalkeepers! Indeed, opposition custodians had to sport a 'This Side Up' sticker before getting on the field with him, making it easier to straighten them up after he had left them in a mangled heap. Back then, by the way, keepers did not need to be in possession of the ball to be assaulted. That law wasn't passed until 1894, probably at the behest of the Coalition of Robert Donaldson Victims.

Newton Heath were lucky to obtain Bob's signature from Airdrieonians, especially as FA Cup holders Blackburn Rovers tried to hijack the deal, promising him the world - £50 for his autograph and a whopping £2.50 in weekly wages. It took the intervention of the FA to sort Rovers out. Not that Bob had any qualms about joining the Heathens. When he arrived, near his 20th birthday on August 27th, he did not ask his new employers to match Blackburn's outrageous offer. Why make a fortune when you could earn as much as the average Football Alliance footballer? Donaldson was not in it for the money, rather to fulfil his destiny at Newton Heath, which transcended mere roughness. Although he was big on hard play, he had a soft spot for scoring, and he used that to great effect. In seven years at North Road, he outscored all

Heathens before him or after. Soon his goals would finally steer the club to its Holy Grail, the Football League. In Bob Donaldson, Heath had truly found the man to complete the hard work of Jack Doughty.

A SEASON OF NEW

BY 1891-92, football was starting to assume a form that is more recognisable today. Two new rules were passed in the close season to make the game more armchair supporter-friendly. The first was the introduction of the penalty kick, an Irish invention that the English authorities finally came around to. The second was that goal nets, already pioneered, were now deemed a 'must'. Some would say this was done in response to penalty kicks or, at least, the way Alf Farman took them. The Brum Bomber, with his blistering blasts that included one shot hammered home from the touchline, was the ideal Newton Heath candidate to assume spot-kick duties. At the time of inception, interestingly, goalkeepers were allowed to hare towards the kicker, though you would think that running away from a Farman fireball would seem like a more sensible course of action. Alf, incidentally, would soon carve his name in history by converting the first spot kick in English football while simultaneously earning his club a 1-1 friendly draw with Blackpool on September 5th, 1891. Nine days later, the first Football League penalty was also scored by Heath – John, that is – representing Wolves against Accrington.

A new feature was present at North Road. A stand had risen from the mud for the benefit of the 1,000 best dressed clients. Ground improvements were surely welcome, what with at least one bumper gate expected for the visit of local rivals Ardwick, now that they had finally made it into the Football Alliance. They were only one of three replacements for League new boys Stoke and Darwen and Sunderland Albion; the others being Lincoln City and Burton Swifts. And it was against the latter that Newton Heath kicked off their Alliance programme on September 12th. Despite Bob Donaldson, with a debut goal, and Alf Farman scoring, Heath still lost 2-3. The clues for the defeat were in the line-up: Slater; McFarlane, Clements; R. Doughty, Stewart, Sharpe; Farman, Edge, Donaldson, Sneddon, and Henrys. Five Heathens were making their Alliance bows while William Sharpe and Willie Stewart found themselves in midfield. Sharpe had been Heath's top scorer in the league last season. The directors, however, were not too impressed with his paltry return of six goals and asked him to assume the role of jack-of-all-trades for now. It took them until November to realise he was master of none. By December, he was playing against Heath in Ardwick's colours. Sharpe further endeared himself to the Heathen fans by turning up for Arsenal during 1894-95 before returning to Lancashire with spells in Oldham and Wigan.

By contrast Stewart took to centre-half like a Cantona to a Theatre of Dreams. He had proven himself up front, but now he evolved into a ball winner and fine passer while still retaining a liking for the odd goal or three. It is a good job Opta statisticians weren't around at the time for Stewart would have overworked them. With a simple switch he had become one of the best centre-halves in the business, and he would continue to render his services there until 1895.

Positional adjustments aside, there were a lot of new names for the Heath players to remember on that opening afternoon. Donaldson we have already met, but there were a few others to get to know. The most prominent was arguably inside-right Alf Edge, who had ominously came from Stoke treading the same path as Bobs Milarvie and Ramsay. Born in Goldenhill back in 1864, Alf had experienced a long association with the Potters. In fact, when they originally turned professional in 1885, Alf was the first player to pocket the princely sum of half a crown and repaid them by scoring their first competitive hat-trick when he banged five FA Cup goals on the same afternoon as Newton Heath's infamous tie with Fleetwood Rangers in 1886. When Stoke won their place back in the Football League in 1891, Edge was left behind in the Alliance. The Heathens picked him up in the hope he would work the same charm for the second year running.

The other new inside-forward, the well-built John Sneddon, was not burdened with so many expectations. His only previous role of note had been a very brief stint with Accrington last season. Next to him at outside-left stood Arthur Henrys - the 21-year-old Geordie came from Gainsborough Trinity. Although a forward, he did everything but score. The Heath committee finally cottoned on and relocated him to midfield.

With as many as four strikers signed, picking up someone for the defence seemed like a nice gesture. Bob McFarlane duly arrived to fill J. Mitchell's vacant right-back slot and find love in Manchester. Bob was so in awe of the Doughtys he married their sister, Ellen. A Great British lass, Ellen was. Born in England to an Irish father and Welsh mother, she ended up marrying a Scot. The Scot in question was born in Airdrie himself and played for Airdrieonians before moving to England, first with Bootle and, lately, Sunderland Albion. Clearly the committee liked Bob's commitment for he was handed the Newton Heath captaincy faster than he could say 'I love you'.

HEATH v. ARDWICK

WHEN THE NEW season's fixtures list was first released, one match in particular was circled for close attention by footy-mad Mancunians: the Alliance tussle between Newton Heath and Ardwick on October 10th. This was going to be the first competitive match between the two sides. Sure, they had met several times in the Manchester Cup. In fact, Ardwick had only recently defeated Heath in the final after years of the Heathens using previous encounters for shooting practice. This proud city, like Birmingham, now boasted dual representation in the Alliance.

The funny thing was, this fixture was gazumped to all the glory when the randomness of the FA Cup draw dictated that Newton Heath and Ardwick square up in the first qualifying round a week earlier. Now, this was going to be the first real competitive meeting, and 11,000 overexcited Mancunians congregated at North Road. Jack Owen was back in the line-up by now as the newcomers were starting to better understand each other's exotic style. The best initial understanding was of Alf Edge's runs, and he benefitted to the tune of a home debut hat-trick in a 4-0 thrashing of Bootle. Then Birmingham St George's - with Thorpe sent off - lost 1-3 at their own patch thanks to a Donaldson double. Bob, however, had the luxury of sitting out any FA Cup involvement this season as a consequence of his late registration with Heath. In his absence, these Heathens took to the field: Slater; McFarlane, Clements; R. Doughty, Stewart, Owen; Farman, Edge, Sneddon, Sharpe, and Henrys.

Fittingly, it was an encounter that had nearly everything. For a start, none of the 22 players kicked off. That was undertaken by the local MP, Sir James Fergusson. Goals, there were aplenty, though the majority easily belonged to Heath. There was also enough derby-style rough play to soothe the blood-seekers among the audience. First, Bob Milarvie's return to Monsall was made into a painful one. Then, Roger Doughty broke a finger that required him to manfully shriek on the sidelines for about ten minutes and, on top of all that, there was one of those innovative penalty kicks. It went Ardwick's way and was taken by Joseph Davies, a Welsh international though not the ex-Heathen. Slater, however, superbly fisted the ball away to keep the game scoreless. Eventually, John Sneddon put enough bobble on his shot to wrong-foot Ardwick's keeper: 1-0 at half-time. The Heathens piled forward after the break, Sharpe's pass was missed by Edge, only for Farman to come steaming in and send a revenge-seeking missile into the net. Roger Doughty, recovered from his snapped digit, notched from another Sharpe pass to ease the pain before Pearson fired home a free-kick for the visitors. This so riled Heath that Farman and Edge took turns hammering goals high into Ardwick's net. 5-1 was the final score though it could easily have been more, the Heathens apparently facing Ardwick's keeper William Douglas on one of his good days. Douglas would later have many bad days in Heath colours.

First spoils had gone to Newton Heath, flavoured with revenge for last season's Cup final loss and topped off with a record FA Cup win. As for Ardwick, they were once and for all accorded their place in Manchester football's pecking order. The last thing they wanted was a return to North Road the following week for confirmation of their inferior status. This time they had to handle their own kick-off too, the politician having seen enough and stayed away. Roger Doughty was the only change for the Heathens, his finger injury exacerbated by a damaged shoulder. It doesn't require a qualified physio to determine the cause of that knock. In Roger's place came Bob Donaldson who wasted little time notching his fourth goal in as many Alliance appearances. He was starting to settle at Monsall, not only in terms of goals, but also in general play. Later on in this match, he went on a typically bullish run which helped earn him the reputation of being a ball-hog. Retaining possession, however, was crucial for him: the longer he held on to the ball, the more he absorbed his opponents' knocks, the more powerful he became.

Alf Farman, meanwhile, concentrated on obtaining another brace to go with the one from the earlier FA Cup tie. It helped that Weir had tried to double up as an auxiliary goalkeeper, giving Farman the chance to teach Ardwick how a spot kick should be taken. Their bigger lesson, however, was the bitterness of a 1-3 loss. From that day, they swore never to venture near North Road again.

GOODBYE… HELLO

TEAMS LOOKING TO go on a successful run should try whipping Ardwick a couple of times. It certainly gave Newton Heath a tonic. Unlike in the first two seasons, Heath were experiencing life at the trendy end of the Alliance table this time around. The form they showed in the late pre-organised football days was now being reproduced on a stage that mattered, the only game they failed to win was a 2-2 draw at Grimsby, and they would have – courtesy of another Donaldson double – had the referee blown for time on 89 minutes. Burton Swifts, on the other hand, were punished for turning up half an hour late with a 3-1 beating. There was a special treat for the patient North Road crowd: Jack Doughty was making his first Alliance appearance in over a year. And, yes, being Jack, he got on the score sheet.

By the end of October Heath were in second place in the standings with nine points from six matches. The leaders were Nottingham Forest, who were discovering the benefits of turning professional. They had played seven games and won them all but the Heathens did not care. Their form and reputation were working wonders, especially in the FA Cup. The second qualifying round opponents, Heywood, arrived in Monsall a quivering wreck, barely able to stutter the words 'we forfeit'. Suddenly, Newton Heath found themselves in a cup run that did not involve breaking sweat. They eventually got a workout when a friendly was contested instead, and that was when 'forward' Arthur Henrys chose to convert his only goal for the club. When South Shore were seen off 2-0 in the subsequent round, Heath's suspicions were confirmed: to enjoy an extended run in this competition you need to start off at the qualifying stage and draw all the fodder. Indeed, despite their three victories so far, the Heathens had not even reached the first round proper yet.

One man would remember this tie more than most: the club's longest-serving player; that man Jack again. This was Doughty's last game for Heath, and he signed off with his 116th and final goal. He was now retiring from first-class football – later spells at Hyde and Fairfield are a testament to that – and the grateful Heathens rewarded him with a benefit in April with a team of Welsh internationals, providing the opposition.

Around this time there was the first sighting of another monumental name from the club's history. In the Alliance fixture at Crewe, the Heathens came up against Harry Stafford, who would play a key role in the creation of Manchester United 10 years on. For this match, he gave a brief preview of his services by scoring an own goal to help Heath along to a 2-0 victory.

While waiting for Harry's arrival, the club made a more immediate signing. Ashton-born Billy Hood was only 18 years old when Heath snapped him up. Billy represented Heath in all five forward positions, both wing-back spots, as well as right-back, though not during the same match. Unfortunately for Hood, his debut was as it good as it got. Entertaining Lincoln City on November 21st, Newton Heath plundered four goals before the interval then added six afterwards for a club record Alliance win of 10-1. Hood scored twice, as did Stewart, while Donaldson helped himself to a hat-trick. It was downhill after that as they were only able to beat Walsall Town Swifts 4-1 the following weekend. Only Donaldson maintained any scoring consistency when he notched a second successive hat-trick. He had now accumulated nine goals in the space of eight days, having scored another three in two midweek friendlies.

It was a shame then that he could not be unleashed in the FA Cup. Both Bob and Billy Hood were able to put their feet up as Newton Heath hosted Blackpool. And, with Jack Doughty having hung up his boots altogether, reserve right-back J. Denman was forced to masquerade as a forward. At least Heath managed to find a way out of the interminable qualifying rounds, albeit through a 3-4 loss.

One team to take advantage of Heath's FA Cup commitments

was Sheffield Wednesday, who rose to second in the table while Heath had other plans. The Alliance's inaugural champions had emerged from their season long strop at being overlooked by the Football League and had recently handed leaders Nottingham Forest their first league loss of the campaign. Coincidentally, Newton Heath were up next at Olive Grove, Sheffield, where one of the matches of the season unfolded – at least as far as Mancunians were concerned. Goals from Sneddon, Farman (2), and Owen gave them a 4-2 victory – their eighth in nine matches – taking them back to second spot. They still trailed Forest by five points, but they now had three spare games with which to catch them.

THE TITLE CHASE

In victory or in defeat, Newton Heath were making the net wish it had never been invented. Friendly results, for instance, widely ranged from a 3-6 loss at Bolton to a 5-1 pummelling of the Canadian touring team. These were the same professors and doctors who had visited North Road in 1888 and won 2-0. All they could do on this occasion, however, was to go in hard on reserve inside-forward O'Shaughnessey, then diagnose him with a broken leg. On the contrary, they could not get anywhere near Alf Farman, especially when he picked up the ball outside his area, sold half his opponents dummies to take back with them to Canada as souvenirs, and crashed home a dazzling solo effort.

This was the second time in a week that Alf had brought the house down. On Boxing Day, Newton Heath went in to grab their half-time tea trailing Small Heath 0-3 at North Road! A brace from Edge edged the home team towards an incredible comeback and, in the very last minute, Farman equalised to send the delirious crowd leaping into the air. And it was quite the superhuman achievement too, considering there were as many as 7,000 fans at North Road – the ground's record attendance for an Alliance match. For now! Mancunians had gone footy-mad this season: the rivalry with Ardwick; the title drive; goals galore; and not to forget the new stand. Heath's average gate for the first two Alliance campaigns had been 3,000. This year it had nearly doubled to over 5,000.

By the most generous estimates, 16,000 fans crammed into

NEWTON HEATH, 1891-92.

This selection walloped Walsall Town Swifts 5-0 on March 5th, 1892, in a Football Alliance fixture. Back row, left to right: Mr. Peddy (trainer), Mr. Jones (director), Mr. Bird (occasional club cook affectionately called 'Father'), Bob McFarlane, J. Slater, John Clements, Mr. Smith (club's umpire before linesmen became neutral), and an unknown. Middle row: Roger Doughty, Willie Stewart, and Jack Owen. Front row: Alf Farman, Billy Hood, Bob Donaldson, John Sneddon, and Alf Edge.

North Road on New Year's Day, 1892, for the top-of-the-table clash with Nottingham Forest, not only creating the ground's greatest attendance ever but possibly the largest congregation of mud-wrestlers in one place. The interest was understandable as Heath had cut the gap to three points with a game in hand. Yet despite being subjected to a physical onslaught on the pitch and a verbal one off it, Forest held on for a 1-1 draw, Edge netting for Heath.

Sheffield Wednesday were scheduled at Monsall on January 23rd and anyone arriving at the ground fifteen minutes late would have been shocked to find Newton Heath four goals up. The bigger surprise would have been to see the opposition wearing the royal blue of Small Heath rather than blue and white of Wednesday. Having sneaked ahead of the Heathens by playing two extra matches, the Owls planned to prolong their second-place experience by cancelling their North Road appearance at the last minute. The riled up Heathens arranged a friendly with the Brummies instead and proceeded to wallop them 7-2. Bob Donaldson, who tormented Small Heath with a hat-trick, was a fair fellow. Crewe were accorded the same treatment a week on and another treble in a 5-3 triumph took his tally to 16 goals in 15 Alliance outings.

113

Newton Heath were back in second now on 23 points, still three short of Forest. Sheffield Wednesday finally summoned enough courage to turn up in Monsall on the 20th of February. They brought along a well-prepared plan too to go in one goal up at the interval. The Heathens rallied in the second half and secured the most crucial equalizer through Billy Hood: it kept Heath ahead of the Owls while setting a new record for the Alliance of 15 games without defeat. There is a reason I mention this now. The run inevitably came to an end a week later at the hands of Small Heath. Walsall Town Swifts, however, immediately presented themselves for a backlash. Five-nil they were battered, with a brace each from Farman and Sneddon, and a rare contribution from McFarlane. Jack Owen was unavailable to do any back lashing as he was concentrating instead on gaining international recognition at long last. Wales were hosting England in Wrexham and, when he lined up alongside his brother Bill, Jack became Heath's first capped player in two years.

It had to happen one day and, on March 12th, 1892, it finally did: Newton Heath were eliminated in the semi-final of the Manchester Cup! It required the summoning of the Wanderers from nearby Bolton to finally halt the Heathens after they had won all of their previous 20 ties outside the final. For seven years it had been easier to touch your right elbow with your right hand than to prevent Newton Heath's appearance in the final. But, this season, the Heathens had a shorter skirt to chase. Not the Lancashire Cup – that was dumped after a one-night stand – but rather the Alliance title, with an ulterior motive in mind: penetrating the Football League's sacred ring.

Appropriately, Newton Heath had the hottest of dates coming up next: away to Nottingham Forest on March 19th; first versus second, now separated by only two points, nothing that a Heath victory wouldn't take care of. You could tell Mancunians – if not Sky Sports – were excited when 3,000 of them packed their lunch boxes and travelled to Nottingham. Soon they wish they hadn't. So much congestion caused delay and the Heathen masses arrived at Forest's Woodward's Field to find their team already one goal down. By the 14th minute, it was two; by half-time, three. The Heathens had frozen! Was it nerves? Tiredness? Not of roughness – for that they had plenty of reserves – but for producing the sort of comeback that had lately become their party trick. For the rest of the game, they applied pressure but their best efforts were wasted by Donaldson shooting high and Sneddon straight at the keeper. That this 0-3 defeat was their worst of the season was the consolation. The really bad news was that their hopes of winning the Alliance were virtually over.

ACCEPTED

FATIGUE MAY SOUND like a cheap excuse for Newton Heath folding at Nottingham Forest, but it was actually the main reason. How else can you explain the committee's decision to freshen up the team with two new faces for the final three fixtures of the Alliance programme? Most stale was Slater, apparently. Since joining in the summer of 1890, the keeper had been ever-present appearing in all but one league match: the early season visit of Bootle. That appearance had been credited to Cash, the reserve team goalkeeper. Unfortunately for Slater, his 'goals allowed' setting had been stuck on '3' for the last few games. He was duly given a rest which remains indefinite to this day. John Davies was obtained from Burslem Port Vale with orders to mind the net until the season finished. Heath also signed the Glaswegian Mathieson brothers: 22-year-old William, a left winger from Clydeside, and 18-year-old John, a right winger from Irvine. Tiny but cool under pressure, William went straight into the first team while John was saved for reserve football and the odd non-competitive outing.

The additions had the desired effect. Indeed, when Newton Heath defeated Birmingham St. George's in the last match of the programme, they were able to overhaul idle Nottingham Forest. It had taken three years and 66 matches, but the Heathens were finally at the Football Alliance's summit. They were champions-elect... with one proviso: that Forest lose their remaining three fixtures! There was some hope, for all three were away, but, alas, Heath's first appearance on top of the Alliance table would also be their last. Forest beat Small Heath 2-1 on April 16th to guarantee the championship before adding another point from their other two matches. Newton Heath were consigned to the runners-up spot.

Strangely, the Heathens were not too downbeat about this

narrow failure. It was a similar situation to the one in May 1968 when Manchester United ceded the Division One title to neighbours City on the ultimate day of the league campaign. It should have been the worst time to be a Red - but it wasn't; for there was something considerably more important just around the corner. Back in May 1892, that something was a golden opportunity to gain Football League status for, this year, change was in the air. Having been a resounding success since its inception, the Football League was constantly pressurised by a host of envious clubs wanting in. Some kept bugging, others begging, most bigging themselves up until the League could take it no longer. Finally, a radical solution was found. The League would expand again – to 16 clubs – by scooping up the two best candidates on the market; additionally, all the leftovers would be rounded up in what would constitute the Second Division of the Football League. Now, everyone would be happy.

Happiest, of course, would be those admitted to the new Division One itself. As Alliance runners-up, Newton Heath fancied their chances of securing one of the five tickets to the big time. It should have been six but an exception was made for the new FA Cup winners, WBA. Nowadays, such an accolade grants you qualification into Europe. Back then, it simply afforded you a 'Get Out Of Election' card. The rest of the League's bottom four – Accrington, Darwen, and Stoke – had to wait for the election process to determine their fate. Soon the results were out: Sheffield Wednesday, 10 votes; Forest, 9; Accrington, 7; on 6 votes were Stoke; also on 6… were… Newton Heath! By a single vote, possibly a misjudged one, the Heathens had nipped ahead of Sheffield United to finally become a Football League club, and a First Division one at that. Even Darwen missed out, not to anyone's displeasure. After blagging promotion the year before by using their prestigious connections, they realised that whoever lives by the vote similarly dies by the vote.

In truth, this was a deserved reward for the season Newton Heath had enjoyed. 31 points was the highest any Alliance runner-up had ever gathered. They had gone unbeaten for 15 matches and had scored 129 goals overall, 69 in the league – easily the division's best tally. Of those, the books show that Bob Donaldson was responsible for 20 in 22 matches, though he might have possibly nicked more. In the penultimate game of the season, the Heathens visited Lincoln City whom they had earlier thumped 10-1. On this occasion, they only managed a 6-1 win. This so under whelmed the newspaper reporters they could not be bothered to list all the scorers. Just the goals by Sneddon and Mathieson have been traced, the other four subsequently earning the honour of being the only unknown competitive goals in Manchester United's entire history. There is a conspiracy theory that claims the identity of these scorers is hidden somewhere in a vault underneath the North Stand at Old Trafford, along with other secrets, such as why Jaap Stam was sold and where it wrong for George Best! With that being so far-fetched, a more viable suggestion is to allocate some of these goals to Donaldson on the grounds of probability. This too should be rejected once the following piece of trivia is taken into consideration: in 1927-28, Everton's Dixie Dean set a record of 60 league goals in one season. Yet during the campaign, Everton thrashed West Ham 7-0, and none of the goals were Dean's!

Regardless, Bob's tally was outstanding for a debut season, his overall total reaching 34. Also prolific was Farman, who probably provided more goals from the wing than crosses: 28 overall and 16 in the league. This meant he finished as Heath's all-time Alliance top scorer with 25. Missing one match since his Alliance bow obviously helped. Three other forwards also reached double figures: Edge 16, Sneddon 14, and Hood 10. Surprisingly, two of them never kicked a ball for Newton Heath again. The unlucky John Sneddon was let go and absolutely nothing is known of him thereafter. He had one successful season then disappeared out of North Road. Alf Edge had enjoyed an even better year but he was offloaded too, though only at the second attempt. Both Alf and Arthur Henrys had supposedly been sold to Notts Jardines until the FA detected some creative accounting in the paperwork. They promptly banned the Jardines official and suspended the pair for three months. Heath were stuck with them until November! Eventually, Henrys proved useful in a few Football League matches before departing to Leicester Fosse. As for Edge, Heath realized they still had his receipt so they returned him to Stoke City.

Sadly, after six years of shoulder-barging all comers, Roger Doughty bid farewell to Monsall. 215 times he had donned the famous green-and-gold jersey, scoring half a century of goals. He had a nice collection of three Manchester Senior Cup winner's medals. He also helped the Heathens to top spot in the Football Combination and, more significantly, runners-up in the Alliance. The club thanked him for his services, ushered him off to Fairfield, and asked him if he could take goalie J. Slater with him. Roger's departure signalled the end of the Welsh influence at North Road. Newly-capped Jack Owen remained at the club for next season, but he was largely confined to the reserves. The principality's stars had played a glorious role in the history of Newton Heath up to now, but, from this moment on, a new era was about to begin.

1892-93

THE LIFEGUARD

FOURTEEN YEARS AGO, they had been kicking balls in their spare time in a deserted yard outside the Newton Heath LYR depot. Now, this railwayman's team was a member of the country's footballing elite. The club's rise to the First Division of the Football League not only reflected greatly on the local area, but on the entire Republic of Mancunia as well. You could imagine then the citizens of this republic's surprise whey they opened the papers one summer day in 1892 to discover that Newton Heath LYR was no more! The name, that is, had been amended to exclude the trailing 'LYR' part. Newton Heath, the club, had decided it was time to break away from the railway company. It should have been an emotional break-up but the two parties opted to go with childish instead. The company reacted to the news by evicting the Heathens, who misinterpreted the eviction order for 'anything you can carry, you may take with you'!

You could understand the LYR's point of view. For years they had housed the Heathens, hauled them around, and put them on the schedule. As soon as prestigious League status was attained, however, the railway were discarded. Yet it is possible to relate to Heath's side of the story as well. The railway did help – to a certain extent – while the running of the club was a relatively small operation but if the club were to compete against the League's top outfits then the LYR suffix would be like a ball and chain around Heath's ankle. Eventually, tempers cooled and the Heathens gave the missing items back. In return, the railway company allowed them the use of North Road… for a nifty £530 a season! Heath agreed but not without the proviso that some ground improvements were made. The Heathens weren't asking for advances in hygienic convenience, per se, just the instalment of baths and dressing rooms to sort of point the stadium in the general direction of Division One standards; and raising the ground on both sides of the pitch to bump the capacity up by five thousand or so.

Once Heath decided to fly solo, they announced their plan for world domination. They were turning into a limited liability company, to be floated on the market. Two thousand shares were accordingly issued at £1 a pop. Oh, to have two grand in hand and the chance to zip back in time! All you had to do to own one of those shares was hand in the completed form to Newton Heath's brand new secretary. Alfred Harold Albut was the name, or 'A.H.', as Heath's first paid official was generally known. At the time, the secretary oversaw most aspects of running a club. Albut had honed his administrative skills at Aston Villa. For how long is not known, but he was spotted as early as 1887 in their FA Cup-winning team photo. He had been a sportsman himself in his younger days in Birmingham, excelling at cricket.

From the day he was hired by Newton Heath, Albut faced an uphill task. The shares did not prove as hot an item as the club had hoped, meaning they were floated on insufficient capital and the club were doomed to struggle for the rest of their history until Manchester United came along. Albut's role was to keep them from sinking. It was like being given a basket with some fish and bread in it and implored to feed the entire village... for the next eight years!

Luckily, if there was one man who could perform any duty big or small, it was AH Albut. He was a wily, bubbly character – a know-it-all who could do it all. If you can imagine Bob Hoskins' personality allied to MacGyver's gimmickry, you've got Albut in a nutshell. Tales abound of his legendary deeds. At first he was holed up in a tiny cottage at 33 Oldham Road, but soon Heath could no longer afford the rent of 30p a week! Albut moved to a disused classroom in a school off Silver Street in Miles Platting called the 'Institute'. This was soon converted by the innovative Albut into a social club were all Heathens – players and fans – could be brought together to hang out and mingle. Building the club's spirit, he termed it, and he talked the directors into purchasing a billiard table to aid the process. It proved a success... until someone came up with the idea of offering cues as trophies to game winners. This scheme came to an end once the number of available cues dropped

THE NEWTON HEATH FOOTBALL CLUB COMPANY
LIMITED.

SHARE CAPITAL - - £2,000

In 2,000 Shares of £1 each; payable as follows: 2s. 6d. per share on application. 2s. 6d. per share on allotment, 2s. 6d. per share two months from allotment, 2s. 6d. per share four months from allotment, and the balance as required in calls not exceeding 2s. 6d. per share at intervals of not less than two months between each call.

FORM OF APPLICATION FOR SHARES.
(TO BE RETAINED BY THE SECRETARY.)

TO THE DIRECTORS OF

THE NEWTON HEATH FOOTBALL CLUB COMPANY, LIMITED.

GENTLEMEN,

Having paid to the Company's Secretary the sum of £   :   : being a deposit of 2s. 6d. per share on an application for   shares of £1 each in the above Company, I request you to allot me that number of shares upon the terms of the Prospectus, and I agree to accept such shares or any less number allotted to me, and I agree to pay the further sum of 2s. 6d. per share on allotment, 2s. 6d. per share two months from allotment, 2s. 6d. per share four months from allotment, and the balance as required in the terms of the Prospectus, and I authorise you to place my name on the Register of Shareholders in respect of such shares. In the event of the shares not being allotted to me the amount of the deposit to be returned in full.

Name (in full) _____

Address _____

Occupation _____

Dated _____ *1892*

THE NEWTON HEATH FOOTBALL CLUB COMPANY
LIMITED.

SECRETARY'S RECEIPT.

Received this _____ *day of* _____ *1892, from*

_____ *of* _____ *the*

sum of _____ *being the deposit of Two Shilling and Sixpence per share required on an application for an allotment of* _____ *shares of £1 each in the above Company.*

£   :   :

STAMP.

SHARES: Just fill in one of these to purchase a share of Newton Heath.

below that of snooker tables.

Eventually, Newton Heath fell behind on the room's rent too, the corporation cut off the gas supply and served the Heathens a summons. A directors' meeting was doomed to darkness, only for Albut to step in and turn it into a romantic rendezvous lit by three candles affixed to beer bottles. However the summons itself provided the material for Albut's greatest stunt. He had been monitoring developments at another club where a certain player had not been getting paid lately. The slick Albut took him to the side and concocted an elaborate ploy. Soon the player was in his secretary's office, the blue paper in hand, demanding he received his wages or he would serve the summons! Absurdly, the embarrassed secretary fell for it without verifying the wording. Next thing you know, Albut had snapped up the released player who subsequently put an extra tenner on the next gate. Neither the club nor the footballer's identity is known, but there is no denying his excellent acting skills.

Albut was not afraid to get his shoes dirty. When Newton Heath moved to their new home at Bank Street, he could be seen in clogs washing the goalposts and the perimeter fence in preparation for the ground's opening. That, incidentally, was the setting for another famous Albut gimmick. To raise extra money, he placed an ad in the match programme inviting the fans to come hear "Michael the Bank Street Canary in full song" – for a small fee, of course. Sure enough, about a hundred additional spectators showed up for the next fixture… only to be greeted by the honking of a goose! Why anyone would pay to hear a canary in the first place is beyond me but late 19th century Mancunians must have liked that sort of thing. It is worth reporting that the plucky goose met with a sad end, disappearing shortly before Christmas from his special sty at the ground. Word on the street was that an irked fan had exacted revenge. The truth, however, was that this was the work of Albut himself, who had been beefing the poor creature up for his festive dinner all along.

A SQUADRON OF SCOTS

THEY WERE EXCITING times as usual at West Craigie Park, home of Dundee Our Boys, in mid-June 1892. The club was hosting their

10th Annual Amateur Athletic Sports, but it was threatening to be their last. The cause of concern was that mysterious fellow prowling through the crowd, observing with studious interest, and diligently taking notes. By the time they figured out he was a Newton Heath scout, he had convinced three of their players to migrate south. Jimmy Coupar won the dribbling contest; Fred Erentz was the sprint master; and James Brown joined them, just for the sake of it. By the following year the club would have changed its name to Dundee, its obsolete suffix making more sense if it were tagged behind Manchester instead.

Frederick Erentz was born in March 1870 in Broughton Ferry, right outside Dundee. He blamed the un-Scottishness of his surname on his father, who was Danish, and that is how he explained his blond mane too. A 5'10" left half-back, he was lured to Monsall with the promise of £2. 10s a week to fill Jack Owen's void. When he arrived in Manchester, he caught the pheromones from the air and at once decided he was staying here for the long haul. Indeed, Erentz would still be around ten years later when Newton Heath played their last match. Jimmy Coupar was also born in Dundee, was a year younger than his team-mate and stood just 5 feet 6 inches high. He was perfectly proportioned to play inside-right, where he combined craft with elusiveness and topped them off with a tendency to whack the ball goalwards on contact. Coupar was a primitive Dennis Viollet prototype, if you like. Not much is known about James Brown, who moved in at Rose Villa on Stanley Street, except that his brief sojourn at left-back was notable for awry distribution.

This trio was but a portion of Newton Heath's shopping spree in the close season of 1892. A whole squadron of footballers were dragooned as the club prepared for League life. A recruitment policy that seemed like good insurance once the team captain, Robert McFarlane, hoofed it to Airdrieonians as 1892-93 approached having studiously collected his wages all summer long. Miffed no end, the Heath directors instructed their Scotland scout to head on to Airdrie and sign their left-back out of spite! Andrew Mitchell was duly purchased then converted to right-back, a position that had been Mitchell-free since J. left the year before. While Alf Farman's claim to fame was that he had scored the first penalty in English football, Andrew Mitchell could counter that claim: in the summer of 1891, he had given away the first spot kick in Scottish football! In Manchester he would slump to an even lower nadir when he would notch a brace of own goals to help Aston Villa along towards their 1893-94 title success. Nonetheless, the solid, 5'11' defender with the powerful shot was an excellent acquisition for the Heathens, an improvement on his predecessor, even. For Bob

JIMMY WARNER

Jimmy Warner put more effort into posing for portraits than he did catching trains to games.

McFarlane fate caught up with him when he caught pneumonia in 1898 and pass away soon after. Just in case there was not enough Tartan flavour in Monsall, one more Scot's signature was secured, that of Adam Carson. And it required terms of £10 down and the not-too-shabby £3 per week. The wee inside-left came from Glasgow Thistle, bringing along his repertoire of intricate moves.

Sated by Scots, Heath added the odd Englishman or two into their shopping basket. Most prominent was 27-year-old Jimmy Warner, born in Lozells, Birmingham, a goalkeeper's punt away from Aston Villa's headquarters. Coincidentally, that was his position and Villa were his club of six years after an initial spell with Milton. While some of his new team-mates were gleeful with their Manchester Cup medals, Warner could have walked around dangling the big one around his neck – an FA Cup medal won with Aston Villa in 1887. Yet he preferred not to, just in case the topic of conversation got round to his 101st and last appearance with the Villains. They had again reached the FA Cup final in 1892 and were favourites to beat WBA after they had swatted them 5-1 and 3-0 in the League. When Albion produced a 3-0 final upset, the Villa hierarchy placed the entire fault at Warner's door. He was accused of having bet on an Albion victory and promptly sacked before the accusation could be proven false! That is when Heath pounced to secure a superior replacement for Slater.

NEWTON HEATH, 1892-93.
Newton Heath of the First Division gather for the start of the 1892-93 season. From left to right, back row: Mr. Massey (groundsman), Jimmy Warner, and John Davies. Middle row: Mr. Taylor (director), Mr. Albut (secretary), Mr. Fairbrother (director), Andrew Mitchell, George Perrins, Willie Stewart, James Brown, Fred Erentz, John Clements, and Mr. Lateward (director). Front row: Alf Farman, Jimmy Coupar, Bob Donaldson, Adam Carson, Billy Hood, and William Mathieson.

Finally, George Perrins, also a Brummie, was signed from Birmingham St. George's. They had been alone among last season's Football Alliance teams to refrain from joining the Football League, eschewing centuries of mediocrity by folding instead. Consequently, several of their players drifted into the League, the speedy Perrins being Heath's catch. Only nineteen but with a ferocious tackle, he was a dashing fellow – he smiled when he flattened you. Though it may seem an exaggeration that nearly every other Heathen was a tough nut, Perrins certainly liked to put his retaliation in first, third, and fifth. In the company of Bob Donaldson and John Clements, Perrins found his spiritual home in Monsall.

SEPTEMBER 3RD, 1892

IT WAS TIME! Years of fighting tooth and nail – and the odd shoulder-barge – to drag the club to its destiny; application upon application for acceptance by the elite; and every drop of sweat shed by the Sam Blacks, the Jack Powells, and the Doughtys; had converged into one historical moment: Newton Heath were about to kick their first ball in the First Division of the Football League. At the extreme end of optimism, the Heathens could ostensibly win the whole bloody thing. But seeing as that would take another 15 years, for now they could settle for a place in mid-table. If that were to fail, then a narrow escape from the drop on the last day of the campaign would do. Irrespective of all these possibilities, the 1892-93 season promised to be an extraordinary adventure.

Excitement and anticipation filled the air on September 3rd, 1892. It was the opening day of the season for a league that was now bigger than ever – 16 teams were to fight for the title. And there was a Division Two as well. Champions Sunderland were scheduled to stretch their legs at Accrington. Nottingham Forest, winners of the Football Alliance, had a tricky trip to Goodison Park, where Everton had just moved from Anfield. Another promoted team, Sheffield Wednesday, faced Notts County. But the toughest task of all awaited Newton Heath: an away trip to Blackburn Rovers! That is *the* Blackburn Rovers. Preston may have had their 'Invincible' year and Sunderland may have been the reigning champions, but Blackburn were simply the most famous club in football. Five times they had won the FA Cup, including three on the trot. They were founder members of the League and they boasted more internationals than some entire countries. Newton Heath's league bow was a fixture from hell, devised by Satan himself.

It seems his minions were about too, one setting the Lancashire Rain Gauge to 'torrential', another doing his evil work at Salford Station. Despite the rain, a fire broke out there costing the Heathens half an hour in detours. It wasn't the ideal preparation for such a momentous match neither did it get better when they walked onto the field at 4pm. The greeting committee consisted of 8,000 partisan fans and just as many raindrops per second. Then there was Rovers' line-up: Pennington; Murray, Forbes; Almond, Dewar, Forrest; Chippendale, Walton, Southworth, Hall, and Bowdler. Not all were international players, just seven, with one destined for future honours. As for Heath, now that the Welsh connection was over, they could not muster one cap even if the selected eleven underwent a comprehensive strip search. This was Manchester United's historic first league line-up: Warner; Clements, Brown; Perrins, Stewart, Erentz; Farman, Coupar, Donaldson, Carson, and

Mathieson.

Six of them were newcomers. The seventh summer purchase, Andrew Mitchell, was not yet eligible, so he was selected as linesman! At least he stopped short of refereeing the game himself, leaving this task to Mr. T. Holme of nearby Farnsworth. When Manchester United kicked off their inaugural Premier League match in 1992-93, it took them five minutes to fall behind to Sheffield United. A century earlier, they did not even wait that long. Barely three minutes in, Rovers' England centre-forward, Jack Southworth, collected a pass from Forrest, barged past Heath's wide-eyed defenders, and shot straight into Warner's hands. He fumbled the ball then watched in horror as it rolled over the line. Was Heath's most experienced player nervous, or had he put a fiver on the time of the first goal?

It was a terrible start and soon things got better – for Rovers. After the ball had struck his hand, Hall stabbed it home, the referee ignoring the visitors' complaints. It can only be assumed Mitchell was manning the opposite line. 2-0, still Blackburn held the momentum. In the 13th minute, Chippendale darted to the byline and pulled the ball back for Hall to a wallop a third. Blimey, at this rate it would finish 18-0! Welcome to the First Division.

To say Heath were shell-shocked was an understatement: Jitters, inexperience, bad luck - these won't do in the top flight. After all Bob Donaldson was facing a club he turned down, could they be so superior if they wanted him in their ranks? In the event Donaldson initiated Heath's response. After a nice move, he took a mighty swipe and notched Manchester United's first ever league goal. Heath were now in the ascendancy and hemmed Rovers in. Shortly before the break, Jimmy Coupar pulled another goal back after finding space when his marker, Forrest, ran into a strategically-placed Donaldson shoulder. There was still time to complete a stunning comeback when Farman crossed, but Mathieson's header was superbly blocked by Pennington.

Having got over their obligatory nervy start, the Heathens dominated for a full half hour of the second half. Blackburn could not create much, especially as, every time Southworth darted forward, he found himself flattened by Clements or Perrins, or both. But Heath were made to pay for failing to capitalize when on top as, with just over ten minutes left, Bowdler's cross was cushioned by Hall for Chippendale to bang in and the crowd were jubilant. Heath attacked again, Farman's shot well saved by Pennington. But he now knew what was needed. A minute later, Alf tried again, his howitzer packed so much power that the goalie didn't bother. With time almost up, Mathieson broke down the left and sent in a dangerous cross. All heads rose to meet it... but it was a Blackburn one that got there first. The home team that had begun so splendidly was now reduced to frantic defending to prevent an equalizer. But Rovers held on to win a cracking match 4-3 and Heath had more than played their part, initially through nerves then through verve. Barring the opening quarter hour, for 75 minutes, they had made the most of their first ever league match.

FIRST AND FOREMOST

ONCE NEWTON HEATH had set the ball rolling on the league era, there was no turning back. Forever, perhaps? One match was out of the way and 29 were left of this season's programme, the next of which was equally important. On September 10th, Heath faced Burnley in the first ever Division One fixture to be held in Manchester. It was only apt then that their selection consisted of eight Scots and three Brummies! Andrew Mitchell put an end to his days in black by replacing Clements at right-back. A Bob Donaldson goal in front of 10,000 fans secured a 1-1 draw and the club's maiden point.

Heath's initial bite of top flight football, however, had a bitter aftertaste. In the return game at Burnley they lost 1-4, then a 0-6 hammering followed at Everton. This is what the First Division was all about. Yet the Heathens bounced back two days later when it was Everton's turn to travel. For 75 minutes they held their guests at 1-1, but what they could not do was hold the sun in the sky. Darkness decreed that the match be abandoned and Heath's chance of an improbable recovery dimmed. The Heathens then earned their first away point with a goalless draw at WBA, only to succumb to them at home (2-4).

The Heathens had already worked their way to the bottom of the table. The Football League was proving to be harder than anything Mancunians had previously encountered. It was easy to see what the problems were. The papers were busy detailing them.

The forward line was elaborating. Carson and Mathieson's finesse was all dandy, but they were so lightweight you could fuse them together and the hybrid would still be too fragile for this division. In defence, James Brown's kicking verged on the abject, and even the North Road faithful were ignoring manners when addressing the referee! As outlandish as it may sound that team tactics are based on newspaper suggestions, this is what appears to have happened next. Brown was demoted to the reserves, Clements coming in to become Mitchell's partner for a year; Billy Hood was preferred to Coupar at inside-right; and Mathieson's injury was used as the perfect excuse to draft James Hendry, a new Scot freshly delivered from Alloa Athletic.

Additionally, daily training was cranked up a notch. If cross-country running is not original enough for your liking, Newton Heath beat even the continentals to this one: hammer throwing! What purpose it served is unclear, but what is apparent is that most in need of practice was Willie Stewart. His best effort was so wayward it arrowed straight towards the side of Bob Donaldson's temple. For once Bob could not head it away, reacting instead by dropping to the floor unconscious. The blow was feared to be fatal at first, but Donaldson was not made from solid rock for nothing. He was back in the line-up two days later, the incident having indirectly achieved its initial aim of team bonding: Donaldson scored in the loss to WBA while Stewart was man-of-the-match!

Hopes were high for a first league win when fourth-placed Wolves came to Monsall on October 15th. The Manchester skies rained all day in preparation. Had this been your first trip to North Road you would not have needed to ask for directions, just follow the mud trail that led straight to the ground. Inside it was worse, the pitch puddles were so deep groundsman Charlie Massey doubled up as lifeguard on duty. The Wolves' players were stunned, all bar ex-Heathen Joe Davies who was probably responsible for one or two of those puddles.

The rearranged Heath took to the field thus: Warner; Mitchell, Clements; Perrins, Stewart, Erentz; Farman, Hood, Donaldson, Carson, and Hendry. The instructions were clear – shoot to score. Most attentive was James Hendry. Barely thirty seconds into his debut, he smashed the ball home with his first kick in English football to seal a place in the record books! And to think he would have made his bow a week earlier had he not been held behind in Scotland by the illness of a close relative. On four minutes, Stewart put Heath 2-0 up and, when shortly after Farman added a third, the club could finally start dreaming of a victory. Wolves' biggest mistake was to pull a goal back because that enticed the Heathens into grabbing three of their own… in the first half! The visitors did not score after that, but little did it matter as Heath still piled forward, driven by desire and the forces of nature. It was as if six games' worth of frustration exploded in one outing. Donaldson, always up for personal accolades, produced the club's first league hat-trick, closely followed by Stewart. Hood also scored and even wee Adam Carson. The final result was an emphatic 10-1, which made Heath unique in that their first league win is also their biggest ever. Had the players known that then they might not have bothered again. As it is, they have had over 4,000 attempts since and we're still waiting…

KILLER KNEES

THIRTEENTH! THAT IS where a record double figures victory takes you. The league title did not interest Newton Heath. Mid-table mediocrity translated to stability in their language. Now that they had figured out how, the Heathens added another three goals in the rearranged fixture with Everton. How they wished they had assigned someone to man-mark the visitors' outside-right Alex Latta. He alone struck four times, and what originally was destined for a draw morphed into a 3-4 defeat. Then they were unlucky to succumb to a narrow 0-1 reverse at Sheffield Wednesday, the cold-stricken Perrins and Stewart manly insisting on playing and sneezing their way back to 15th spot.

Soon, however, there was worse news. On the same afternoon as the savaging of Wolves, the Newton Heath Reserves took to the field at Darwen with the instructions to take no prisoners. Newly demoted to the reserves, James Brown took it literally. Just ask Joseph Aspden, Darwen's 18-year-old fringe player. He was on the sharp end of a typical Brown tackle and kneed in the stomach! Apparently, Brown's balance was as refined as his kicking, and that added a dash of slip into his slide. Although Aspden was able to continue the game, after peeing red for eight days, he sadly died from undetected internal bleeding. Brown was devastated. Luckily, the court deemed the incident accidental and Brown, despite causing the killing, was allowed to continue making a living. He was actually called up to the first team a couple of weeks later for a hastily-arranged friendly with Darwen in memory of Aspden, whose older brother was a regular starter for the club.

Ever since their groundbreaking league win over Wolves, all Newton Heath had been dreaming of was a second one. That finally occurred on November 19th with a fine 2-0 defeat of third-placed Aston Villa. The Heathens were back in heady 13th themselves. Disappointingly, they could only muster a 2-2 draw at bottom of the table Accrington, though both their goals were provided by the brand new left-wing partnership. Tommy Fitzsimmons and James Colville had recently been signed because, with just the nine names at the latest count, the Heathens evidently did not boast enough Scots on their books. Just a few weeks earlier, the pair had been marauding down Annbank's left flank. Although Annbank were not a league team, they were reportedly the best outfit in Ayrshire, so that made them ideal for the English League in the eyes of the committee. In truth, the directors had had enough of Carson and Mathieson's miniature act.

The bulky Fitzsimmons took over at inside-left having just turned 22 last month. He had made his debut the previous week, scoring a cracking individual goal in the victory over Villa. As for Colville, even at 5'7" he was already a one-inch upgrade on Mathieson at outside-left. This had been a problem position for the club these last few years, the directors presumably yearning for a left-footed Farman to fill the void. Alf's displays had attracted so many lucrative offers from rivals teams that he must have been tempted but he turned them all down to stay at North Road.

Sadly Colville proved to be no left-footed Farman. His size never struck fear into opposition backs although his uncanny resemblance to a young Saddam Hussein may have done. Unfortunately, he hurt his ankle shortly afterwards and only turned out in a few games thereafter. The void at left-wing was symptomatic of the club's continued struggle. A 0-2 defeat at Wolverhampton on December 17th sent them back to the basement, before Sheffield Wednesday handed out a 5-1 pasting on Christmas Eve. Two days later leaders Preston edged out a Boxing Day tussle 2-1 to leave Heath three points adrift at the bottom. All those years they had dreamt of reaching the heaven of the First Division only to discover that, once they got up there, it turned out to be hell.

SEVEN AND ONE

ONE GAME REMAINED in 1892 for Newton Heath, Derby County came to North Road looking to extend the home team's losing streak. But this turned out to be as hard a day to explain as when Wolves were hit for ten. Heath played tremendously and behaved impeccably (even Mr. Jope, the referee, said so) in a 7-1 rout. Donaldson notched his second hat-trick of the season to make it 12 goals in 17 league matches and Farman helped himself to a treble too, the odd goal being scored by Fitzsimmons. If it hadn't been for County's splendid goalie Robinson and the referee chalking off a further 4 goals, a new record victory would have been achieved.

The mood going into the New Year was as you'd expect following a 7-1 win. True, Heath were still three points adrift of Derby at the bottom but a few more results like that and the club would creep up the table. For despite their lowly position, Heath had easily the best home scoring record in the division. The following Monday, Heath played cross-town rivals Ardwick for the first time in over a year and struck five goals to make up for lost time. Unlike future United-City tackle fests, this friendly was played as 'friendly' as possible. And friendliest of all was goalie Warner whose kindness allowed Ardwick to grab three goals of their own in front of an estimated 10,000 crowd. The very next day, the Heathens continued their hot scoring run in another local friendly against Fairfield, at the same time taking the opportunity to catch up with old boys Slater and Roger Doughty. The 5-4 win meant the team had scored 17 times in four days.

On the Wednesday, Heath decided to take a break, the committee sending the players to Matlock Bath for a few days "with a view to the approaching cup tie". Well, with goals galore and a nice, albeit short, winter break, hopes were high for the trip to Stoke on Saturday. And then fate stepped in to deal a severe blow to any hopes of a revival. The railway had created Newton Heath but now it stabbed it in the back. Jimmy Warner missed the train to Stoke and left the other ten to face their hosts alone. The versatile

SPOT THE KEEPER

The famous Newton Heath team photo with the missing goalkeeper. It was taken in January 1893 shortly after Jimmy Warner was suspended by the club for missing the train for a match in Stoke. Back row, left to right: Arthur Henrys, and John Clements. Middle row: Timmins (trainer), Jimmy Coupar, George Perrins, Willie Stewart, Fred Erentz, and Andrew Mitchell. Front row: Alf Farman, Billy Hood, Bob Donaldson, Tommy Fitzsimmons, and James Colville.

Willie Stewart had already performed in seven different positions for the club, now he was asked to add goalkeeper to his collection. So Tommy Fitzsimmons retreated to centre-half leaving his wing partner Coupar alone on the left. Evidently so did his Stoke markers as, before you knew it, Coupar had given Heath the lead! But there was no way that those ten men were going to resist seventh-placed Stoke for long. Soon the eleven men equalised. Then they took the lead and started adding to it. The brave Stewart did his best in his new position but soon he'd had enough. So Fitzsimmons gave it a try in goal. That didn't help. Clements had a go too and by the end the Heathens had reversed the score line of the previous weekend, 1-7. It was a new record defeat in their fledgling Football League history, and it would remain so for the next 33 years.

Back in Manchester, the directors were furious. That's what playing one man short (a goalie, no less) does to you, they reckoned, and they knew exactly who to blame for this calamity.

Some may have inquired as to why the team played four games in eight days. But it was Warner who got it in the neck. The goalie had compounded an inept performance at Ardwick in midweek by carelessly missing his train for the next match, the seven goals conceded was the last straw for the committee. Warner was suspended and reserve custodian, John Davies, was given the chance to add to three first-team outings he had made at the end of last season's Football Alliance programme.

Which brings us to the case of the perplexing picture: the team photo of 1892-93 that has caused a mystery. There's Henrys and Clements at the back. There's Coupar, Perrins, Stewart, Erentz, and Mitchell in the middle. And seated you have Farman, Hood, Donaldson, Fitzsimmons, and Colville. But wait, there is no goalkeeper! The photo was published on January 28th as card number 15 and many historians believe it was taken the day of the Stoke match. But I don't think so. Firstly, why would you take the team portrait on an away trip? Secondly, and most importantly, if that was the same day, then either Colville or Henrys could have played when Warner did not show up. It is more probable that the photo was taken a day or two after the Stoke match, by which time the directors had suspended Warner but not yet decided with whom to replace him. That would explain Davies's absence from the picture. Equally, he might have simply missed the train!

ECHOES OF RONALDO

Davies' re-introduction to the first-team only emphasized why he shouldn't have been there. As the goals kept leaking in, Stewart might as well have continued between the posts. A further five more league matches were lost with aggregate goal figures of 2-19. Even Warner was allowed back after apologizing for his disappearance. But following two 5-goal showers, he was dropped for good and, come the end of the season, banished to the wilderness of Walsall Town Swifts.

The FA Cup visit of Newton Heath to Ewood Park struck fear into the hearts of Blackburn – the local medical board trembling at the thought of hundreds of Mancunian spectators spreading an outbreak of smallpox into the town! The doctors even advised Rovers to postpone the match, but, wary of being kicked out of the competition, Blackburn ignored doctors' orders. In the event, the Rovers could not treat the Heathens' infection, but they did relieve them of the headache of having to combine a relegation fight with an extended cup run. The 4-0 score line was replicated one week later by Bury in the first round of the Lancashire Senior Cup.

Things were now looking very bleak for Newton Heath. Out of two cup competitions, they had barely scraped through the Manchester Cup third round thanks to a Fitzsimmons brace at West Manchester. While Sunderland surged to a second successive league title, the Heathens slid towards relegation. Or not quite. In this first ever season of having two divisions, the Football League had not agreed on automatic promotion and relegation. Instead, a novel idea was hit upon: a series of one-off test matches between the top division's bottom three and the lower division's top three. Heath, bottom of top, still had hope!

The directors realized they still had one shot at survival and did the sensible thing by recruiting new talent for the battle ahead. Suitably, the reinforcements came from the unlikeliest of places. On February 4th, the team played their first ever game outside English soil when they visited three-time Irish champions Linfield for a friendly. And just as Manchester United would absolutely have to buy a mesmerizing youngster called Cristiano Ronaldo when he starred for Sporting Lisbon in a 2003 friendly, history preceded itself some 110 years earlier. Linfield defeated the English visitors 2-0 but those tourists were so impressed with the local forwards that they decided to take two back with them to Manchester as souvenirs. Souvenir number one was James McNaught, a tiny Scotsman who, for a change, came to England without crossing the border. A two-time champion in Scotland with Dumbarton, he was enticed with a job as a boilermaker and terms of £4 a week, while in the summer he would get £2 a week for doing nothing.

But the bigger catch was outside-left Jack Peden. A folk hero in Ireland, he was set to become the first of his ilk to represent Newton Heath in League football. Peden's similarities with Ronaldo did not end there. He too was a crowd pleaser and a decent goal scorer. When Linfield won the inaugural Irish championship in 1890-91, he scored 19 goals in 14 matches. By the time he had retired a few years into the next century, he had added five more championships and four cup medals with both Linfield and Distillery. McNaught and Peden were registered on February 23rd. A week later, another forward was signed, and in time he would develop into Newton Heath's greatest-ever striker. Twenty-year-old Joseph Cassidy, a Lanarkshire-born Scot, was signed from modest Blythe F.C., a small town club in the northeast of England.

So on March 13th, all three lined up in the new-look Newton Heath forward line: Coupar, McNaught, Donaldson, Cassidy, and Peden. The occasion was a friendly at Bootle and the hosts were trounced 4-1. Both ex-Linfield men scored, but as Heathens fans looked forward to an exciting end-of-season, little did they know that neither of the two were going to play a part in it! Proud Irishman Peden was the owner of 12 caps already, and he certainly intended to add to them in the upcoming British Championship. Since England-based players were not selected for Ireland at the time, Peden opted to postpone his Manchester experience until the following season. Now the comparisons become less akin with Ronaldo and more with Gabriel Heinze, the Argentine who delayed his United bow to represent his country in the Olympics. Meanwhile, the 22-year-old McNaught was the unlucky casualty of one friendly too many, dislocating his shoulder at no-good Ardwick on March 27th. Like Peden, he would not show Manchester his true potential until the following season.

CLASH OF THE HEATHENS

So, ONLY JOSEPH Cassidy remained of the new recruits, making his league bow at the end of March. Almost four weeks had elapsed since the last Division One outing and, in the meantime, other results had confirmed that Newton Heath could no longer escape the bottom three places, the test match beckoned. With the pressure removed, or perhaps buoyed by the new recruit whose presence had attracted a five figure gate, the Heathens managed to stop their losing streak and gain revenge on Stoke. Again Heath took the lead (through Farman's 10th league goal) but, assisted by an 11-man contingent on this occasion, they shut up shop thereafter. The 1-0 score line confused Newton Heath. Mr. Albut inquired about the meaning of that circle after the '1' and was informed that it meant a 'clean sheet'.

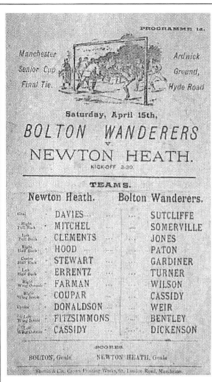

PROGRAMME 1d.

Manchester
Senior Cup
Final Tie.

Ardwick
Ground,
Hyde Road

Saturday, April 15th,

BOLTON WANDERERS
v
NEWTON HEATH.
KICK-OFF 3.30

TEAMS.

Newton Heath.	Bolton Wanderers.
DAVIES	SUTCLIFFE
MITCHEL	SOMERVILLE
CLEMENTS	JONES
HOOD	PATON
STEWART	GARDINER
ERRENTZ	TURNER
FARMAN	WILSON
COUPAR	CASSIDY
DONALDSON	WEIR
FITZSIMMONS	BENTLEY
CASSIDY	DICKENSON

SCORERS

BOLTON, Goals   NEWTON HEATH, Goals

Shortis & Co., Cross Printing Works, 97, London Road, Manchester.

MSC FINAL PROGRAMME, 1893.
The programme of the 1893 Manchester Senior Cup final, played on April 15th. Newton Heath defeated Bolton 2-1.

It had certainly been a Good Friday. Cassidy had performed admirably at outside-left, raising hopes that this problem position could now be fixed. Almost everybody had had a try out there throughout the campaign, and since Peden was taking his time coming over, Cassidy filled in. The next day North Road hosted Preston North End, the only team still capable of catching Sunderland at the top. The Heathens surprised even themselves by winning back-to-back league matches for the first time. Two goals from Donaldson did the damage, handing the championship to Sunderland. The Wearsiders thanked the Heathens by tanking them 6-0 three days later! But this was just a blip in an ever-improving season climax for Heath. Another point was obtained in the final fixture against Accrington on April 8th. In what proved to be Newton Heath's last match at North Road, the division's bottom two teams fought out an exciting 3-3 draw. Now both had to wait a fortnight before the test matches that would decide next season's status.

Before then, Newton Heath had their old friend the Manchester Cup to fall back on. They reached the final with a 3-1 victory against Bury when Fitzsimmons notched another brace in the competition. Now the opponents were Bolton Wanderers, Heath's conquerors last season and a Top Five side this one but this did not bother the Heathens too much. They were the masters of the Manchester Cup and they wanted their trophy back. In a closely-fought tussle, Heath won 2-1. Cassidy notched his first competitive goal for his new club but the other strike would never win a 'Goal of the Season' award. It was obtained in what can only be described as Newton Heath style. Following a melee in front of goal, Bolton's custodian John Sutcliffe, and England's new Number One, got hold of the ball, only to find himself barged past the goal-line by a crazed posse of Heathens! It was a perfectly legitimate tactic back then and a favoured mode of scoring of one Bob Donaldson. So perhaps the posse consisted of just Donaldson in a whirlwind of dust. The goal, though, can be best classified as an own goal by Sutcliffe. It was he, after all, who was kind enough to carry the ball over the line. The Mancunians never forgot his lovely gesture and signed him... ten years later.

April 22nd was the date set for the test matches. Six teams in England still had one game to fret about. Notts County faced Darwen, Accrington squared up to Sheffield United, and Newton Heath were left with the hardest task. For finishing last in the First Division, they were paired with Division Two champions Small Heath Alliance. The Birmingham club had lost just three league games all season and scored an astounding 90 goals in 22 matches. They were favourites but Heath clung to the hope that their recent improvements that had seen them lose just once (against champions Sunderland) in the last 12 games, would see them through.

The venue was the Victoria Ground, Stoke. The weather was sunny but there was a strong wind; and about 4,000 fans filed into the stadium. Newton Heath were represented by the heroes of the Manchester Cup final: Davies; Mitchell, Clements; Perrins, Stewart, Erentz; Farman, Coupar, Donaldson, Fitzsimmons, and Cassidy.

The Heathens of Manchester kicked into the wind in the first half and soon found themselves under the cosh from the Heathens of Birmingham. Gradually they picked up the pace and soon enough were playing their part in a very exciting encounter. Both teams excelled and both keepers were doing a decent job. Now Farman set off on a tricky run leaving four Brummies in his track. It came to no avail; only for a short matter of time. Soon Cassidy zoomed down the opposite flank and put in the perfect cross. Farman cut in from the right and smashed the ball diagonally into back of the goal: 1-0 Newton Heath. The Mancunians were lifted and remained on top until the interval. Small Heath came out stronger in the second half and, despite determined defending from the Mancs, the Brummies pulled level with a rasping Wheldon shot. The rest of the match was played at full speed but neither team was able to take the lead. 1-1 it finished and the outcome was still undecided. The two teams had to play again. Newton Heath had refused to die.

The results from the other two test matches saw Notts County and Accrington beaten and relegated. Would Newton Heath make it a trio of teams to lose their First Division status? The following Thursday, Heath travelled to Sheffield to face their fate. Thousands of railway workers accompanied them across the Pennines to Bramall Lane. Heath made one change: the injured Stewart dropping out, Perrins sliding across to fill his place and Billy Hood coming in at right-half. The game started and it was only polite for the Mancunians to let the Brummies take the lead this time. Immediately they regretted it and pinned Small Heath in their own half, only allowing them the odd counter-attack. The trapdoor to the Second Division was wide open and Newton Heath had no other option than to pour forward. Eventually the pressure paid off when one of the Brummies, struggling to keep up with the barrage of Newton shots, fisted the ball away when it was heading to goal. No, the culprit wasn't Hands the outside-left but rather Barley the right-back! Farman, he of the rocket shot, stepped up and fired home despite the goalie rushing six yards out in an attempt to block. In the second half, the rejuvenated Mancs simply took over. Cassidy, Coupar, and Farman (twice) found the net and by the final whistle, Newton Heath had triumphed 5-2. Despite finishing five points adrift at the bottom of the table, despite conceding 85 goals in the process, and despite winning just six matches (none of which came away from North Road), Newton Heath stayed up. A big thanks was due to the new man Cassidy. And what about Alf Farman? His four goals in two test matches had more than repaid the benefit match (Ardwick were the opponents) the club had granted him a couple of weeks earlier.

Heath's survival had surprised most observers and even impressed some. Well, one team, at least: Celtic. The champions of Scotland had noted Joe Cassidy's role in keeping the Heathens up and decided that he was good enough to lead their attack for next season. Initially he moved on loan but soon permanently. It was a great loss for Newton Heath. Cassidy had been made club captain upon arrival, and he soon galvanized his troops to a rousing end to the season. The fans would not forget his deeds and would be thrilled when he returned two years later. However, he would never play in the First Division again for the Heathens. His departure also meant that the three stars signed in mid-season – Cassidy, McNaught, and Peden – would only ever play one friendly match together.

Cassidy aside, the rest of the end-of-season releases highlighted what still holds true today: the only way after Manchester United is down! Goalie Warner was ditched to Walsall Town Swifts before he migrated to America to work as a Boxing promoter, Colville went to Fairfield, and Brown, still affected by the death of the Darwen player, returned to his hometown Dundee. Adam Carson, like Warner and Brown, had been there when Heath took the very first step in League football. But he had been discarded long before them. Back in March, not only did he transfer to Ardwick, but worse, to Liverpool a short while later. Another March departure was half-back Henrys, destination Leicester Fosse. Two other players disappeared without a trace but not before scribing their names forever in the statistical history of Manchester United. One was James Hendry, the scorer of that quick-fire goal against Wolves in the first-ever victory. He managed one more match before getting injured. In his absence one Joe Kinloch was picked for the visit to Nottingham Forest at the end of October… and never again. He lacked pace, or experience, or something.

As for Jimmy Coupar, another test match hero, his case was more complicated. The troublesome injury he picked up in October kept him out for three separate spells, but the club did not want to lose his services. The popular Scot had performed rather consistently when fit and even contributed five league goals. The directors, using the full extent of medical assessment available to the physio, told him to take some time off back home in Scotland to recuperate. One whole year, in fact. Not only that, they even agreed to pay him £1.25 per week until he recovered. And they say today's stars are pampered! So Coupar took the money and rode into the summer sun. The fans too drifted away into the summer break, chatting about this eventful season and the narrow escape. In a few months they would return to a new home.

1893-94

THE END OF THE (NORTH) ROAD

Nortth Road had seen the birth of the club. It was there that the first Manchester United footballers kicked a ball. For 15 years they gathered there after long hours of work and washed their blackened faces off with North Road's mud. Mud? Yes, it was everywhere. But only from October to May. The rest of the time it was hard as rock, with craters and divots left behind when all the stud-marks had dried. It was not up to top flight standards, so said visiting teams. Heck, even Heath's own players complained. They were tired of changing half a mile down the road at the Three Crowns pub. As for the supporters, they had had enough of trekking back and forth in ankle-deep puddles. Emotional attachment aside, everybody wanted a move to another home. And not because the grass was greener on the other side, but simply because it was existent on the other side.

By the end of 1892-93, it became imperative that the board find another ground, partly to escape the appalling facilities, but mainly because the club was being kicked out! North Road was the property of the clergy of Manchester. The Lancashire and Yorkshire Railway had always covered all costs of using the ground. When Newton Heath decided to go solo, the railway company hiked up the rate and kept the biggest chunk. Only 'a nominal fee' was passed on to the Cathedral authorities. In fact, the Dean and Canons did not deem it right that fans had to pay to get into North Road. Heard the one about the professional club that had no source of income? The Heathens were banned from charging admission. The situation with the landlords got so bad that a notice to quit was issued. The directors, having spent considerably on North Road improvements, had no option but to relocate the club.

Mr. Albut and the directors skipped their summer holidays in

BANK STREET FUMES - CAPTURED ON CAMERA!
Bank Street's noxious fumes can be seen during a match. The stench helped to provide Newton Heath with a great home record.

1893. They were busy finding Newton Heath a new place to call home. For a while it seemed that they wouldn't have a place to play when the season started. But by mid-June the worrying was over. The search had stumbled upon Bank Street, in Clayton, three miles south of North Road, and situated along the railway. The Heathens had cut the umbilical cord, but they were still mummy's boys. The Bradford and Clayton Athletic Company Limited owned the stadium and agreed to let Newton Heath use it every year from September to April.

The directors were thrilled with their find. Bank Street was more spacious than North Road and could accommodate larger crowds. Along one side ran the main stand, which was upgraded in time for the new season. It was divided into separate sections with respective ticket prices. The highest payers among loyal fans would even have cover over their heads, but alas, no prawn sandwiches were provided. The opposite side had a stand too, while the ground was elevated behind one of the goals to fit more spectators. Facilities extended to a wooden hut where the lads could put their kit on without getting stuck in traffic. And no one could have been happier than Mr. Albut when headquarters moved from Oldham Road to the stadium: a table was placed in the wooden shed where the **Manchester Evening News** conducted its correspondence, and now Albut could call it his office. In a unique occasion in the history

JACK PEDEN
Newton Heath's first Irish star

of United, the management and press were roommates.

With Bank Street located in an industrial area, a typical chemical works stood adjacent to the ground. Day after day, the chimneys belched out toxic fumes that poisoned the air and left a hellish stench for the entertainment of ground guests. The Heathens, by mutation or otherwise, would soon get used to these stinky conditions and utilize them to their benefit when facing unprepared visiting teams. Soon the legend grew that if Newton Heath were trailing at half-time, a message would be urgently relayed to diehard fans at the works. More coal would duly be dumped onto the fire so that when play resumed, the visitors would find themselves surrounded by choking smoke. The accustomed Heathens, meanwhile, would take advantage and storm to victory.

Results over the years provide statistical proof to this tale. By the time Manchester United moved to Old Trafford in 1910, the club had played 281 League games at Bank Street. Only 42 were lost – a rate of 15%, as good as any era in United's history. Another problem that visitors were liable to encounter was with directions. The club left the Newton Heath part of the city but held on to the name. This was too confusing for some of the southern teams, and there are one or two incidents of teams travelling up to North Road only to find an abandoned, unkempt stadium. They then had to dart through Manchester towards the source of the stench, barely in time for kick-off.

Most importantly Bank Street had that green stuff the Heathens had seen at away pitches: grass so good it was rated one of the best in the land. Inaccurately, as it turned out. A few matches in and the pitch turned into a quagmire. So, Bank Street's field ended up being just as bad as North Road's, but with more people to view it. But in the bigger picture, Newton Heath had a new ground now, and in the next 17 years their stay at Bank Street would see a

League title, the FA Cup, new ownership, and some of the greatest stars of their day, in short it would see Heath grow into United.

THE GARDEN OF PEDEN

Jack Peden was one of the stars of his day, in Ireland at least, where the biggest guarantee of success in the title race was having him in your line-up. Six Irish championship medals with Linfield and Distillery attest to that. His cup exploits were not bad either: four winners' medals and enough goals to put him in the top dozen cup scorers in the world before 1900! By that time he had been capped an astonishing 24 times, scoring seven goals. And he was currently the toast of the whole island having just banged a hat-trick against Wales, the 4-3 win being Ireland's third ever victory. And now he was finally coming to Newton Heath. No, not as a guarantee of title success, but perhaps in the hope that his weaving, crowd-pleasing runs down the wing would complement his new non-dribbling team-mates. At least his temperamental nature would fit right in with the Heathens: he could count to ten and still retaliate.

Peden's debut was on Bank Street's opening day: September 2nd, 1893, the first day of Newton Heath's second season among the country's elite. Burnley, sixth last term, were the visitors along with a five figure crowd that put to rest fears that locals would not accompany the team to its new location. Peden was instantly to the fore on the left wing. Twice he put in splendid crosses but Donaldson and Clements met them with shots of the 'shoot-first, aim-later' variety. Just before half-time, Peden was off again, a thrilling run ending with a cross from which Farman made the score 2-2. More mesmerising moments in the second half and the crowd had seen enough. When the final whistle blew to signal a 3-2 home win, the fans headed straight towards Peden, carrying him shoulder-high from the pitch. Spare a thought for Farman on the opposite flank. In the previous game, at the end of last season, he had struck three times to save the club from relegation. Today he claimed another hat-trick to make Bank Street's unveiling a victorious day. Yet he had to walk on his own two feet to the changing hut.

Three other players made their debuts on the same afternoon. Like his old team-mate Peden, McNaught was finally making his league bow – only six months after joining from Linfield. Known as the 'Little Wonder" – for being tiny yet possessing silky skills and superb passing ability – he played at inside-right and almost scored on his debut. However, and strangely considering his 5'6" size and non-aggressive style, by the end of his first season in Manchester he would be converted into a centre-half!

Filling in at left-half was newcomer Will Davidson, the latest talent to be whisked from Annbank in Scotland. Davidson would soon earn the respect of the fickle Bank Street crowd and make the left half-back position his own. Previous incumbent Fred Erentz had to go all over the pitch in search of first-team action, eventually settling at left-back, where he would be found for the next nine years. And Heath had a new goalkeeper! Jimmy Warner had caught the permanent train to Walsall, while John Davies took a one-way ticket to the reserves. So between the sticks stood 21-year-old Joe Fall. He came from Middlesbrough Ironopolis but he hailed from Miles Platting and thus became the club's first local Football League player.

One player who would not be back at Newton Heath for 1893-94 was Jimmy Coupar. Remember him? The popular Scot was deemed in need of a year's rest with weekly pay. Well, he returned briefly to Manchester having miraculously recovered but only to inform the First Division club that he would be joining non-league Scottish outfit St. Johnstone instead! Fancy that happening today. Obviously whichever miracle remedy he had used to heal his leg caused cranial side effects as well.

THE PEAK

Newton Heath's line-up at the outset of 1893-94 was invariably as follows: Fall in goal; Mitchell and Clements as full-backs; Perrins, Stewart, and Davidson forming the half-back line; and Farman, McNaught, Donaldson, Fitzsimmons, and Peden up front. It could be argued that this selection saw Newton Heath at their peak. Since the kick-abouts in 1878, the club had continuously risen in status. Now, after cementing their place in Division One, the Heathens entered a period of about six to seven weeks when they were at their zenith. It was the moment for which men such as Black, Powell, and Albut had strived. Of course it wouldn't last for long, as fate again would butt in with a defining blow...

The second match of the season was lost at West Brom, and then Farman scored the only goal of the game as Newton Heath won at Sheffield Wednesday. Let me say that again: Newton Heath won at Sheffield Wednesday. Yes! A short while into their second season in the Football League, the Heathens had finally obtained their first ever away league victory. Not only did that stop a nine-game losing bender, it also secured the first imported points since November 1892 – a 10-month embargo. And most importantly, it took Newton to joint second in the table. Well, eleventh to be precise, but on the same number of points as all the other ten bar Aston Villa who were top with five points having played a game more. A draw with Nottingham Forest inched Newton up to ninth, and that is where they stood after nine matches when, following defeats at Darwen and Derby, they trounced WBA 4-1 on October 14th. Having played a game or two less than all the teams above them, Newton Heath could, for once, dream of challenging at the top of the table. But this is where the bubble burst and the seeds of gradual demise were sown. Those two last games, against Derby and West Brom, were the ones to blame.

First stop: October 7th. The Heathens were away at Derby and, boy, did they live up to their nickname. Perhaps provoked by their hosts, or maybe just victims of a conspiracy, the Mancunians played a rough, brutal game; at least according to the referee Mr. Tranter. His biased match report made the Derby players, rightly or wrongly, look like saints. Apparently Donaldson had assaulted Leiper, his trusty boot being the sharp weapon in question. Derby's emerging England star Steve Bloomer had to settle for emerging from the mud having been put there repeatedly by Clements. Several players used 'very strong epithets'. The horror: colourful language on a football field! To cap it all, Perrins whispered sweet nothings in Mr. Tranter's ear after the game, the exact words being: "It licks me why they send men such as you to referee, who knows nothing about the game".

The FA commission was quickly on the case. The Heathens had to be punished. Clements, Perrins, and Donaldson were each suspended for 14 days, despite the fact that tattletale Tranter had only found their actions worthy of a booking. Derby got away scot-free, protected by the skewed report. Yet the commission cottoned on to the exaggerated comments, branded the referee incompetent, and banned him from officiating for the rest of the season... which justifies Perrins' complaints and makes the suspensions all the more puzzling. They were especially cruel on Clements. Having missed just one match in over a year, he had to sit out the Darwen and Wolves fixtures. Fred Erentz, searching for a first-team spot, gleefully accepted the left-back position. Clements, automatic choice for the last three years, would never regain his place again. He played a few more times during the season before leaving for Rotherham Town.

ONE FARTHING

Saturday, October 14th, proved to be an even more significant day for the Heathens. They put in an excellent performance to thrash highflying WBA 4-1. Donaldson got one while Erentz and Peden opened their goal scoring accounts for the club, with Peden making an extra deposit. But the story began to get interesting on the following Monday. The **Birmingham Daily Gazette** published an astonishing report by William Jephcott. Peeved by the drubbing his local team had endured, still shedding tears since Small Heath's promotion failure, and sensing the possibility of a further public outcry similar to the Derby encounter, he attacked the Heathens and their style. Writing under the pseudonym 'Observer', he produced another list of offences, either fictional or exaggerated, but mostly biased. The West Brom keeper accidentally getting caught became a deliberate kick by Tommy Fitzsimmons. Geddes being injured without complaining meant Perrins had made 'a lump the size of a duck egg' in his back, as revenge for an earlier love-in. It was easy to focus on the previous week's culprits. Clements was accused of charging Barton violently on several occasions, whereas the flammable Peden had entertained with dirty tricks. In brief, Jephcott demanded that "the FA deal severely with them for the better of the game generally". For the better of the West Brom points total, more likely.

Soon Mr. Albut received a cutting and all he could see was the most pertinent of the following three choices: a) a bundle of sour grapes; b) an accurate description of Heath's tactics; or c) a lawsuit. 'C' was the correct answer. We're no Heathens, he countered, before deciding to sue the newspaper for libel, what with all the damage the report had done to the club's reputation. £200 should repair that damage, he reasoned. He even talked the referee into enlisting on his side. Mr. J.R. Strawson sent a letter to the **Manchester Guardian** refuting all the report's allegations. "Untruthful... groundless" he vented before proclaiming it "one of the best games [he] had ever controlled". So there you have it: the cleanest match ever according to one side, an excessive display of brutality according to the other. And neither was willing to back down.

So, a play-off was arranged at a neutral venue: Manchester Assizes courthouse. Date: March 2nd, 1894. Referee: Justice Day. It's safe to say the case generated a sensational story with the media eagerly attending. The way present-day author Richard Kurt describes the scene in his book 'Red Devils' you'd think he was there too! And most probably he would have spent the two days in court giggling. For the case soon took a turn for the farcical as each side decided lying and partisanship were as good as any argument to adopt. One Brummie described how a 'grinning' Newton Heath player had kicked him where it really hurts. Another apparently had to rub oil on a bruise on his back. He didn't, however, disclose whether he needed to apply moisturizing lotion to his dry skin as well. The Heathens, despite the best grace-preserving attempts by their esteemed briefs Shea and Bradbury, were not to be outdone in the mockery-producing claims. Jack Peden's defence for kicking an opponent in the stomach was that the sun had blinded him as he aimed at the ball. As for Mr. Albut, when questioned about past misdeeds, he explained that he "was too drunk to know if [he] was too drunk to remember."

At length, Jephcott's claims were countered by a Mancunian journalist, E.H. Davies. Then another local figure, Reverend Reid weighed in with some much-needed holy testimonial to sway the verdict in Heath's favour. Newton Heath thought they had scored the decisive goal... only to see it quickly disallowed for offside. Yes, they won the case, but Justice Day had seen through the shambles and awarded them the princely sum of... one farthing! Aka the smallest coin around. Aka nothing. Newton Heath could have won four such cases and came out with just a penny. Furthermore, since the defence were able to prove that Jephcott's article had not greatly affected Newton Heath's business operations, the judge ordered each party to pay their own costs. This was tragic for Albut and his club. He had hoped £200 would bring financial stability to the struggling club, but instead he now had costs of £145 to contend with. The court case, if not entirely bankrupting Newton Heath, knocked the stuffing out of it instead. From now on the club would struggle to survive and would barely sustain its existence until Manchester United came along.

MESS OF A SALESMAN

The chaos that ensued following the Derby and West Brom matches greatly disrupted Newton Heath's decent start to the season. What with the suspensions enforced on the troublesome trio, changes had to be made to the line-up, and that proved to be very unsettling. Apart from recalls to Fred Erentz and Billy Hood, several new recruits were tried all over the front line. Journeymen, rejects, Bellion types. They came, they saw, they were quickly forgotten. But let me tell you all about them. William Thompson came from table-toppers Aston Villa, only he had never played for them. He had appeared for the then powerful Scottish outfit Dumbarton, though. As soon as Newton Heath signed him, he broke down in training. Eventually he was picked for three consecutive matches, all ended in defeats, and Thompson never played League football again.

Big John Graham arrived from Blyth without an 'e', as compared to Blythe with an 'e' from whom Joe Cassidy was signed a few months earlier. Following a winning debut against Wolves, Graham was accused of being decent, but he was quickly proven innocent. A few more appearances could not save him from the end-of-season clear out. Outside-left Prince left such a mark on the club's history that only the initial of his first name is remembered: D. His debut against Darwen saw the Heathens lose at home in the league for the first time in eight months. He too did not survive the cull. At least he outlasted William Campbell, who joined in November and departed in March probably in an attempt to uphold his 'much-travelled' tag. Newton Heath were his sixth club in three years! In fact, after failing at his last club Blackburn, Campbell decided to pack it all in and move to South Africa. Those plans failed too and he was indeed working as a cigarette salesman – still travelling then – when Newton Heath decided he was the long-term solution to the inside-right berth. He was given a five-match run and, unlike the aforementioned 'strikers', he actually scored a league goal for the Heathens! His reward was a transfer to Notts County where the FA stepped in to put an end to his wandering. He was banned for two years after trying to 'recruit' an ex-team-mate from Blackburn.

It is not surprising that all those enforced changes derailed the Heathens' season. Their unfair reputation for rough play was accompanying them everywhere they played. They were, however, attempting to clean up their act, much to the appreciation of their loyal fans. Despite the ground switch, the original die-hards were still prepared to walk the extra distance to support the Green-&-Golds again. In fact, despite a dismal first season at Bank Street, the Heathens still enjoyed the fifth highest attendance in England. But the results only got worse. After that narrow 1-0 victory against Wolves on November 11th, four consecutive defeats saw the Heathens in the all-too-familiar position of 16th: bottom, like last season.

When a further two defeats followed before the end of the year, the directors decided it was time for a break. What's better to revive the spirits and refresh the limbs than five friendlies in one cold winter week? The highlight was a foreign tour to… Scotland. Yes, Scotland, that exotic faraway place that Newton Heath had never visited before. It is surprising that, despite hosting Tartan visitors on numerous occasions and practically living on the tracks, the Heathens had never ventured past Hadrian's Wall (except on scouting missions). Obviously the costs had been deemed prohibitive for a poor club, but this was now a reflection of the bigger status Newton Heath had attained. Last season's excursion to Linfield had whetted the appetite for adventure, and now a triple header was arranged. The first match was at Hampden Park (not the present one) where the Mancunians pitted their skills against Scottish Cup holders Queen's Park, narrowly missing out in a five-goal thriller. Next was a New Year's Day trip to Division One Dundee where Erentz and Stewart met up with their old chums. And the last exhibition was in Stirling where King's Park were beaten 3-1.

THREE MORE SCOTS

While the Newton Heath players were busy introducing the natives to the intricacies of Route One football, the scouts took advantage of their stay in Scotland and went shopping at their favourite Tartan talent factories. Spring was coming with its second annual fight to escape the test matches, and the Heathens wouldn't contemplate turning out in the same outfit. For soon a 0-2 reverse at Everton meant the losing-run had reached seven. That inaugural victory at Wednesday in September proved a false dawn as the Heathens had now lost all nine league aways since. So, just as last year's trip to Ireland had unearthed Peden and McNaught, the Scotland odyssey saw Heath pick up a new right wing partnership. John Clarkin was signed from Glasgow Thistle, where he had excelled in a short stay. Heath truly lucked out with this purchase as Clarkin took over at outside-right and made the position his own for several years. In the process, he accelerated the end of Farman's great career at the club.

On the same day, Sam Parker joined from Hurlford F.C., a small town just south of Kilmarnock. The history of Manchester United is brimming with a vast array of forwards. The likes of Denis Law and Ruud Van Nistelrooy inevitably sit at the very top of that list with astonishing scoring rates. Sam Parker sits at the very bottom. In 11 outings he scored absolutely nothing. No forward in United's entire history has played more matches than Sam and not found the net. Instead he found the reserve team and, in October, a one-way ticket to Burnley.

Clarkin and Parker made their debuts on a sunny day at Bank Street but the team narrowly lost to Sheffield Wednesday 1-2, Jack Peden scoring for Heath. They were ineligible for the next match, the Lancashire Cup Round One, instead turning out for the reserves where Clarkin gave a brilliant glimpse of his ability and scored four goals in an 8-1 rout of Beswick. The first team almost replicated that score line... in reverse. John Clements went down injured after five minutes and the other ten went down 1-7 to Everton in front of 8,000 fans. The defence of the Manchester Cup did not outlast the first round either, Bolton seeing off the Heathens' reserves 3-2 on February 23rd. On the same day, the first team visited league leaders Aston Villa boasting a new goalie –

presumably quaking in his boots. William Douglas was signed on January 24th to help ease Joe Fall's burden of picking balls out of his net. Douglas, yet another Dundee product, came from Ardwick where he had played in that first-ever competitive United-City derby, the FA Cup tie in 1891. The Heathens had put five past him that day. The Villains did the same this time. At least being cup-tied spared him from conceding a further five in the FA Cup Round Two replay at Ewood Park after the first game had seen a record 18,000 fans at Bank Street. Joe Fall was back in goal as Blackburn ended Heath's cup run for the second year running. This also meant that, in the space of four weeks, the Heathens had been removed from all three knockout competitions. Now they could really concentrate on the battle for survival in the First Division, as well as participate in a crack new Lancashire county trophy: the Palatine League.

THE PALATINE LEAGUE

A LONG CHAMPIONSHIP programme, three separate cup competitions, test matches, and endless friendlies were not enough to deter the Lancashire FA from launching an additional league. It wasn't a breakaway European Super League, per se, but an 'experiment', they claimed, to fill the clubs' fixture list with 'league' matches. In other words, an attempt to kill the friendly a century before Sven Goran Eriksson.

Significantly, this was perhaps a demonstration of how far along Newton Heath had come. After the early factory kick bouts, Heath's programme for years consisted largely of friendlies against other local sides. Now the fixtures were mostly competitive, and this trend was to continue in upcoming years. By the turn of the century, the club's total of friendly exhibitions would dwindle to four.

So, the top Lancashire teams were split into two groups. Teams in each group played each other home and away for league points. At the end, the leaders of the two groups would meet in a final to decide the Palatine champions. Newton Heath were placed in Group B along with Accrington, Bolton, Bury, Darwen, and Everton. They would have fancied their chances against this lot, but already they were busy complaining about too many games!

Not just a modern day excuse, then. The sequence of matches ran from January to April, sometimes conflicting with Division One obligations that wouldn't go away. The solution was to field weakened teams at times or simply not bother with certain games altogether.

The Heathens kicked off their programme on February 6th against Accrington, losing 1-3. Only Mitchell, Perrins, and Farman could be described as first-teamers. Some forgotten men, such as Clements, Fitzsimmons, Hood, and Mathieson, got to stretch their legs for a change. The second match clashed with the FA Cup replay at Blackburn, so the stiffs were selected again. Not surprisingly, they fell 0-3 at Bury. But five days later, the mighty first-team finally decided to see what this new competition was all about. I say first but, although George Timmins appeared in the photo, he did so in his club trainer capacity. His selection at left half-back against Darwen was not such a shock for he had represented WBA there in three consecutive FA Cup Finals in the late 1880s. Poor Darwen did not know what hit them until it emerged Bob Donaldson had smashed five goals in a 6-1 win. It was the first time the Newton Heath fans could remember anyone scoring that many. You couldn't blame them muttering under their breath how come he hadn't performed such feats in the two 0-1 defeats to the same opponents in the league. Donaldson, like the rest of the ever-changing forward line, had struggled to maintain any scoring consistency. His grand tally up to this moment stood at three league goals, one behind joint leaders Peden and Farman. The wingers!

When the Mancunians won the return fixture at Accrington on April 11th, they jumped to second place in the group, three points behind Bury but with a game in hand. However, within the next five days, any dreams of glory were ended. First Bury and Everton gained two points each, then the Heathens found themselves having to face both those teams on the same day – exactly the kind of full programme the county had in mind with this Palatine idea! The fixture congestion arose when Newton Heath realised they had to squeeze in six Palatine games in under two weeks before more pertinent matters at the end of the month. So, on April 16th, the first team entertained leaders Bury at Bank Street, a 2-2 draw failing to reel them in. Meanwhile, the reserves travelled to Everton where the home team replicated the Lancashire Senior Cup score-line (7-1, if you were not planning to turn back a few pages). With no hope of making the final, Heath only completed two of the remaining fixtures, which means, as we speak, the return matches with Bolton and Darwen are still waiting to be fulfilled. With six points from eight games, Newton Heath finished third, ahead of Bolton only because the Wanderers did not complete half their programme.

Obviously, the Palatine experiment proved unpopular (except with Donaldson). It would be contested one more time the following season after which any ideas of a league within a league were shelved for a hundred years until the advent of the European Champions League.

BOTTOM AGAIN

On March 3rd Newton Heath resumed First Division duties after a one-month break with a contest against reigning champions Sunderland. It was the first of six consecutive home matches in three weeks, enough, surely, to save Heath from a prolonged relegation struggle. True, the team was languishing nine points adrift from safety. Yes, they had lost the last nine league matches. And, of course, confidence had just been tried by the disappointing outcome of the court case. However, there was still the slim hope that an improved effort in those upcoming six fixtures – and additional assistance from Bank Street's noxious stench – could wheel the Heathens away from the test match zone. If Heath wanted to remain among the country's elite, and justify the dynamic progress of the previous 15 years, this was the moment to seize their destiny and shape it.

They battled gamely against Sunderland but lost 2-4. Then Sheffield United handed them their 11th defeat on the trot. Eleven was also the gap to thirteenth-placed Bolton now. The outlook appeared very grim. For the next match, against Blackburn, James McNaught was moved from the forward line to replace the injured Davidson at half-back, with Farman the beneficiary of the reshuffle as he came in at inside-right: Fall; Mitchell, Erentz; Perrins, Stewart, McNaught; Clarkin, Farman, Donaldson, Parker, and Peden. Somehow it all clicked. Not only did Newton Heath end their record dismal run and earn their first points in four months, but they also destroyed their nemesis 5-1. Donaldson – with a hat-trick – and Farman claimed their first league goals since September, whereas Clarkin opened his scoring account at his new club. McNaught, excelling in his new position, would remain permanently there from now on. Despite being lightweight, he would serve the Heathens at centre-back for the next four years. Of course, the centre-back in those days was positioned higher up the field and was regarded as the team's pivot, having license to join attack or defence - the 'Little Wonder' McNaught, with a shrewd footballing brain, would thrive in such a role.

The following weekend, two goals from John Clarkin were Heath's consolation after Derby put six past them, but a reversal of the score line left Stoke feeling bad on Good Friday. Clarkin scored for the third match running, while Farman and Peden nabbed a brace each. Last season, remember, Newton Heath thrashed Derby 7-1 only to lose by the same score against Stoke next. Now, symmetric results had guaranteed revenge for the losers. The bright side was that the Mancunian forwards had finally rediscovered the path to goal. In three matches they shook the net 13 times. It had taken them the previous 18 matches to do as much shaking.

Now came the crucial four-pointer against Bolton. With five matches left, Bolton had 21 points, Newton Heath 13. In between, Darwen had 19 points and Preston 17. Both had played more matches and both needed Heath to beat Bolton if any of the bottom three wanted to do without the test matches. A nervy, topsy-turvy encounter ensued with obligatory end-to-end stuff and all. But the final score was two-each: there was to be no automatic survival for Newton Heath. The test match escape route would have to be used again.

It was no surprise the Heathens abandoned any energy-sapping efforts for the remainder of the league programme. All four matches were lost, three of them away to make it 14 out of 15 throughout the season. Relegation statistics by miles. The final afternoon saw Preston North End win at Bank Street in a match between two outfits with test matches on their minds. Heath must have felt honoured to be in the presence of such exalted test match companions. The original 'Invincibles' had spent the first five Football League seasons in the top two spots. Now they preferred Heath's company. Given their abysmal home form of late, few

Heathens present that April 1894 afternoon could have predicted that, after this defeat, the home team would only lose four more league matches at Bank Street for the rest of the century.

So, with a measly 14 points, Heath finished bottom again. Just five home wins, six altogether, constituted an unwanted club record. They even refused to draw: just the two all-squares all season. And on top of that came a morale sapping finish to the season with those last four matches all lost. Not ideal preparation for a make-or-break first encounter with a soon to be deadly rival.

BIRTH OF A RIVALRY

They've met in FA Cup finals. They've met in League Cup finals. They've contested title deciders and relegation scraps. They've shared Charity Shields. They've even fixed a match. Their encounters have grown into the fiercest rivalry in English football, with fans, players and managers unwilling to yield an inch and this is where it all began: April 28th, 1894; the test match to decide which team would earn the right to play amongst the crème de la crème. No television windfall as incentive perhaps, but prestige, status and bigger gates were on the line. On one side: Newton Heath, laden with thoughts of Accrington Stanley who, after losing in last year's playoffs, dropped out of the League completely. On the other: Liverpool – a club created to fill a stadium following the departure of Everton to Goodison Park in 1892. In response, Anfield landlord John Houlding founded Liverpool so he wouldn't lose out on ground rent. They were professional from the start and had been elected to Division Two just a year after their formation. For over a century the rivalry between Mancunians and Scousers had grown as the two cities commercial ambitions clashed. Now their two clubs met in mortal football combat on the pitch for the very first time.

The two Lancashire clubs had been on amicable terms… up to now. They'd met in numerous friendlies throughout the season, including a benefit for Willie Stewart at the beginning of the month. The Heathens had won 2-0, and they would have no doubt been heartened by that result. But Liverpool had swept to the Division Two championship with an even better record than Small Heath, last year's opponents. In fact, Liverpool hadn't lost all season, whereas Newton Heath hadn't lost in 14 days. And there was no worse omen than the choice of Blackburn's Ewood Park as the venue for the test match. Four times the Heathens had visited that cursed stadium these past two seasons, and on each occasion they were swatted away with a least a four-goal drubbing.

Into the fray they entered: Fall in goal, preferred to Douglas; Mitchell and Erentz, the regulars, at full-back; Perrins, McNaught, and Davidson in the middle, with Stewart missing for the second test match in a row; and up front, the best five available – Clarkin, Farman, Donaldson, Hood, and Peden.

Both teams were at it from the off, exchanging offensive moves in the hope of drawing first blood. After 15 minutes Liverpool lumped the ball into the Heath goalmouth where Gordon headed home. Then Liverpool hit the woodwork. They almost doubled their lead with a blockbuster but were denied by the spring of Fall. Eventually McQueen (one of seven Macs in their line-up) scored with an even stronger shot. Half-time came to the relief of the Heathens, but it was obvious they were affected by nerves - with 6,000 watching, the Heathens ground to a halt. In the second half they simply failed to build any momentum as their First Division light started to fade. The closest they came to scoring was with a wasted effort from Donaldson late on. Two-nil it finished, only Fall's heroics keeping the 'two' in the score line. Newton Heath were relegated.

The top flight fraternity breathed a sigh of relief. No poisonous excursions to Bank Street in 1894-95. No rough scrambles and no courtroom drama. For Newton Heath, however, this was a sad moment. Perhaps they deserved the drop after such dismal displays, but they were now on a slippery slope towards bankruptcy. Little did they know that they were never to see the First Division again in their current guise. It would require a takeover, a name change, and a dozen years of struggle to resurface in the top flight again.

One player would be left behind in Division One: Jack Peden, the mercurial, enigmatic, temperamental winger. He was too good to be turning out at lowly slums like Walsall and Lincoln. He would try English football for one more season, helping Sheffield United to the dizzy heights of sixth – their highest position up to then. Eventually Peden returned to Ireland to further cement his legend. Newton Heath were lucky to have had him in their ranks, albeit for the one campaign. He had notched seven league goals from the wing to finish as the club's second top scorer, one goal behind Alf Farman.

Another forward who somehow retained a place in the top flight was hotshot Sam Parker who ended up at Burnley despite eleven games and no goals. The committee had other problems too: they could no longer afford John Fall's wages, but after his test match super show surely some First Division suckers could. So, Fall was put in the shopping window with a £60 price tag hung around his neck! Obviously no one came in for him at such a ludicrous amount, and the directors' plan backfired. Poor Joe was left club-less. Of course it was cruel what the directors did, this however was the norm at the time. The players had to be re-signed by their clubs on a yearly basis, yet they couldn't move without their club's permission even if they were out of contract. Poor Joe indeed. He sat on his backside and waited a year before Small Heath bought him.

The club also bade farewell to five men who had served Newton Heath during that first season in the Football League. John Clements and William Mathieson remained team-mates, but at Rotherham Town. The former had lost his place to Erentz while the latter was never able to dislodge Peden from the left wing... to the relief of the team selectors – the 10 times Mathieson appeared in the first team, Newton Heath failed to win! Tommy Fitzsimmons had also lost his place halfway through the season. He had scored in his first and last league matches for Newton Heath. It was just in the intermediate 25 games that he mostly abstained. The symmetry was extended when he returned to his previous club Annbank. Another forward, Billy Hood, half of whose six goals came in 12 days in October 1892, wandered away to Stalybridge Rovers. And Andrew Mitchell, right-back, spite-signing, and occasional linesman, went to Burton Swifts in search of new challenges. From his debut on he appeared in 53 consecutive games. Now though, Newton Heath would have to do without him in their new adventure in Division Two.

1894-95

PETERS... AND SMITH

In June 1894, Newton Heath's secretary AH Albut and vice-president Harry Jones got on a train and headed to a small town called Halliwell, just north of Bolton. They were on a mission to sign a player. It wasn't a secret mission, yet Mr. Jones wore a long cloak. He always wore a cloak. Observe any Newton Heath team photo from 1890 to 1895 and you'll see a mysterious figure, heavily clothed, lurking in the background with a big hat that covers half his forehead. That's Mr. Jones – a very nice man. Mr. Jones was responsible for creating the Newton Heath circular. It was a smart scheme that involved going around to people's houses and asking for support for the Heathens' cause, either by attending games or, preferably, with straightforward cash donations.

This time, though, Jones and Albut had a recruiting assignment: destination the Halliwell Mill, to meet an employee of that pub, who happened to be a decent left winger. Jack Peden had taken the first train to Sheffield and the Heathens sought to replace him with someone with the same initials, Heywood Central's James Peters. Heywood Central were an average Lancashire League outfit but were beginning to fall apart. Sheffield Wednesday had just raided the club to pluck England's future centre-half Cramshaw, and Newton Heath decided to follow suit. The meeting went very well. Peters agreed to the move and the trio began drinking in earnest to celebrate the coup. While chatting away into the evening Peters recommended his Heywood wing partner – and Halliwell native – Dick Smith. Albut and Jones must have been into their umpteenth round because they agreed on the spot to sign Smith as well, without the inconvenience of a trial.

When they sobered up to the reality of the situation, there was nothing to justify their fears. Smith – and Peters – turned out to be excellent acquisitions. Smith grabbed 20 league and cup goals in his first season, becoming along the way the first player in Manchester United's history to score four league goals in one match. He achieved another feat that only two men (one of them George Best) could equal. And he served Newton Heath in two lengthy spells. Peters, not to be outdone, had a smashing first season as well, his claim to fame being Manchester United's first ever-present player in a Football League campaign. He would top that in his second year by banging a hat-trick against Liverpool. From the wing!

Suitably impressed with their double delight, Newton Heath decided to re-use the formula again that summer. So they raided Scottish Second Division side Cowlairs and relieved them of a couple of Macs, one of whom was definitely from the Big Mac menu. John McCartney had eaten all the pies at Cowlairs, not to mention previous clubs Rangers and Thistle F.C.. In his Manchester United bible, The United Alphabet, Garth Dykes politely described him as "built along hefty lines". The newspapers of the day were blunter and simply called him fat. The Newton Heath directors were thoroughly impressed and promptly made him captain. The other capture, however, was not able to pull his weight as tellingly. David McFetteridge came boasting the experience of First Division football with Bolton, but he was unable to make the Heathens' first team more than once. However, there was another Scot who began the season as a new member of the forward line. Newton Heath had tried him out in a couple of games late last season. To protect a trialist's anonymity, it is usual to label him "John Doe". But what do you do when his real name is indeed "John Dow"? The Heathens gave him the pseudonym MJ Woods, and he performed well enough to earn a contract. Dow was signed from, you've guessed it, Dundee. He was very versatile and could play full-back or centre-forward. He was also reliable and possessed a splendid kick. And, as if there wasn't enough Tartan influence at Bank Street, Heath tried to sign Partick Thistle's goalkeeper John Crozier. They had been tracking him for a while but, luckily as it eventually turned out, they missed out when he chose to join Woolwich Arsenal instead. One year and one game later, he was back with Partick.

New faces, new division, all that was missing was a new kit. Perhaps the historic green-and gold halved kit did not have a size

XXL shirt for John McCartney, or maybe it was simply time for a change. These colours, after all, were not descriptive of Newton Heath – Bank Street had no green grass nor was there gold in the club coffers. Nonetheless, the brand new outfit was based around the same colours. The shirt was all green now but had gold cuffs and collar. The black 'shorts' were removed, to be replaced by long white ones.

It's a shame that the green-and-gold kit was binned. It will always be symbolic of the club, especially those innocent days when Newton Heath emerged from the Football Alliance to become a Division One team. A century later, Manchester United revived the colours in a commemorative third kit. It was a stylish piece voted greatest ever Manchester United kit by its designer. Seriously, though, it is time United brought it back and established it as a permanent away kit. Enough meddling with white, blue, black or even grey. After the traditional red, nothing pertains more to the meaning of Manchester United than green and gold.

YOUNG OLD SKINNY

The Heathens took one look at their 1894-95 fixture list, saw that their first league match was away, and proceeded to lose 0-1. It did not matter that this was the Second Division, nor that their opponents, Burton Wanderers, were playing their first ever league match. A 14th consecutive away league defeat was attained. Back at Bank Street, Crewe Alexandra were blown away 6-1. The new guys did most of the blowing. Dow got two, Smith got two, and even full-back McCartney weighed in with one. It was certainly a pleasant home debut for the last two. The following weekend, Heath travelled to Leicester Fosse (now sensibly Leicester City) where Dow notched two more goals while Smith added another in a 3-2 win. Not only did the victory prove significant come the end of the season, it also broke the away day hoodoo. From now on the club would go forth and prosper.

The line-up was pretty much stable in the early months of 1894-95. Douglas was an immovable object in goal; captain McCartney and Erentz provided big obstacles at the back; Perrins and Davidson complemented McNaught's finesse in the half-back line; and the forward five of Clarkin, Donaldson, Dow, Smith, and

BILLY MEREDITH
'Old Skinny' was still young when Newton Heath first came in contact with Billy Meredith in November 1894.

Peters were proving to be a goal-grabbing machine. Even Farman and Stewart were restricted to the odd start.

The Heathens entered November on the back of an unbeaten run. Though they were only eighth in the standings, they had played much less than anybody else in the division. Then on November 3rd, they met the team one place below them, Ardwick. Their Mancunian rivals had always been a step behind, but now the two rivals met face to face for the first time in League football. Out of the dozens of clubs sprinkled all over the area, these two had emerged as the giants of Manchester football. Ardwick, in fact, had sprung a first on their Heathen foes by converting to a more cosmopolitan name, Manchester City that very summer following the bankruptcy of the old club. I could, of course, proceed to call them 'The Team Formerly Known as Ardwick' throughout the rest of the book, but all clubs deserve respect whether they were great or massive.

So, one of the biggest ever crowds the city had witnessed, estimated to be over 14,000, converged on City's brand new home at Hyde Road to watch Manchester's first league derby. After 13 minutes, Dick Smith swerved in and cracked a grand shot that whistled in the net: 1-0 Heath. He got another before half-time and two more afterwards to become the club's first four-goal star in a competitive match. Clarkin scored too to give the Heathens a 5-2 win.

Both City's goal came from a 20-year-old outside-right making his home debut called Billy Meredith. The original Welsh Wizard would go on to establish himself as the footballing name in Manchester, serving both clubs with incomparable distinction and creating sensational news both on and off the pitch. He was a dribbling king, a rebel, an entrepreneur, a clairvoyant, and a fitness freak. No one has done more to put the city on the footballing map. Meredith played in the first Manchester league derby. He was there when Newton Heath played their last ever match. He was there when United won their first championship and their first FA Cup. He was still there for City 30 years after his debut. 'Old Skinny', he was known by then, toothpick in his mouth, chatting away to the crowd while the ball was at the other end. I could write an entire book about Meredith, but John Harding already did. It suffices to say that he belongs amongst the truly world class footballers in United's history, namely Edwards, Charlton, Best, Law, Robson, Schmeichel, Cantona, Giggs, and Van Nistelrooy. This is a purely subjective list of 10 players and, as I write, Rooney and Ronaldo are pestering me into changing it to 12.

SECOND SPOT

THE WIN AT City was Heath's third away success already this season. In the meantime, they had only won one home match. The last two fixtures at Bank Street had finished in draws with the prawn sandwich brigade barracking Douglas and his full-backs. Obviously they saw McCartney as a threat to their nutritional needs. On November 10th, though, the Heathens put their home record back on track with a 3-2 defeat of Rotherham Town, John Clements and all. That took their goal tally to an impressive 25 in 9 matches, though 15 had been conceded. One of the scorers against Rotherham was left-half Will Davidson. It was only his second goal for the club, a year after his first had earned a 1-0 win against Wolverhampton. It was also his last goal in first level football. Three weeks later, Heath won another away game, at Crewe, but lost their left-half to a career-ending injury. It was a terrible blow for the club and the player. Davidson had been a reliable, consistent servant who had missed a mere two matches since joining the club in July 1893. He was also a popular chap. The directors, perhaps coining the phrase 'better late than never', decided in September 1896 to give him a benefit. They billed it "English XI versus Scottish XI" and asked several adjacent clubs to provide players. But with such a long time having elapsed since Davidson's retirement, the interest was not as hoped. Only Bury and Fairfield sent players, forcing Heath to supply the remainder – God knows they had enough Scots! And only a few hundred appreciative fans turned up to see the 2-2 draw.

One beneficiary of Davidson's misfortune was Willie Stewart. He won his place back in the first eleven as Heath let out their frustrations on Burton Swifts with a 5-1 spanking. Heywood alumni Peters and Smith administered two lashings each. Most importantly, the Heathens had climbed to third spot in the table, i.e. the test match zone. The club was aiming to bounce straight back to the big boys band. A hard-earned draw at fourth-placed Notts County followed before Heath recorded three consecutive victories, all in the space of five days around Christmas. Second spot was Santa's gift for the Heathens. The Yuletide losers were Lincoln (3-0), Burslem Port Vale (5-2), and Walsall Town Swifts (2-1). A common scorer in all three matches was newcomer George Millar. Snapped up from Glasgow Perthshire, he made an instant impact ten minutes into his debut with a bullet header. He wasn't the only on-form forward at the club. Smith took his tally to 13, Donaldson reached double figures, and Clarkin was now on six. Their rich scoring vein meant that the Heathens had lost just once in 16 games since the opening day defeat at Burton Wanderers.

Now was probably as good a time as any to put an end to that run. So, to leave 1894 on a negative note, an exhausted Newton Heath fell 0-3 in the return fixture with Lincoln. The directors were not too impressed and rang the changes for the New Year's Day visit of Burslem. In came two players from the reserve team, the first being centre-half Herbert Stone. He had made his debut towards the end of last season following a convincing media campaign. He failed, however, to displace McNaught and, after a few more first-team outings, left to Ashton North End. The other was young amateur Charles Rothwell. A lucky lad, Charlie, turning out for Newton Heath just for the fun of it. He scored a ton of goals for the reserves and was almost always on the score-sheet whenever selected for the first-team. He notched league goals, cup goals, Palatine goals, and friendly goals. So much so that he didn't leave any for his brother, Herbert, who made Manchester United's first-team in 1902-03. It goes without saying that he was on the mark against Burslem as Heath triumphed 3-0 but George Millar upstaged him with a double to make it five in five in his personal tally. Yet surprisingly both men were dropped for the next game, as Albut sought experience in the return derby against City. Bragging rights were already proving an incentive and the

Heathens obliged, underlining their neighbourhood supremacy with another goal glut. Clarkin (2), Donaldson, and Smith sent the green half of the 12,000 spectators home massively happy. Then on January 12th left-back Erentz performed his early day Gary Neville impersonation by scoring his annual goal. Despite losing to Rotherham, Heath clung on to their number two position as they took a six-week break from the rigours of the promotion chase.

THE SECOND COMING

It was now time to cram as many different competitions as possible to disrupt the promotion charge. First off, Heath headed to Bolton because that's what the Lancashire Cup first round draw dictated. The draw seemed to have something against poor Heath. For the fourth year in a row they've had to face strong opponents at the first stage, mostly away, and for the fourth straight year they took the quickest way out of the competition. A week later Heath returned to Burden Park, this time following Manchester Cup first round orders. That's where Heath had been eliminated in two of the last three years. So, with the beloved Palatine League kicking off on the same day, and considering that the first-team did not fare much better the previous week, the Heath directors sent over the reserves. A 0-4 drubbing demonstrated that the Heathens' love affair with the old cup had waned, stalwarts Alf Farman and Will Davidson playing their last competitive games for the club.

The first-team players, meanwhile, went chasing that younger attraction whose prize they had yet to savour. The Palatine League was here again and Heath decided to give it another try. Again they found themselves in Group B, which now contained just four clubs. Two were last year's group mates Bury and Bolton; the newcomers being Liverpool, the test match victors from the previous spring. No wonder the directors saved the first-team for this. Revenge was in the air as the Heathens tore forward. And how sweet it smelled after a 3-0 demolition. The scorers depended on which newspaper you chose to believe. According to one, Smith, Millar, and McNaught got the goals. Another claims Smith did all the damage by himself. The third had no idea. But this was as good as it got for the Mancunians in this tough group. Liverpool and Bolton were, after all, top flight teams whereas Bury were the runaway leaders in Division Two. Soon they put the Heathens in their place with home and away wins in February, and when the return fixture at Anfield finished 1-1, Heath could no longer reach the final. So, having already faced Bolton in both the Manchester and Lancashire Cups, the Heathens opted to do without the two Palatine games against the same opponents. Considering Wanderers had thrashed the Scousers 7-2, Heath's decision seemed a wise one.

By this time the FA Cup glory quest had been quashed too. First Division Stoke came to Bank Street and triumphed 3-2 in a genuine cup tussle, Smith and Peters netting the home goals. So, all that was left to play for was a place in the test matches. Two years ago, in an attempt to secure a Division One slot, the directors had enlisted the help of young Joe Cassidy. He scored in the test match replay victory against Small Heath and Newton Heath stayed up. Now, to the delight of the Bank Street masses, the directors dialled the same helpline. Cassidy had been with Celtic where he won the Scottish League title in 1894 and the Glasgow Cup in 1895. But he felt the dressing room atmosphere wasn't too harmonious so he was pleased to return to Manchester. It was an excellent coup by Albut and co. Blessed with adhesive ball control, a ferocious shot, and an alertness to link-up play, Joe Cassidy would go on and establish himself as Newton Heath's greatest forward and become the first player in Manchester United's history to score a century of goals.

Two more purchases were done, where else but at Heath's first feeder club, Dundee. Just how many decent footballers could one team produce? Albut didn't bother to check. Based on the Law of Averages it was obvious that they would turn out to be duds. George Campbell never got near Heath's first-team while William Longair appeared in the ultimate game of the league programme which was a surprising disappointment since he came with a highly-regarded reputation, having just been capped by Scotland. And, boy did Heath need international players. The days of the Welsh contingent were long gone, and, since Jack Peden's departure last summer, the club didn't have a single international in their ranks. Longair and Campbell's episode brings to mind the anecdote about the time Manchester City were facing a crucial relegation-deciding match in the mid-eighties. They obtained special dispensation from the Football League to sign Maradona, Platini, and Zico on loan just for that game. They still lost! The reason? All three new signings were sat on the bench.

23 PAST WALSALL

JOE CASSIDY MADE his comeback in a phantom match. It was a record-setting, credibility-defying mystery in history. It has a legendary place in Manchester United folklore but no statistical presence. "Is it true?" young Reds ask their fathers. Bewildered, the fathers have no answer. They can find no mention of it in the record books. But at one time it did exist. It was Newton Heath's greatest contribution to English League football, and on March 9th, 1895, it did take place.

It was a typically rainy Manchester Saturday afternoon. Walsall Town Swifts visited Bank Street for Heath's 23rd league match of the season. Walsall, languishing third from bottom in the standings, saw the muddy state of the Bank Street pitch and came up with a fiendish idea. A few years earlier, when both clubs were still in the Football Alliance, Walsall had visited Newton Heath at North Road in two consecutive seasons, but the weather had wreaked havoc with the playing conditions, and both matches were abandoned. Sensing an easy way out of a probable loss, they immediately handed in a protest. But Newton Heath spread another layer of sand over the quagmire, and the referee, Mr. Jeffries, deemed the pitch playable. Walsall reluctantly took to the field to face a home team represented by Douglas, McCartney, Erentz, Perrins, McNaught, Stewart, Clarkin, Donaldson, Cassidy, Smith and Peters.

Newcomer Cassidy was soon in the thick of the action. Not before long, he released Donaldson, and the latter crashed the dam. Walsall fought back momentarily, but soon enough Dick Smith put in a brace, first from a Donaldson pass then pouncing on Cassidy's blocked shot. It was 3-0 at the interval with the Heathens in excellent form despite the heavy ground. In the second half, Walsall gave a comprehensive lesson in the skill of the kick-off. Twelve times they demonstrated it: once to start the half and eleven more times as Heath piled the goals. There were lovely goals, there were route one goals. There were headers, scrambled efforts and

NEWTON HEATH, 1894-95

The Heathens pose in their new kit of green shirts and white shorts. This selection was unchanged from March 16th to April 12th, 1895. Left to right, back row: Mr. Albut, F. Paley (trainer), John Dow, William Douglas, Mr. F. Palmer (director), Fred Erentz, Will Davidson, and Mr. G. Faulkner (director). Middle row: Mr. Crompton (president), George Perrins, James McNaught, Willie Stewart, and Mr. Jones (vice-president). Front row: John Clarkin, Bob Donaldson, Joe Cassidy, Dick Smith, and James Peters.

rebounds. Smith possibly farted one in! There was a shot by Cassidy that stressed the elemental importance of the net in preventing fatal injury to fans directly behind the goal. Even John McCartney, the full-back, put his pie down and waddled up front to chip in. In the end, 14-0 was the final score. Yes, that's FOURTEEN. Cassidy had helped himself to four on his second debut. The other forwards all scored. Donaldson, Clarkin and Peters got one each, while Dick Smith claimed the remaining six! Six goals in one match. Now who else has done that in Manchester United's history? There was the Charity Shield match against Swindon Town in 1911 when Harry Halse got a half dozen in an 8-4 victory. And decades later, in 1970, a fired up George Best turned in as many as United demolished Northampton 8-2 in the FA Cup. That's how rare Smith's achievement was. The 14-0 victory itself was a new record score in the Football League. In fact, it remains unequalled to this day. Even Manchester United have not been able to reach 14 goals in any subsequent competitive, wartime, or friendly game of any kind.

For a few days Newton Heath basked in the glory of their mammoth win and their second-placed position. Then grim news started to emerge that wiped the smile off their muddied faces. The Football League had seen the skewed result, taken into account Walsall's pre-match complaint, and decided the match should never have taken place. Even Mr. Jeffries, who had given the go-ahead and refereed the game, was now backing Walsall's whines. It didn't matter that the two teams were separated by almost the entire division, nor that Heath were undefeated at home in the league while Walsall had lost every single away game since October. Nor that the Heathens had to play in the same conditions as the mud-o-phobic Swifts! The authorities declared the match null. Just like that, Heath's record-breaking success became void, and Smith and Cassidy's exploits were wiped from the scrolls.

The club was shocked. But disappointment soon gave way to anger. "A rematch? Bring 'em on!" they might have growled, injustice in their souls, revenge in their nostrils. On April 3rd, Walsall sheepishly returned to the scene of the grime. The pitch was still muddy, but they dared not glance a peek at it let alone voice an opinion. Again Heath's front line went on the rampage, taking the lead in the first half then adding eight in the second! The goals were a bit more evenly spread this time. Cassidy, Smith, Donaldson and Peters got two each, and Clarkin scored one in a 9-0 drubbing. If only he could have got another like the rest, the record win would have been attained. Instead, it was left to the Busby Babes to achieve some sixty years later. But the message to the authorities was clear: it wasn't the pitch. It was the players.

NAILED ON EASTER

The smiting of Walsall came at the right time. Heath's inactivity had seen them slide down to fifth in the table. But in one week they turned things around. After putting nine past Walsall, scoring five against Newcastle was a walk in the park, as compared to a doddle in a puddle. Cassidy and Smith again claimed a brace each. In five games together so far, they had equally shared 20 goals! Heath were back in second again, trailing only Bury, who had just secured a test match berth. Four matches remained, but three of them were against the other teams in the play-off zone. As many as five further teams could still catch the Heathens.

First up was the top-of-the-table clash with Bury. With it being Good Friday, the two teams divided the points in a 2-2 draw before a bumper 15,000 crowd. Then Newcastle gained quick revenge with a 3-0 drubbing on Not-So-Good Saturday. That was only understandable. Both McNaught and Erentz were missing, injury casualties of the day before. Bob Donaldson came back to full-back, his place up front taken up by debutant David McFetteridge – the lighter half of the pre-season double swoop that had also seen McCartney signed from Cowlairs. McCartney himself had been out for a month, replaced by the early season goal-machine Dow who had been successfully converted to right full-back. He would perform admirably in his new permanent position. The press averred though, often criticizing Dow's constructive approach. Enough with the dribbling of the ball out of defence, they lectured. He should be lumping the ball up field at the earliest opportunity. Oh to have had Martin Buchan around, to give him a whack around the ears. So both starting Heath full-backs at Newcastle were converted forwards, and soon one of them – Donaldson – got knacked himself. He hobbled to the wing while McFetteridge had to spend the rest of his debut at full-back. He did well, preventing Newcastle from adding to their early three-goal lead. This, however, proved to be his only first team game. The injury curse struck him too on Tyneside and he never played for the club again.

Heath were down to third now. Then on Monday came the return tussle at Bury, and out of generosity the Heathens declined to spoil the Shakers' perfect home record. Bury won 2-1, somewhat fortunately, to make it 15 wins out of 15 home games. The encounter featured yet another debutant. A proper full-back was used this time. James Cairns, signed three years before from Ardwick, finally made his league bow while simultaneously bringing his first-class career to an end. Now things were as exciting as it can get going into the final afternoon of the league programme. Notts County were second on 38 points; Newton Heath third on 37; Leicester Fosse fourth on 36; and Grimsby Town fifth on 35. All four could make the playoffs. Leicester had just beaten Grimsby to leapfrog them, but Heath and County still held the upper hand. They faced each other at Bank Street knowing a draw would be enough for County, and could be for Heath – provided Leicester didn't win their last game against champions Bury 26-0.

However, Newton Heath were not taking anything for granted. Buoyed by 12,000 fans that paid £250 record receipts, they went after County. What followed was one of the tussles of the season, and it was only a coincidence that the match finished in a draw. The 3-3 score line meant County had secured second spot and Heath third, ahead of Leicester on goal average. This showed how significant that first away win of the season at Leicester had been. Poor Grimsby, meanwhile, finished just a point behind. Dick Smith scored one of the goals to end his first season at the club as the leading scorer with 19. Clarkin notched another to finish third on 11 goals, four behind Donaldson while Cassidy contributed another to make it an impressive eight goals in eight matches since the voided Walsall encounter.

With so many forwards having prolific campaigns, it was no surprise Heath ended 1894-95 with a total of 78 goals in 30 league matches. That averaged 2.6 goals a game – a stunning season-long average that Manchester United have never bettered to this day. When one bears in mind the Walsall rematch removed five goals from that total, Heath could have reached 83 goals, averaging an even more remarkable 2.77. And just for fun, if the void match was simply added to the number of league matches Newton Heath played that season, then 92 goals in 31 matches would average 2.97! In other words, almost three goals per game. This means that, statistically at least, the forward line of 1894-95 was the most prolific in United's history. Another historic achievement following the draw with Notts County was that Heath had remained undefeated at home throughout the league programme. A special 'thank you' note was duly sent to the boilerman at the gasworks.

A TESTING MATCH

THE ONE TEAM that did beat Newton Heath at Bank Street in a competitive match this season was Stoke, who had knocked the Heathens out of the FA Cup in that topsy-turvy tie in February. They had finished off the season with five wins and a draw in the last six games but failed to escape the First Division relegation playoff zone. Now they were the only thing blocking Heath's hopes of an immediate return to the top flight.

So on April 27th, 1895, the two met again. It was the third year in a row that the Heathens had been involved in the end-of-season test matches yet they approached this one with some apprehension. The match being at Stoke's neighbours Burslem meant it wasn't going to be on neutral territory and Heath were missing two of their most reliable defenders, Erentz and McNaught, the victims of the Easter injury outbreak.

The Mancunians took to the field just like they'd done all season – with the ever-present Douglas in goal. Dow was now firmly established at right-back, but the previous incumbent McCartney had to be patched up after missing the last eight games and stuck at left-back. The consistent Perrins and Stewart continued at half-back, but filling in at centre-half was the inexperienced Herbert Stone, playing only his seventh match for the club. The front five, meanwhile, rolled off the tongue and into the mayhem: Clarkin, Donaldson, Cassidy, Smith, and Peters.

The match proceeded along the lines of the earlier cup tie, with both teams pouring forward at full tilt. Douglas and McCartney were clearing everything that came their way, while Cassidy was causing all sorts of bother at Stoke's end. Eventually Dow was struck down by a brutal tackle, but manfully played on. Stoke took advantage and forced the action into Heath's half. The pressure was mounting; at one point McCartney headed away the kitchen sink. But just before the interval, Stoke took the lead. The Heathens tried hard in the second half but their scoring form deserted them. If only they could have one or two of those Walsall goals back. A while later, Stoke doubled their lead, Heathen heads started to drop, and Stoke tripled it. 3-0 was the result and Heath's dreams were destroyed. All their season's work unravelled in 90 minutes, and now they had to stay in Division Two.

Ten thousand spectators had seen the match, at most 9,999 of whom had paid to get in. One mischievous fan had apparently snuck in. A full year and a half later, in December 1896, when Heath's financial situation had become rather dire, Mr. Albut received an apology note and 20-penny stamp. It was 'conscience money' from the Heathen who obviously felt remorse for the club's plight.

One more match was played on April 29th before turning Bank Street over for the summer: Bob Donaldson's benefit against Blackburn. Then Newton Heath bade farewell to a number of prominent names. The saddest departure was that of likeable Brummie Alf Farman, the club's longest servant. He had been at the club since February 1889 and had amassed almost a century of goals in over 220 matches including friendlies. He scored in the Football Alliance, the Football League, the FA Cup, the Lancashire Cup, the Manchester Cup, and the test matches. He had a rocket shot and on one occasion, which surely would have earned goal-of-the-season had a camera been around at the time, he scored from the touchline with a torpedo of a drive. It was no surprise then that he was assigned penalty-taking duties. He did, after all, convert the first penalty kick in English football. Other successful spot-kicks included the 1893 test match and the Bank Street opening match. But now he was retiring from professional football, leaving fans with the fondest memories of his dribbling skills.

Also retiring was Will Davidson, his career abruptly curtailed by injury. He would become the landlord of a pub on Oldham Road. Like Farman, Willie Stewart had been at Newton Heath since 1889 and had played – and scored – in the club's first Football Alliance fixture but now his stay was coming to an end, Luton being his next destination. He had played over 240 matches for Newton Heath in nine different positions, including goalie. He even chipped in with a couple of hat-tricks, including one from centre-half in that 10-1 record win against Wolves. Sport ran through Stewart's blood for he was an excellent cricketer as well, while one of his daughters, Cissie, would win a silver medal in swimming at the 1928 Olympics.

Accompanying Stewart to Luton, much to the dismay of the local chip shop proprietors, was captain John McCartney. Newton Heath was but a short stop in an illustrious career that saw him serve numerous clubs as a player and, later, manager. He certainly left his mark on Hearts in Scotland where he was 'the gaffer' for a decade, eventually replaced by his son William.

Mid-season scoring sensation George Millar was also on his way. Five goals in six games were apparently not good enough for the directors. He may have been ditched to Chatham, but his contribution to the club's record-setting goal average should not be ignored. And last as well as least, William Longair packed his Scottish cap and headed back to Dundee. After one match in three months he'd had enough of Division Two. Newton Heath, on the other hand, were doomed to a much lengthier stay.

1895-96

S. O. S.

WHEN NEWTON HEATH were relegated in 1894, they were of the belief that they would soon bounce back. 1894-95 was supposed to be just a brief roundabout on the route back to the big time. So, attendances were still superior to a lot of clubs from Division One and Heath actually reported a profit for the season, slicing their debts from £593 to £323. In fact, if either Deloitte or Touche had bothered to check, Newton Heath would have made the '20 Richest Teams in the World' list. Of course they would have been included in a '20 or so Professional Teams Around at the Time' list as well. But after the playoff failure, they had to adjust to the reality that they were indeed a Second Division club. And the reality was that 'Second Division' things would start to happen to them. Things like dwindling crowds, bargain bin buys, freak injuries, extreme management decisions, full-backs in goal, fixture lists with teams such as Loughborough on them, and even fatal experiences in the rain. This was what awaited Heath in 1895-96.

It was inevitable that the directors would answer the close season S.O.S. calls emanating from north of the border: 'Sign Our Scots'. However, the days of picking the crème de la crème from Dundee's ranks were gone. Now it was more about scraping the crap de la crap from the non-league scene. Mind, the locals who turned up at the stadium on December 26th must have thought the club had unwrapped the greatest Christmas gift ever when they saw a bevy of Dundonians on the pitch. Turns out the whole team had come over for a friendly match. Or was it a cunning plan by the Dundee management to put their players off the desire to join Heath once they got a first hand look at the Bank Street swamp?

Instead, Mr. Albut turned to that other source of Tartan talent,

Annbank. Tommy Fitzsimmons had been one purchase from that club back in 1892. Three years on, his younger brother, David, took the same train to Manchester. The Heathens needed a half-back to provide competition to George Perrins, whose form had diminished of late. Fitzsimmons Mark II, "sturdy, skilful, and hard-working", seemed able to offer the same Perrins qualities minus the brutality. Joining him from Ayr Parkhouse came William Kennedy, a decent inside-right with a good scoring touch. While John Aitken was signed from the mighty 5th King's Rifle Volunteers. Apparently the directors figured his pace and powerful shooting were a better replacement for left-winger James Peters, who had 'only' scored seven league goals the previous season. Aitken did score on his debut, but the directors quickly realised he had nothing else on Peters. He got picked one more time before disappearing without a trace.

Walter Cartwright was not Scottish, but Heath signed him anyway. Over the years it became obvious how lucky they had been in overlooking his birthplace when obtaining his signature from Crewe Alexandra. He took over from the departing Willie Stewart and developed into one of the best left half-backs in the division. He was also very versatile and, by the time he left the club nine years later, had played in every position except outside-right. Yes, that includes a stint between the sticks. When Manchester United played their first match in 1902, he was the club's longest-serving star. A year later he played in a match that had eerily similar echoes to that infamous 1996 clash against Southampton at the Dell, when the United players changed their grey kit at half-time because they 'blended into the crowd'. United were playing at Everton in a cup game and emerged for the second half in different colours. The bad weather conditions were a more reasonable excuse in this instance. Just as in 1996, Cartwright and co came out in blue and white striped shirts, United were beaten, and the result was 3-1! Of more significance to our story, a few months after his arrival, Cartwright was instrumental in introducing a certain Harry Stafford to the club.

Joe Ridgway was a rare local signing. Born across town in Chorlton-cum-Hardy, he joined the Heathens from West Manchester to provide cover for goalie William Douglas. His description of 'adventurous' goalkeeper did not refer to an innate passion for safaris, rather for his propensity to wander up field, a century before a great Dane made that the club's official desperation signal. This was, by the way, a long time before the 1912 change of rules that restricted a goalkeeper to handling the ball in his penalty area rather than his own half of the field.

Oh, and Newton Heath also bought John Grundy from Wigan County but immediately sold him to Halliwell Rovers because he was considered not good enough for the club. In 1900, he was signed again by which time Newton Heath had become bad enough for him.

FIVE A SIDE

HEATH COULD NOT have wished for a better opening to the season. No matter how many coins have been thrown down the wishing well since, they've never managed a better start. Last year's bottom club Crewe came to Bank Street, Walter Cartwright finding himself in direct opposition to his former club on his debut. But it was the other debutants, Kennedy and Aitken, who made the bigger splash scoring a goal each in a 5-nil pasting. Dick Smith notched one while Joe Cassidy, starting his first full season at Clayton, topped that with a double. The fans were thrilled to see Newton Heath top of the table and, for the first time, they didn't have to hold the paper upside down. If only the team could maintain that spot, they wished. Just eight months to go. Next Heath became the first Football League guests of Loughborough. Buoyed by the occasion, the newly-admitted club fought the table-toppers all the way to earn a thrilling 3-3 draw, despite two more goals from Cassidy. Why stop there? Cassidy then claimed a third brace in a row when Burton Swifts were swiftly burnt 5-0 at Bank Street. He had now found the net 18 times in 12 League games since his return from exile, including the voided Walsall 14-goal massacre. He was quickly becoming the fans' hero. An older hero also got two in that game: Bob Donaldson. He was playing his first match of the season but it emerged he was not yet fully fit. Back to the sidelines he went for another three months.

Despite the 13 goals in three matches, the Heathens only found themselves in fourth place. Burton Wanderers and freshly-relegated Liverpool still had one hundred percent records, while Manchester

City were also on six points having played an extra game. Soon it was time to face the big boys with consecutive matches against City and Liverpool. With both Manchester clubs excelling, the derby was so eagerly anticipated that the directors bought a stand from a nearby rugby club, expanded Bank Street's capacity by 2,000, and rubbed their hands with glee. Perhaps they ought to have purchased a roof as well as heavy rain kept the crowd down to 12,000. Nevertheless it would end up being the highest home league gate of the season, but it had been only a few months before that 15,000 had welcomed Bury. For the third derby in a row John Clarkin scored for Heath, but an improved City were able to sneak away with a 1-1 draw.

Newton Heath could only wish the next game finished 1-1 as well, as they succumbed to a record-equaling 7-1 defeat at Liverpool. But there were mitigating circumstances - Heath were rubbish. This was also one of the few occasions that the diminishing Perrins was given an outing. The rest of the team were practically picking themselves, Douglas was unchallenged in goal while Dow and Erentz had a lock on the full-back positions; McNaught and Cartwright were beginning to build a promising partnership in the middle; while the front line was taking shape as follows: Clarkin, Kennedy, Cassidy, Smith and Peters. So, the directors dropped Perrins, reinstated David Fitzsimmons, and prepared for revenge when Liverpool came to Clayton three weeks later.

Bang! Bang! Four minutes into the return and the Scousers were two up! Another record loss beckoned. But Heath had had enough. They lit fireworks of their own, and, propelled by a James Peters hat-trick, they replied with five goals to inflict Liverpool's worst loss of the season. It could have been the worst of their history but the referee disallowed another four Heath goals! He was obviously adhering strictly to the five-goal quota that Heath were maintaining at home. This was the third occasion that season that they had struck five at Bank Street, and they would do the same in the upcoming two matches. The next visitors, Lincoln, were well aware of the mandatory five conceded goals, and they reacted accordingly. Trailing 3-1 at half-time, they fought back to 3-3. Soon it was 4-4. Then a thrilling encounter ended in a unique score line in Manchester United's history of 5-5. It was the draw to end all draws. And it nearly did: Heath didn't draw another league game for 11 months!

One of the goals against Lincoln came from a 19-year-old making his league bow. Jimmy Collinson was born in Newton Heath just two years before the club itself. His breakthrough season was at full-back, but over the next few years he would become a crowd favourite at inside-forward. Though small in size, he was as tough as they made them in Newton Heath and packed a blistering shot.

FAIRFIELD FIASCO

On the last day of November, Heath had a home match, so they did the sensible thing and put five goals past Woolwich Arsenal. Half-back Cartwright even contributed two as the team leapfrogged the Gunners into fourth. It seemed they couldn't rise any higher as Liverpool and Manchester City were slowly edging away at the top. The problem was obvious: Heath refrained from importing points from their travels, preferring instead to produce them at their own ground. A similar embargo was placed on goals. In fact, by the time Rotherham Town were swept aside 3-0 on January 11th, the Heathens had scored 56 times in 14 home league matches stretching back to the end of the previous season. That's an astonishing average of four goals a game maintained over a 10-month period. Everybody was chipping in. Take the Rotherham encounter, for instance. Two of the goals came from Bob Donaldson, recently returned from injury. The other came from the unlikeliest of sources. Missing from the line-up was Dick Smith, who was off getting married. Last season's top scorer had not been as prolific so far this campaign, though, it is worth noting, after he tied the knot he started scoring more frequently. Also absent was John Clarkin, his particular ailment being short-term compared to Smith's: he was injured. So, the directors called on an amateur recently signed for the reserves, R. Stephenson. He was a student at nearby Owens College. Obviously not invited to Dick's ceremony, he put his books and cheat sheets down for the afternoon, set up the first goal for Donaldson, and scored the second himself. He also picked up a minor foot injury and disappeared from the club's history just as swiftly as he had appeared.

Yet the players were struggling in the fresh air of away grounds and fell further behind the front two. That was a concern this year for the authorities had decided to tamper with the promotion and relegation test matches. No longer would the third-placed team play off against the third from bottom of Division One for a place in the top flight. Only the top two teams would make the test matches, where they would be joined by the bottom two from the First Division to contest a mini-league.

Any hopes of making it to the playoffs for the fourth year running received a double blow in the space of one week at the end of January. Bury had already ended Newton Heath's Lancashire Cup involvement when Fairfield came to Clayton for a Manchester Cup tie. The Heathens had stopped caring for that trophy a few years back, but not so much Fairfield. Especially not when their line-up included three discarded ex-Heathens – Adam Carson, William Mathieson, and Tommy Fitzsimmons (facing his younger brother David). See, while Newton Heath tended to frequently acquire players from Dundee and Annbank, they also had a habit of shipping flops to Fairfield. Fairfield were Heath's waste disposal unit. The likes of Slater, Roger Doughty and Colville had previously been sent there, while in the near future Dow, David Fitzsimmons, Whittaker and Vance would follow. So perhaps a determined visiting contingent – and an indifferent home selection – could go someway toward explaining why Heath got walloped 5-2. However, the sheer magnitude of this home reverse had profound repercussions. Most affected was keeper William Douglas who endured a really, really bad day at the office. Apart from hearing five shots whistle past him, he was subjected to the ridicule of his own fans behind the goal. The ref even bullied him into changing his jersey due to a clash of colours, no doubt prompting some wisecrack remark from the crowd: "The kit's not the problem. Change the goalie!" Confidence shattered and pride demolished, the overly sensitive Douglas packed his bags and cried off to Dundee in a flash. The directors, not to be portrayed as the sane party in all this, suspended him immediately.

How about some reason? "Nah, we'll sack the trainer as well!" What of Douglas' indispensability after 48 consecutive league matches? "Bah, we'll toss crazy Joe Ridgway into the fray". Just like that, Newton Heath rid themselves of a first class goalkeeper.

A week on they found themselves without a first class goal

scorer as well. While the good news from a laboured 2-1 victory against Kettering Town in the FA Cup was a plum draw with Derby County in the next round, the bad news was that Joe Cassidy got injured. It was a bad injury – Joe was out for the season. This was a worse setback to the club than Douglas' departure. Cassidy was leading scorer so far with 16 goals in only 19 league appearances. In fact, his tally since his return stood at 28 out of 28 League games, including the infamous 14-0 Walsall wipe-out. Fine, I won't mention that match again. Not because of the annoyance factor of repetition, but because each time I am reminded of it my unnatural hatred of Walsall intensifies, and my blood boils, much like Heath's management felt at the loss of their goal-a-game striker.

BROKEN FINGERS

FUNNY WHAT A couple of years in the doldrums can do to a club's image and self-esteem. It was only just over three years ago when Derby came to Manchester as Newton Heath's First Division equals. Heath spanked their guests 7-1 and only one place separated the two teams. To be precise, Heath were bottom of the table; Derby bottom but one. Yet only 3,000 fans bothered turning up to produce Newton Heath's lowest home attendance of that season. Now that the Heathens were established as a Second Division club while Derby had risen to become one of the Top Two in the land, the FA Cup tie became the must-see event of the year in Manchester. Derby, after all, had just knocked-out the holders Aston Villa in the previous round and were their only realistic challengers for the championship. Up front they boasted two of England's regular forwards, John Goodall and Steve Bloomer, the latter would end the season as the division's top scorer for the first of five occasions. Derby even snapped up William Douglas after Newton Heath had banned him.

The directors decided that Derby's visit was a good enough reason to make some stadium expansions. Such was the interest in this cup tie that a huge crowd was anticipated. So, extra stands were erected on two sides to increase Bank Street's capacity to just short of 30,000. In the event, 20,000 attended and that constituted a new record at Bank Street. In fact, that rough figure was not bettered for the rest of Newton Heath's days. The gate receipts totalled

£500 and gave the club a timely financial boost while Albut and co shrieked with unrestrained excitement.

A mighty roar welcomed the Heathens onto the field: Ridgway; Collinson, Erentz; Fitzsimmons, McNaught, Cartwright; Clarkin, Kennedy, Donaldson, Smith and Peters. They were fired up and poured forward relentlessly, like hounds chasing the lumped balls toward their opponents' goal. Derby tried to play their superior 'pretty game' but McNaught was clever enough for them. Heath's forays kept the crowd entranced, but there weren't many clear-cut chances. Soon the home team paid the penalty for that - a partially cleared Goodall free kick on the half-hour mark fell for Steve bloomin' Bloomer to finish from three yards.

Yet Heath refused to lie down. Collinson hurt one foot but continued on the other. Smith went on an individual run before shooting wide. McNaught saved a certain Derby second. With a quarter of an hour left, Peters crossed from the left wing, Kennedy strained every inch of his body and tucked the ball home. Bank Street erupted. "Hats, capes, and umbrellas were thrown into the air" apparently. Soon they were thrown again when Cartwright slid Clarkin in to score, only for the referee to disallow the goal for offside and order the crowd to pick up their belongings. So, 1-1 it finished and the papers hailed Heath's glorious performance in holding the top division giants. It was Heath's proudest moment in the FA Cup so far, and four days later, they got the chance to go through it all again.

The same eleven travelled to Derby for the replay. This was, incredibly, the first time the club had had to leave Lancashire for any cup tie. Joe Cassidy, of course, was still missing, but the lads readied themselves for another brave display. However, bad luck was also ready for Newton Heath's visit. Keeper Ridgway broke a finger while blocking a venomous Bloomer shot and had to leave the field, much to the satisfaction of William Douglas in the stands, no doubt. Then Clarkin received a nasty knock and was forced off as well. So just nine Heathens faced the might of Derby for a while until a patched-up Ridgway got back on, but the circumstances weighed heavily against them. In the end Heath succumbed 1-5, Donaldson notching their consolation effort. Despite the cup adventure ending, the 20,000 attendance had put some much needed cash in the committee's coffers.

AMATEUR PROFESSIONALS

THERE COMES A time when established organisations, through slackness, indifference, or disorder, take their eye off the ball and allow disarray to creep in. Take the Roman Empire, for instance. It was a dynasty that ruled most of the known world, lasting for several centuries and was so powerful it should have lasted forever. However, misplaced priorities, loss of organisation, and other factors contributed to its crumbling. Sir Alex's Manchester United virtually wrote off the entire 2004-05 Premier League campaign due to a badly managed pre-season. The club shot itself in the foot, so to speak, with an untimely USA tour, late-arriving signings, and an extensive injury list with the result that they couldn't recover. In 1895-96, such an unprofessional attitude undermined Newton Heath. The team should have been challenging Liverpool and Manchester City for a playoff place; instead they found themselves staggering from one embarrassing episode to another.

The directors certainly shot themselves in the foot when sacking goalkeeper Douglas with such haste. A more apt expression would have been cutting their nose off to spite their face. A broken finger meant the only other custodian at the club, Ridgway, was lost too, what with no trainer around to help out. This produced a dilemma as the home game with fellow promotion hopefuls Burton Wanderers approached, and a quick solution had to be found. Mr. Albut walked into the dressing room, looked around for a spare full-back, and decided the idle George Perrins was as good as any emergency keeper. Only he wasn't. How the management regretted their rashness as Burton triumphed 2-1. That the Heathens dropped to sixth place was the good news. The bad news was that the long unbeaten home run had ended. This was, in fact, Heath's only Bank Street league loss in a three-season spell. And all that on February 29th.

For the next match, Walter Cartwright got the chance to show his versatility. He too conceded two goals, but he was deemed a success because the Rotherham keeper allowed three in himself, presenting Heath with their first away points in over three months. Now Perrins wanted another go, the opponents being Burton Wanderers again. But this time it was worse. Perrins let in four by half-time and decided he could take it no longer. Cartwright picked up the gloves and promptly conceded another as Burton wandered off with a 5-1 victory.

Though the directors couldn't be faulted for the injuries to the likes of Cassidy and Ridgway, they could be blamed for maintaining a squad as emaciated as a wannabe supermodel. At this advanced stage of the season all they could recruit were a few inexperienced youngsters. At 17 years of age, goalkeeper Walter Whittaker was as young and inexperienced as you could get. Like Newton Heath, he was born in Manchester in 1878. He was plucked from non-league Molyneaux F.C. and thrust between the sticks at Grimsby Town. At 6'1" and 13½ stone he could barely fit. The Grimsby forwards were not complaining though as they racked up four goals, despite an eye-catching performance by the debutant.

Entrusted with the task of replacing Cassidy's firepower was another teenager, 19-year-old James Vance. The source? Hint: not Dundee. That would be Annbank, then. He scored in his second game, a 1-4 loss at Burton Swifts. He subsequently appeared in the last eight matches of the season and proved to be consistent: he ended every one of them three goals short of a hat-trick. Finally, at 21 years of age, John Whitney was the grandpa of the newcomers. He stepped up from the reserves to provide cover at left half-back in a couple of games. And all this time, of course, 20-year-old Jimmy Collinson was also in the starting eleven. Although the season was '95-96, the club didn't win anything with kids.

A player of any age would have done on March 23rd. The Heathens were due in Burslem to play Port Vale. Back at the station in Manchester, as the lads prepared to board the train, one person was missing: John Dow. The club had obviously not learnt the lesson of 1893 when goalkeeper Jimmy Warner missed the train, and they hadn't brought a twelfth man along. A quick message was fizzed to John Clarkin. He gladly put aside his Saturday chores and caught a later train to Burslem. He made it just in time for the second half but couldn't prevent a 0-3 hammering.

At least Newton Heath's carelessness did not prove fatal like that of Loughborough. They came to Bank Street on April 4th but this time their kit man missed the train. They had no shirts, shorts, or boots. Mr. Albut rustled an assortment of shirts for them to wear, but they still had to take to the field in their regular pants and shoes. If this had been North Road, onlookers might have been forgiven for mistaking this Second Division match for an early kick-about among railway workers. The fact that Newton Heath could not beat lowly Loughborough by more than 2-0 was a blow to marketers of athletic wear. The bigger tragedy, though, was about to unfold. The visitors had to make their way back home in their wet clothes. Their most famous player, Jimmy Logan (who had scored a hat-trick for Notts County in the FA Cup final two years earlier) was the unluckiest. He caught pneumonia and got sick. He recovered temporarily to play again, only for the condition to relapse, and he died shortly afterwards.

HARRY STAFFORD

WITH JOHN DOW incurring the wrath of the directors and Jimmy Collinson beginning to struggle in his debut season, Newton Heath went looking for an experienced right-back. Walter Cartwright remembered an ex-team-mate at his previous club Crewe Alexandra called Harry Stafford, and he recommended that Heath signed him. For a degree of importance in Manchester United's history, this moment ranks with Louis Rocca sounding out Matt Busby about a managerial job in 1944. In biblical terms, it is the equivalent of the Holy Ghost descending on the Virgin Mary to effect the Immaculate Conception. Blasphemous? Perhaps. But reading this book you are more likely to be someone for whom Manchester United is a religion. Stafford was an unremarkable player: a reliable, hard-tackling defender of Second Division standard, but he ought to rank among the club's greatest servants.

What classifies a great Manchester United player? Is it purely an abundance of talent? Peter Beardsley was an outstanding footballer, but his contribution to the club's history lasted less than a game. If a person's status in United's hierarchy is based on the mark he left at the club, then Stafford belongs to a dozen or so of the most influential men to have graced the place. The two sugar daddies, JH Davies and James Gibson, are two such men, of course, for stepping in at crucial times to save the club from bankruptcy and then sustaining it till greater glories were reached. The two master-managers, Sir Matt Busby and Sir Alex Ferguson, are obviously on that list as well. Behind the scenes Louis Rocca and Walter Crickmer can easily be added for giving a lifetime of service (and in Crickmer's case, his life) in the name of Manchester United. Then there are the players. Duncan Edwards, George Best, and Eric Cantona each in his own time left an indelible effect with the supremacy of their footballing capabilities. Sir Bobby Charlton is in there on merit too, both for the appearances, goals, and caps records as well as for the ambassadorial image that he epitomizes. And the early 20th century greats Billy Meredith and Charlie Roberts can, to a certain extent, claim inclusion for their pioneering attainment of onfield success, their trailblazing efforts in the formation of the PFA, and their prestigious off-field aura. Yet all these legends owe their place in United folklore to Harry Stafford.

For he was a man divinely bestowed upon the club to alter its fate at the very moment of reckoning and plant the seed that is the Manchester United known today. Stafford was a fast, energetic full-back when signed from his hometown club Crewe in March 1896, and over the next seven years, his was a steady contribution on the pitch. However, it was his loyalty that shone the brightest among his qualities. He never scored a league goal for the club, but that was because his sense of duty cemented him to his defensive tasks. Not for him personal glory, but a devotion to the well-being of the club emanating from an extraordinary level of unselfishness. Here was a man ready to fight for his country, for he was on 24-hour standby when the Boer War broke out in 1899.

It was inevitable that Harry would be made Newton Heath captain, and this is where his effect began to unfold. When the club's financial health started deteriorating, he embarked on a lifesaving mission. He organised a bazaar to raise funds, inviting the leading politicians of the day for maximum exposure. When the threat of foreclosure emerged from the club's inability to fulfil fixture obligations, he went door to door for a whip-round so that the players could purchase train tickets and travel to a game in Bristol. That he missed days of training while collecting donations was of no concern to him. He travelled from Crewe every day, sometimes uncertain the directors would reimburse him his expenses.

In Newton Heath's darkest hour, when extinction was hours away and everybody at the club's meeting had given up any hope of salvation, Stafford stood up and uttered from his breath the words that saved Manchester United. He introduced Mr. JH Davies, whose takeover group was ready to provide £1000 to clear the club's debts. £200 of that total was from Stafford's own money. He subsequently became the first Manchester United captain in 1902. Shortly after he asked to be re-instated as an amateur since his family business allowed him to decline wages from the club. Mr. Davies trusted him enough to hand him a licensed premises in Wrexham.

Soon he retired, only to become the first former player in United's history to be appointed director. That didn't affect his humility, for he combined his new position with being Bank Street's groundsman as well as being in charge of alcohol sales at the ground. Stafford excelled in his capacity as a director. He did like extravagant clothing – frequently seen in a white hat and a flashy waistcoat – but his work was substantial. As a former player he made a shrewd scout and was instrumental in bringing the likes of Charlie Roberts and Alec Bell to the club to help build the legendary Duckworth-Roberts-Bell half-back line.

It was in the line of recruitment that Stafford made his last selfless act for the club. At a time when maximum wages were enforced by the FA, various clubs participated in under-the-table payments to induce decent players. Both Manchester clubs, United and City, were suspected of such behaviour. The FA cracked down on City, caught them red-handed, and nearly destroyed the club. Directors were punished and players were banned. United actually benefited, signing Billy Meredith among others. But the only reason they were able to do so was due to Stafford's sacrifice. When the FA came sniffing around at Bank Street, Stafford stepped forward and alone took the blame. No harm was to blemish the club. He admitted to the misdemeanour of paying a newly-recruited Scot his wages in advance before he was fully registered with United, and he was suspended from football for two and a half years. As he was being crucified for the forgiveness of United's sins, he defended himself thus: "Everything I have done has been in the interests of the club".

That was Harry Stafford. He served his ban and remained associated with the club to see his efforts bear fruit. No one was happier when Manchester United became champions of England in 1908 then won the FA Cup a year later. By 1911, ill health had begun to affect Stafford. Or was it overexposure to kryptonite? His life's mission finally accomplished, he bid his farewells and headed to Australia. The club gave him £50 for his services. A mere fifty in exchange for Manchester United's existence...

DEATH TO FAIRFIELD

STAFFORD ARRIVED JUST in time for Easter. His debut was against Darwen on Good Friday, Newton Heath were represented thus: Ridgway; Stafford, Erentz; Fitzsimmons, McNaught, Cartwright; Clarkin, Kennedy, Donaldson, Vance, and Smith. The Heathens put behind them a sticky run of five defeats in six outings by crushing their guests 4-0. Showing least hospitality was William Kennedy, who hammered three goals. Loughborough were dispatched 2-0 on Saturday then Burslem Port Vale were overcome 2-1 on Easter Monday. The 5,000 who turned up represented Bank Street's highest league attendance since New Year's Day. Apparently it required a lot of holiday spirit to make the club watchable. One unhappy chappy was Kennedy. On Friday he kept the match ball, but tonight he got to keep his foot in an ice bucket. A knock forced him out of the last match of the season, thus ruining his ever-present run.

Newton Heath lost the last game, going down 0-2 at Lincoln, to finish sixth, a point behind Newcastle. Liverpool were Second Division champions and won promotion via the playoffs. Runners-up Manchester City failed to do likewise, preferring instead to renew derby duals for next season. Heath's only saving grace was another decent goal scoring average. They racked up 66 goals in 30 matches for a 2.2 average, though that had declined alarmingly in the second half of the campaign. Joe Cassidy, who had been out since January with injury, easily finished top scorer with 16 league goals. He could have stopped scoring in November and still remained top, for only Kennedy was able to reach double figures too, ending on 11. Dick Smith got a disappointing nine – 10 less than last season. His excuse? He spent the last part of the campaign at outside-left while the club gave Vance his chance. Clarkin got seven, as did Donaldson, who missed the first part of the season. He could have claimed eight but for bad weather. On December 28th Heath were leading Leicester Fosse 2-0 with goals from Donaldson and Kennedy when the match was abandoned with 20 minutes left. The two teams started from scratch in February. Again the

Heathens won 2-0. Again Kennedy scored once, but that goal thief Smith etched his name rather than Donaldson's on the score sheet.

In the end 1895-96 was a season of frustration. The high 'Goals For' total was almost matched by the 'Goals Against' one. Every Newton Heath game in either league or cup included two goals or more. You'd think that was entertaining enough, but the average attendance had fallen. The sixth-place finish meant the club was moving in the wrong direction. The directors decided that an overhaul was necessary, and numerous prominent players found themselves on the way out of Clayton.

Perhaps the most surprising departure was that of John Clarkin. He had been very consistent since replacing Alf Farman on the right wing. In two and a half years he missed just five league games and contributed a healthy 23 goals – a one in three ratio. Now Blackpool came calling in readiness for their first season in the Football League, and Clarkin obviously fancied some fun in the sun. On the opposite wing James Peters was also gone. His left-wing partnership with Dick Smith was finally broken when he fled to New Brompton. Like Clarkin, he was prolific for a flankman, but a combination of injuries and a drop in form kept him out of the last part of '95-96.

Forceful full-back/leaky keeper George Perrins packed his robust style and headed to Luton. There he met up with two other members of Heath's first-ever league match, Willie Stewart and Jimmy Coupar. He had played around 150 times for the Heathens, including friendlies, but it was not possible to dislodge the new full-back partnership of Stafford and Erentz.

Fairfield had walloped Newton Heath 5-2 in the Manchester Cup. The directors reckoned that if you couldn't beat them, weaken them with your rejects. So, as many as three agents of doom were sent their way. First off was constructive full-back John Dow, never forgiven nor picked after missing the train to Burslem. Poverty cost David Fitzsimmons his stay, on the other hand - the financially-stricken club unable to pay him his summer wages. Finally, young goalie Walter Whittaker was the victim of the management's carelessness. They failed to renew his registration and a capable prospect was lost. On the contrary, they retained the registration of another one of 'the kids', John Whitney, for four years even though he had long since drifted into the non-league domain.

By the way, the ploy to undermine Fairfield worked a treat. The following year they were disbanded! Revenge was Newton Heath's. However it was doubtful that Albut could be heard screaming: "Today Fairfield, tomorrow the world"!

1896-97

THE BIGGEST NAME

There must have been a breakdown in communication between Mr. Albut and his scouts in the summer of 1896. His request for a 'big name' centre-half, got a literal response when they signed the man with the biggest name in football: Caesar Augustus Llewellyn Jenkyns. No, that's not the entire half-back line, that's just the centre-half. The Welsh international from Woolwich Arsenal not only arrived with an extra large moniker but an extra large frame. He may have stood an average 5'10" tall but he weighed in at an intimidating 14st 4lbs. Jenkyns proved that size does matter, either when steamrollering opponents with beastly shoulder charges or when bulldozing them with earth-shattering tackles. Even the leather ball could not escape his ferociousness. One mighty lump and it found itself in a different time zone. Add to that a 'macho-man' nature and a loud mouth, and it's no wonder the directors – trembling at the thought of provoking him – immediately installed him as captain. This way his abrasive tongue would come in handy as he barked his instructions to the forwards haring before him. A gladiator on a chariot, he was Keane-esque you could say, and it's tempting to imagine how similar Keane and Jenkyns would have appeared had the Irishman not given up the junk food diet early in his career.

Jenkyns was not the only heavyweight hauled to Bank Street in preparation for the coming campaign. Tilting the scales at 12st 3lbs, Billy Draycott wasn't as heavy, but, as his height stopped at 5'7", he was just as hefty. At least he had one thing going for him: he was surprisingly speedy for his build. The 27-year-old was born near Derby and had years of Football League experience with Stoke and, lately, Burton Wanderers.

So, Jenkyns and mini-Jenkyns' presence in the half-back line complemented the Little Wonder himself, James McNaught. Only McNaught was set to start the season in his old position of inside-left in a much-changed front five. With Clarkin and Peters gone, two new faces were added. The first was Willie Bryant, a 24-year-old winger who arrived from Rotherham after a spell at Chesterfield. He slotted in on the right flank and wouldn't budge for four years. The same cannot be said of the second newcomer. William Brown came from Chester and was deemed classy enough for the reserves. Somehow he was able to kick-off the new season as first-choice centre-forward until inexperience caught up with him. He would shortly be sold to Stockport County.

Notice anything odd about the new lads? Four signings and not one of them from Scotland. Perhaps the directors decided to give Englishmen a chance to see if they too could play. Well the Scot Joe Cassidy was back from a long injury layoff and, as Sir Alex would say, he was like a new signing. This was, in fact, the third coming of Cassidy in a chequered start to his Bank Street career and this time he would be wearing a third different kit. He had been clad in the traditional green-and-gold shirt during his brief stay in 1893. Now the club was ditching the green top of the last two seasons. This was not a Slippery Pete-style marketing ploy. Fans wearing their team's colours was a fashion concept still a century away, let alone them being proud enough to put on a Newton Heath top. The new colours? A basic white shirt found everywhere, and equally uncomplicated blue shorts to go with it. The Invincibles of Preston North End had donned that combination as they conquered all before them at the dawn of league football, but no one mentioned to Heath that the 'In' prefix had long since been removed from Preston's adjective.

With a shiny new uniform, the Heathens sent the following XI to welcome the new season: Ridgway in goal; the dependable Stafford and Erentz as full-backs; Draycott, Jenkyns, and Cartwright as robust a half-back line as you could put together; and Bryant, Donaldson, Brown, McNaught, and Cassidy entrusted with scoring the goals to get Heath out of Division Two. This was all the more urgent now that a newcomer, Gainsborough Trinity, had been added to an opponents list that included the likes of Burton Swifts, Burton Wanderers, Loughborough, and Darwen. With all due respect to, er, well nobody since none of these teams exist in the League anymore, this was not the kind of company that Heath wanted to keep.

THE GREAT START

NEWTON HEATH MIGHT as well have reattached the L.Y.R. suffix to their name the way they blitzed into the new season. For they resembled a steam train with the midfield pumping and the forwards steaming ahead as no one dared step onto their tracks. Gainsborough Trinity were welcomed into the Football League with the words "Mind the Gap". The 2-0 win secured courtesy of McNaught. Then Burton Swifts were battered 5-3 on their own turf. McNaught was again on the score sheet, as were new signings Brown, Bryant, and Draycott, as well as the 'just-like-new' signing Joe Cassidy. Donaldson was the only one of the forwards not to get a goal but he politely waited his turn and was on the mark as Walsall were beaten 2-0 and Lincoln 3-1. The rest of the goals came from Cassidy who maintained a goal-a-game ratio.

Four games, four wins, four points clear; Heath were in a league of their own. Almost everybody else had inexplicably dropped half their points already. Only Notts County maintained a 100 percent start so far, but they had only played two matches. They appeared to be Heath's main challengers, along with Manchester City and Grimsby Town who had finished second and third respectively last season. The relegated Small Heath also fancied their chances of bouncing straight back up. The next match was Heath's first real test of the campaign: away at Grimsby, one of those aforementioned challengers. However, the opportunity to establish how good the Mancunians were quickly evaporated due to the misfortune of losing goalie Joe Ridgway to a serious shoulder injury. The reshuffled ten men went down 0-2. There was no time to look around for a replacement as the next match was just two days later. So, another Joe, Wetherell, stepped up from the reserve team to face Walsall. But he proved to be just an average Joe as he conceded two goals. The 23-year-old got to play one more time, against Small Heath, when his error allowed the Brummies to take a point from Bank Street.

By this time the directors had found a new custodian. As always in case of emergency, they immediately headed to Scotland.

No more trawling the land for Englishmen. They did what came naturally to them and signed Frank Barrett from feeder club Dundee. It is obvious, however, that they had been tracking him for some time for here was a goalie so good they ought to have renamed him Frank Barr-it. He had been handed two Scottish caps and, to be frank, Barrett didn't drop them. In fact, he remained Manchester United's solitary Scotland international keeper till Jim Leighton was signed in 1988. Although a tad short for a goalie, he made the number one jersey his private possession missing a mere six matches in the next four years. Frank was there for every league, cup, or friendly game. Presumably he went home for the summer. Oh, and also on the odd occasion when a spell of soul searching was required. A neat keeper, he liked his sheets clean. So, whenever at fault for a loss, he would evade the criticism and sulk away to Dundee. Mr. Albut and his staff would then set off hastily to Scotland to appease him and tempt him back. God knows they had had enough bad luck with keepers in the past to lose this good one.

Barrett made his debut on September 26th when the Heathens crushed Newcastle 4-0, thanks to a Cassidy hat-trick. He replicated the feat a month later as Burton Wanderers were swept away 3-0. He added another two in the next league match when revenge was obtained against Grimsby with a 4-2 victory. Having played a dozen games so far, Cassidy had netted a round dozen. Since his return from Celtic he had amassed 36 in 39 league matches. No one in the rest of Manchester United's history comes close to such a stunning strike rate. The great Tommy Taylor grabbed 28 goals in his first 39 matches, and that's as close as anyone else gets. Of course he led Heath's scoring charts by a distance. Three players were next on four goals, one of whom was new right-half Draycott. The club led the Second Division table

NEWCASTLE PROGRAMME 1897
A rare Football League programme of a Newton Heath game. This was for an away trip to Newcastle on New Year's Day 1897.

195

until the thirteenth match when Notts County nipped a point ahead. They had won eight, lost three, and drawn two. The first of these draws was the Manchester derby. Around 20,000 fans converged on Hyde Road only to be rewarded with a 0-0 goal-fest – Heath's first drawn league match in almost a year. At least they kept their neighbours at arm's length. More importantly, the quest for promotion was very much on.

A FULL CUP

AT THE BEGINNING of December, the Railwaymen found themselves involved in Cup play. Wasn't it a bit early to be knocked out? The problem was that, since Heath's stay outside the top flight had been extended, they were now required to participate in the qualifying rounds of the FA Cup for the first time since joining the Football League five years ago. The humiliation! Now they were forced to get through three qualifying rounds before the competition proper.

The Lancashire Senior Cup was coincidently brought forward too this season and, by chance, Heath were drawn to play the same opponents, West Manchester, at home in both competitions on consecutive weekends. First up was the Lancashire Cup and Heath put an end to six straight defeats in that competition by winning 4-1 in front of a five-figure crowd. Bryant (2), Cassidy, and Donaldson grabbing the goals. The FA Cup match went even better as a refreshed forward line inscribed their names in the record books with a 7-0 trouncing. It remained the club's biggest victory in this competition until 1949. Cassidy and Bryant were again responsible for three of the goals, the latter's contribution being a spectacular long-range howitzer. The identity of the other scorers was unusual, though. Two goals were obtained by that fly-by-night amateur Charles Rothwell, whose first team appearances were about as regular as the 29th of February. This was his last competitive game for the club and it gave him the enviable statistic of 'played three, scored three'. By contrast, the other two came from Scottish newcomer Matthew Gillespie who had signed from Lincoln City the month before. He had been catapulted into the starting eleven following a hat-trick in a friendly at last season's Manchester Cup conquerors Fairfield. Yet his promising start proved misleading. It took Gillespie the best part of a year and 21 matches to match his

JENKYNS AND BOYD
Caesar Augustus Llewelyn Jenkyns, the man with the biggest name in football, was signed from Woolwich Arsenal at the start of 1896-97. Henry Boyd followed Jenkyns from Arsenal in February and brought his own ball with him.

tally after one game. Surprisingly, the directors kept picking him in the hope that he would develop an acceptable scoring rate. He was, after all, useful in the air and a hard worker. But that's about it. His shooting would have doubly improved if only he could have kicked with his head.

For now, though, Gillespie was unstoppable in the Cup. He was on the mark as a team called Nelson was swatted aside in the next round, and again against Blackpool soon after. It took a replay to see off the Seasiders but Heath were finally in the first round. When Manchester City were defeated 1-0 on their own patch in front of an enormous gathering of 18,000, talk was suddenly of the 'quadruple'. Promotion and success in three knockout tournaments seems fanciful, but why not? The spirits were definitely lifted by that latest victory – the first in the Manchester Cup since 1893.

However, the extent of the club's ambitions soon had to be revised to just a 'treble'. The visit to Division One Burnley in the Lancashire Cup Round Two began brilliantly, the Heathen forwards hounding the home team into putting through their own goal within two minutes. Unfortunately, the strain of playing four tough cup matches in the space of nine days began to tell, and Newton Heath fell 1-2.

Meanwhile, the FA Cup march continued unabated. All these intermediate ties had resulted in the very same first round draw as the previous campaign: at home to Kettering Town. Then, the Heathens had toiled hard to a 2-1 victory. Now they pummelled their opponents - Cassidy claiming his third hat-trick of the season, Bob Donaldson adding a couple for a 5-1 pasting. The next round draw gave the newspaper headline writers something to drool over: Saints versus Heathens! The Saints in question were Southampton, or Southampton St. Marys, to give them their proper name back then. A 1-1 draw on the South Coast was followed by a 3-1 triumph of evil over good, back at Bank Street, Bryant notched a brace and Cassidy hit the other.

The Mancunians were now in the third round for the first time ever. These days the third round is where it all begins for the big boys. In the Heathens' time, however, it was the equivalent of the quarter-finals. Yes, Newton Heath were in the Last Eight, just two games away from the final! A lucky draw now and they would be halfway there, but the other seven names in the hat were daunting. All were Division One teams, and five of them were from the top third in the table. Eventually, Heath were drawn away to crack outfit Derby County, just like last time around. Though the Mancunians fought manfully, watched by 12,000 fans, their limitations were exposed as Derby triumphed 2-0. But this year's FA Cup odyssey had been an excellent experience. They played eight ties (the same total as the previous four campaigns put together), won five and scored 23 goals. The quarter-final berth may have been the highlight of Newton Heath's cup exploits, but those 23 goals in one campaign have never been bettered since.

A week later, Bury knocked Heath out of the Manchester Senior Cup, winning the semi-final 2-0. It brought the curtain down on an eventful cup campaign and refocused their minds on the essential battle ahead: promotion to Division One.

BUOYED BY BOYD

WHEN OUR STORY last touched on Newton Heath's league escapades, they were doing very well. They had been scoring freely and had maintained a play-off spot. However, while they were involved in all those cup games, a few challengers had made up ground by playing extra matches. Consequently the extended cup run proved distracting as results suffered soon after. They collected just five points in three months, losing four away matches. The lowest point came on December 19th when Notts County 'edged' the top-of-the-table clash 3-0, thanks mainly to the sending-off of skipper Caesar Jenkyns for rough play. The papers sympathized with Jenkyns, explaining how his bulky appearance can compound his roughness. After all, here was a mammoth of a man who could look violent by simply posing for the team photo, let alone over-enthusiastically wading into tackles.

At least the return derby with Manchester City went Heath's way. Bank Street's biggest gate of the season (18,000) cheered on as Heath powered to a 2-1 victory. The most crucial factor in obtaining both points was the deployment of James McNaught at left half-back. His experiment in attack had been a success at the beginning of the season but the goals had dried up lately. On this afternoon he performed such a flawless job in marking the great Billy Meredith that the Welsh Wizard spent most of the afternoon frantically chewing on his toothpick. The home goals came from Bob Donaldson and Dick Smith. The latter had forced his way back into the starting eleven but he was no longer a fixture in the front line. Neither was William Kennedy, another regular marksman of the previous season. Surprisingly, he was unable to replicate his exploits this time around and only made one solitary first-team appearance. By December he was deemed dispensable, as was the man originally keeping him out of the forward line, Brown. Both players were offloaded to nearby Stockport County. And another fallen striker, James Vance, got the boot after just one game in this new season. Newton Heath fulfilled their annual obligations by selling him to Fairfield.

In return Heath signed Henry Boyd from Woolwich Arsenal. These days, £45 would (possibly) get you a decent ticket for a match at Old Trafford. In 1897, that same fee bought you a prolific Scottish forward at the peak of his career. Boyd had suffered a broken leg on his last appearance at Bank Street when Newton Heath had entertained the Londoners back in November 1895. He had been out of the game for a year but returned to lead his team's scoring charts with 13 goals from 22 league matches. Boyd was just the player Newton Heath needed. He had vast top flight experience with Burnley and WBA, was a committed individual, and was excellent at linking the attacking unit together.

On the morning of his league debut, February 6th, Heath stood fourth in the table, six points behind Grimsby Town and the play-off zone. Boyd was selected at centre-forward as Heath hosted Loughborough: Barrett; Stafford, Erentz; Draycott, Jenkyns, McNaught; Smith, Donaldson, Boyd, Gillespie, and Cassidy. Just a few weeks back Loughborough had handed Boyd's old employers Arsenal their record league defeat (8-0), now the Scot turned the tables, marking his debut with a goal and an exceptional overall performance to help his new club to their biggest league victory in almost two years. Even the half-backs Draycott and Jenkyns joined in the rout grabbing a goal apiece in a 6-0 drubbing.

The fantastic win, as well as Boyd's introduction, was like an adrenaline injection to the Newton Heath team. They embarked on a five-game winning run to catch Grimsby and topple them on goal average. Notts County were unreachable at the top, while just behind lurked Newcastle, still in with a chance of stealing second place. On the negative side was an injury to Harry Stafford that would limit his availability in this crucial end to the season. A five-figure crowd congregated at Bank Street for the Top Two clash with Notts County on March 27th. Fits-anywhere Walter Cartwright was now filling in at right full-back while Bryant had regained his starting place from Dick Smith. And it was Bryant who struck for Heath as the two rivals settled for a point each. However this point was enough to nudge Heath ahead of idle Grimsby, who had two games left compared to Heath's three.

Grimsby were getting desperate. They checked out Newton Heath's run-in and saw that the next fixture was at Lincoln City. Lincoln were so far adrift at the foot of the table they were in a league of their own. Seeing as an upset was highly unlikely, they decided to provide the Lincoln players with an incentive. In a fiendish idea that stretched the boundaries of morality, if not breaking the legal ones, Grimsby offered each Lincoln player the princely sum of £2 if they were to beat Newton Heath. On top of that, the club itself would get £20. Might as well motivate the management too. It may not have remotely resembled the Premier

League circus as we know it, but this showed how badly Grimsby wanted to be in Division One.

One man, though, stood between the Lincoln players and prosperity. One mountain of a man, in fact. While his team-mates struggled with the pressures of the promotion chase, Captain Caesar Jenkyns strode forward not once, not twice, but thrice to secure Heath a 3-1 victory. A hat-trick from centre-half. Grimsby could keep their silver pieces, for Heath were keeping the golden points.

When Arsenal were defeated 2-0 on their own turf two days later, Grimsby were out of the picture. Henry Boyd scored against his old club, as he had done a fortnight earlier in a 1-1 draw. This was Heath's ninth undefeated league match in a row since he joined. It all but guaranteed a playoff place. On April 12th, Newcastle fell 0-3 at Burton, and Heath were out of reach. They had finished second behind Notts County and secured a test match ticket.

FOUR FOR TWO

A YOUNG NEWTON Heath fan who had followed the club's fortunes since they had joined the League could have been misled into believing that everybody's season ends by playing test matches. For the fourth time in five years Newton Heath were involved in the playoffs. They had skipped out last season but fear not, the powers that be had changed the setup to where it was now four times the fun. In this new format, the top two teams from Division Two joined the First Division's bottom two in the same group. Teams played home and away against the two teams not in your division to collect points with the top half of the group gaining promotion. Confused? It gets better.

Newton Heath's first opponents were Burnley, the team that had knocked them out in the Lancashire Cup. The other adversaries were Sunderland. Sunderland!? Yes, the champions of 1892, 1893, and 1895 had opted to spend 1896-97 slumming it with the basement dwellers. With such opposition, Newton Heath's task was going to be tough and matters weren't helped by the absence of Harry Stafford. He had tried to make a comeback in the last league match of the campaign (when Loughborough handed Heath their first reverse since New Year's Day) but was not deemed fit enough for the gruelling test match series. Also missing from the first match would be talismanic forward Henry Boyd. In his place, the selectors called up a familiar name from the past, Welshman Roger Doughty; he of the Doughty clan who had carried Newton Heath's flag forward the previous decade. He had rejoined the club this season but was only able to make the first team for the Lancashire Cup match against West Manchester in December. At the very least he would have vast experience to offer as would the stalwart Bob Donaldson – a veteran of three previous test match campaigns. And to spice things up, the directors promised the players £10 each if they could secure promotion.

The situation worsened before it even started! The first match against Burnley was postponed until the following Wednesday due to some shocking news: the Bank Street pitch was muddy! Though both Heath and Burnley were in the same boat, the real disadvantage would most likely emerge towards the end of the series. By the time of the last tussle with Sunderland, Heath would have played four important matches in eight days whereas the Wearsiders' workload would have been spread over a 10-day period.

On Monday April 19th, the following eleven donned their white shirts and took to the field at Turf Moor, Burnley: Barrett; Cartwright, Erentz; Draycott, Jenkyns, McNaught; Bryant, Doughty, Donaldson, Gillespie, and Cassidy. The Heathens outplayed their hosts, showing superior purpose and hunger, yet still lost 0-2. Most sane observers thought Heath should have won, and the Mancunians went out two days later determined to set the record straight. Boyd was fit again, coming in for Doughty and bringing with him his goal scoring boots. Inevitably, the Scot was on the mark, as was Jenkyns to earn the team a 2-0 victory. The promotion push was back on. Notts County had taken three points off Sunderland and led the table. Burnley and Newton Heath were joint second. Heath's next clash was against bottom team Sunderland.

The Mancs descended on Bank Street in their thousands to watch the ground's most important game to date. By kick-off there were around 18,000 fans wailing for Heath to slay the northern giants. One man who would neither slay nor play was Walter Cartwright. His temporary stint at right-back had proved as much a mishap as it had for Stafford. So, in stepped Doughty, the replacement's replacement. Heath's hero was again Henry Boyd with another crucial goal, while Bryant displayed his bravery by limping on his one left healthy leg. But the real star of the show was the Sunderland goalie Ned Doig. With the scores level as the match entered its latter stages, Heath poured forward seeking the winner to all but guarantee promotion. Yet Doig stood in their way, single-handedly saving anything the home team hurled at him, The 1-1 draw suited neither side although the gate receipts of £487 would have pleased Mr Albut. Within hours both teams caught the same train up to Wearside.

Notts County and Burnley had copied the score line, so nothing changed in the placings. With one match left, County needed a draw; Heath could do with a win though a draw just might do it; Burnley and Sunderland definitely required both points.

There were 8,000 spectators present for the last game, one or two of which likened Newton Heath's strip to that of the mighty Preston North End. There, unfortunately, the similarities ended. Playing for the fourth time since the previous Monday, the Mancs performed with the zest of a speeding turtle. Their hosts, on the other hand, suddenly remembered their lofty status and played accordingly. The first quarter of an hour saw one-way traffic, all roundabouts blocked for construction. This period of intense pressure culminated with a headed goal from Gillespie – James of Sunderland not Matthew of Newton Heath. The Heathens were derailed. Their innate roughness began to emerge, no one encapsulating that spirit more than Caesar Jenkyns. There he was hacking a human away. Here he was lashing a shot wide. Next he was heading a certain goal clear. The forwards, however, struggled to create good chances. It didn't help when a bad knock made McNaught take a much longer half-time break than his team-mates.

In the other match, Notts County were leading 1-0. Just one goal for Heath would unlock the Division One door. Consequently, the second half was a tense affair, but fate did not favour Heath. With just 10 minutes left, Gillespie (alas, James again) found the net. It was all over. The First Division giants had preserved their place, and so had the plucky team from the railways.

A HEALING CUP

No one celebrated louder than the folks in Clayton when the Football League pulled the plug on the test matches in 1899 and installed automatic promotion and demotion instead. Newton Heath, along with Notts County, had been involved in the most number of playoff campaigns (four) and had solely played in the highest total of games (eight). And, frankly, they'd had enough. Ask Bob Donaldson, the man who participated in every one of those eight matches. He enjoyed them as much as a scoring record of zero goals indicates.

You see, although the test match success of 1893 had presented Newton Heath with another crack at Division One, over the ensuing years they grew to regret and detest the existence of this hoopla altogether. Their subsequent record would have been less fruitful only if they had not participated at all. True, the escape clause provided by the playoffs came in handy in its first season, but the Heathens would have been relegated in 1894 anyway, then might have returned in 1895 if three teams were allowed back, and would definitely have earned their place back fair and square in 1897. As it was they were doomed by fate – or the gods that sanctioned the creation of Manchester United – to remain a notch below the upper crust.

A small fraction of a minute portion of a tiny piece of consolation came Heath's way in the last game of the 1896-97 season. It happened in a friendly competition so exclusive even Heath could win it. A Manchester and Salford Cup was introduced as the brainchild of the Newton Heath director, Mr. William Healey, who modestly termed it the Healey Cup. All Heath had to do to make the final was flog Fairfield four-nil a few days before the test matches. Then, after spending a fortnight combating First Division opponents with the aim of continuing to do so, meeting Manchester City in the final was a relatively easy if disappointing climax. Stafford returned to right-back while reserve left-back Richard Roylance was drafted into his first-team debut with the cruellest of initiation pranks: man mark Billy Meredith. The Heathens ran out 5-2 winners with goals from Cassidy (2), Donaldson, Bryant, and Draycott. So, Barrett, Stafford, Roylance, Draycott, Jenkyns, McNaught, Bryant, Donaldson, Boyd, Gillespie, and Cassidy collected gongs about as meaningful as Roy Keane's Champions League medal.

Undoubtedly this was poor reward for an entire season of tremendous endeavour. Apart from finishing runners-up, the Heathens were undefeated at Fortress Bank Street in 25 games in all competitions, including friendlies. They possessed easily the best defensive record in the division, thanks to the miserliness of Barrett and his backs, not to mention the highly prominent half-back line. Jenkyns, indeed, had brought some prestige onto the club when he played – and scored – for Wales against Ireland in the British Championship on March 6th. Needless to say, training at Bank Street was not disrupted during international week.

At the other end of the field Joe Cassidy was unique amongst his team-mates in venturing into double figures for league goals scored. The hot striker put the 'heat' in Heathens, as compared to Jenkyns, who focused mostly on the 'eat' part. Cassidy notched 17 league goals even though he started two-thirds of his games on the left wing. He laid claim to eight FA Cup goals as well, while in all first-team matches his total was a nice round 30. Donaldson stopped on nine in the league, though he added six in the cups. None of the others, however, broke the six-goal barrier in league play. The reduction in chance conversion coupled with an enhanced defensive effort meant that Newton Heath curiously had the lowest aggregate goals total in the division: 90; a drop of 33 on the previous season.

What was strikingly different about the end of the season was that the directors refrained from performing their annual random player cull. They observed how the team's stability had almost paid rich dividends, so they decided to experiment with continuity. McNaught, for instance, had appeared in every competitive match, simultaneously becoming the club's trump card without whom they never left the dressing room. A few others, namely Bryant, Cassidy, Donaldson, Draycott, Erentz, and Jenkyns, appeared in 27 or more of the 30 Division Two contests. Also, the likes of newcomers Boyd and Gillespie did not miss a match after arriving at Clayton.

So, the only departure in the close season was Joe Wetherell. He became obsolete when goalkeeper Barrett was purchased and Ridgway's shoulder healed. He simply drifted into obscurity. As for Roger Doughty, his presence remained in the reserve team for one more year, while his legacy lasted a lot longer.

1897-98

TWENTY YEARS AND COUNTING

1897-98 WAS Newton Heath's 20th season in existence, yet none of the players were interviewed in the local papers making hollow promises about marking the anniversary by gaining promotion. Nor did any director climb onto the Bank Street rooftop and babble on about how it was Heath's destiny to win the cup because this year the final was being held in their hometown. Instead, most kept their heads down and thanked their lucky stars they were still around two decades after formation. To say that Heath were financially crippled was something of an understatement. A big reason Heath had been able to preserve their position as one of the top twenty clubs in England for the last half dozen years was that most other clubs were also in the red. The situation was getting to a stage where the Heath players' win bonuses were no longer applicable. Instead, whenever the Heathens won, the directors treated them to an all-expenses-paid dinner at ...the local chippy! The hungrier the players, the more improved was Heath's performance. This might explain why 14st 4lb Jenkyns was constantly snarling and roaring his team-mates on to victory.

If that was impoverished enough, then spare a thought for the transfer funds situation. The management, with astute judgment, had continuously been able to unearth decent prospects that would provide excellent service for the club. The scouts would often travel far and entice players with jobs at the station. However, now the circumstances were so dire the club went sniffing in the streets of Manchester with the deal-clinching slogan of "have boots, will play". And while it was not customary to release transfer fees, "undisclosed" came in as a handy replacement for "insignificant" in this case. So, Newton Heath's reinforcements for the new campaign, drum roll emphatically unnecessary, were: William

Dunn from South Bank, Billy Morgan from Horwich F.C., and Harry Erentz from Oldham County.

The Dunn deal brought a versatile forward to the club. Fresh out of his teens, he was expected to display his enthusiasm anywhere up front. Morgan had been signed earlier in the year, in fact, and tried out in a couple of matches at the end of the previous season. This term he would again be restricted to sporadic appearances in Heath's efficient half-back line. In time, though, Billy would carve a lengthy career at Clayton, eventually donning the red of Manchester United. As for Erentz, his purchase demonstrated that if you couldn't afford scouts to travel to Dundee, have the players come from there by themselves. Much like Fred Erentz, Harry was born in that city and played for the team, albeit just the once. He spent one season with County, who were Oldham's premier club at the time, before fulfilling the destiny of all Dundonians by joining Newton Heath. Also like Fred, he was of Danish ancestry and operated as a full-back. They were, as a matter of fact, brothers.

Both Dunn and Morgan were considered ready to appear in the first team for the start of the campaign. Dunn's inclusion came in place of long-serving stalwart Donaldson at inside-right. Donaldson must have known his days were numbered, his return of 15 goals in 1896-97 surprisingly didn't suffice for the directors. Or perhaps they looked to justify spending their last few quid on Dunn. In either case, the management opted on this selection to get the campaign going: Barrett; Stafford, F. Erentz; Morgan, McNaught, Cartwright; Bryant, Dunn, Boyd, Gillespie, and Cassidy. At least Donaldson wouldn't feel lonely now that heavyweights such as Jenkyns and Draycott were selected for the stands alongside him. On the other hand, one man was taking his first steps on the tortuous path that would fulfil his destiny. With Jenkyns excluded from the starting eleven, a new captain had to be picked. In a moment of divine intervention, or plain old luck, Harry Stafford was the chosen one. From this day on, he would lead and they would follow.

NOT ENOUGH HAT-TRICKS

IN THE FIRST game of the season, Newton Heath beat Lincoln City 5-0; Henry Boyd scored a hat-trick. In the second, they beat

Burton Swifts 4-0; Henry Boyd scored a hat-trick. In the third, Heath lost to Luton Town 1-2; Henry Boyd was out of hat-tricks. The directors, meanwhile, were out of their senses. Not as a show of solidarity with Boyd, but because this wasn't any ordinary defeat. This took place at home, and Newton Heath just did not lose league games to Second Division teams at Bank Street. In the preceding three years, it had happened just once, and that was because a full-back was playing in goal. On this occasion, Heath had Barrett between the sticks, but the usually reliable custodian had a game to forget. Up front, the Heathens had a great opportunity to preserve their unbeaten run when they were awarded a penalty. However, Boyd, probably thinking ahead to another three-goal haul, didn't focus on the immediate task at hand and missed from the spot. The directors were furious with this home reverse and brought out the axe. Chop! Chop! But it wasn't Barrett whose name was chopped from the first team. After all, it was sacking their goalie that led to that home defeat two years ago and, thankfully, the directors had learned from that lesson. Apparently, they weren't proficient in other subjects for they elected to make wholesale changes throughout the rest of the team instead. Out went the new lads, Morgan and Dunn. They were the unlucky scapegoats of one bad result, their efforts in the first two victories suitably ignored. Also out was inside-left Matthew Gillespie, the precursor of the Alan Smith-type 'forward'. He put himself about with abundant enthusiasm and came in handy in the air, but he boasted the scoring prowess of a 30-year-old virgin.

Into their places slotted the tried and trusted trio of Donaldson, Jenkyns, and Dick Smith, fully equipped with a figurative apology from the management for even considering dispensing with their duties in the first place. No one was more pleased than Smith who notched the solitary goal of the trip to Blackpool. Then Boyd made it eight goals in five matches by grabbing a brace in the 2-0 defeat of Leicester Fosse. Despite the great start that saw Heath collect four wins from five matches, they were only fourth in the table. Manchester City, Burnley, and Small Heath had made better starts and played more times.

The next three matches were all against Top Five opposition yet Heath did their best to prove they did not belong among them. They earned one point out of six, and that came from holding leaders Manchester City to a 1-1 draw on October 16th. Matthew Gillespie was recalled at the expense of Smith to face his brother Billy in the opposition's attack, and it was the Heathen who represented the family on the score sheet. The Derby was watched by another 20,000-strong gathering at Bank Street. It is quite impressive the level of support that Heath enjoyed at that early and inglorious stage in the club's history. Even today, teams with a significant past struggle to attract such a huge following outside the top flight. This goes to show how loved Manchester United have been throughout the generations, a devotion that started with those rugged, cavalier Heathens then swelled during the Mangnall, Busby, and Ferguson eras.

The month ended with Heath putting six goals past Walsall, the eternal whiners. That goal haul was not enough to cause voided matches on this occasion, much to the relief of Donaldson. He helped himself to a brace in one last hurrah, as we'll shortly see. Cassidy, in a desperate plea not to be forgotten by the fans in all the hoopla surrounding Boyd's early exploits, duplicated Donaldson's tally to reach five goals for the season. He was still as prolific as ever. Also on the score sheet was William Bryant. He was developing into an accomplished winger who dribbled like a baby and crossed like a true Christian. His consistent form so impressed the international selectors that, the following weekend, he became the first Heathen to appear for the Football League when he was selected at right wing against the Irish League. This was back in the days when the different leagues played each other for the sake of representative competition; what with just the four international teams in the entire universe.

THREE STARS DOWN

A WISE PERSON once postulated that two wrongs do not make a right. Some wit countered that three rights make a left. While the Newton Heath directors may have chuckled at the latter, they certainly didn't heed the former. After throwing the mother of all fits and ringing the changes when Luton Town won at Bank Street, they threw the grandmother herself when Newcastle United repeated the feat two months later. It did not matter that Newcastle were developing into a very good side – they would win promotion this coming April. A home defeat, and the failure to score at home after 55 consecutive league matches dating back to early 1894, meant heads had to roll again, with the management concluding that the players who were recalled in the aftermath of the first setback were the same ones that had to be dropped now. Only 'dropped' wasn't the actual action applied. Sir Matt Busby preferred the term 'rested' whereas Sir Alex 'rotated' his squad. The Heath directors were blunter: the culprits were suspended! And we're talking about some of the club's most prominent players here, and Matthew Gillespie. The likes of Donaldson, Jenkyns, and Smith were placed on the transfer list, their 'conduct' having irked the powers that be. Yet even the papers were questioning the directors' sanity, especially when they opted to retain Gillespie of all people. True, Jenkyns was now all bark and no bite, but Donaldson was still a name to be feared and trembled at. While Bob exuded power and hard work, Matt Gillespie's activity during matches, in comparison, was so minimal that Mr. Albut considered charging him an entrance fee like the rest of the spectators. Yet with the directors restricted to keeping one low-scoring big lad up front, they placed their financial needs above the footballing ones. While Donaldson was two years younger than Gillespie, years of barging into opposition keepers and defenders meant there wasn't much gas left in the tank. And more importantly in these hard times, there was no way that the £80 fee Luton were offering was going to be turned down. The directors would have been lucky to have received a pound for every league goal Gillespie had bundled in at Clayton.

So Newton Heath and their longest-serving stalwart parted company, Donaldson discovering that even in those early days the club's coach waits for nobody. He was Heath's last link to the Alliance days, his 20 goals having propelled the team into the Football League in 1892. In truth, that was when he was at his most lethal. He netted 16 times in Heath's inaugural First Division season, but after that defences tightened a grip on his free-scoring vein. However, a rocket here and a shoulder barge there kept adding up until his tally reached 125 goals in all first-team games. No one else has gathered so many Newton Heath goals. As a matter of fact, he would remain Manchester United's leading scorer (including friendlies) for another 30 years after his departure. Only 1920s hero

Joe Spence scored more in the club's first 65 years in existence.

His pickup line, of course, would always be that he scored Manchester United's first Football League goal ever, while his clinching sweet nothings were that he also registered the first hat-trick. He wore Newton Heath's colours in over 250 contests, of both competitive and friendly nature. His contribution, however, far exceeded mere digits. For he foraged and battled in Heath's cause, quite often literally. He was feared yet respected by his opponents, who flattered him for flattening them. Football was a physical war in those days and, luckily for Heath, Donaldson was their great gladiator.

The other player of considerable physical presence, Caesar Jenkyns, was sold too, his destination Walsall. The Heath directors were hoping to exchange him for his weight in gold but had to settle for £45 instead. The regret for Newton Heath was that Jenkyns' time at Clayton was too brief. He had spent most of his early career with Small Heath, facing the Heathens, in fact, in the test match series of 1893. He represented Wales on eight occasions and, although just one coincided with his spell at Bank Street, it made him the last Newton Heath player to gain full international recognition. When he eventually retired, he put his bark to good use by becoming a policeman (like his father) in Birmingham. The Heathens cheered for him even more now that his chief occupation was putting Brummies in jail.

Dick Smith lasted a couple of games longer, but he too was soon shown the door. His demise had been the most baffling. After cracking 19 league goals in in his first season at Clayton, he spent the next three years slowly collecting a further 13. Perhaps he sulked when he was separated from his erstwhile wing partner James Peters, while his goal return was understandably affected when the management started using him as a stopgap all over the pitch. Their argument was that his hot streak had already diminished, but the reality could be that the 'Second Season Syndrome' had not entered soccer terminology yet for them to demonstrate patience. So Dick returned to his hometown club Halliwell Rovers where he developed the habit of changing clubs with the frequency he had for changing positions. Within three and a half years he would play for Wigan County, Bolton, Wigan United, and Newton Heath again. Consequently, future generations of Heathens fans could also claim to have spotted Dick.

IN.OUT. REPEAT

WITH SO MANY line-up changes it was inevitable that Newton Heath would stutter through a spell of indifferent results. The departure of key players left some gaping holes that would now have to be patched up, but something had to be done. The Newcastle setback left Heath in seventh, which, as a shirt number, is feted like no other at the club; but not so much as a league placing. The directors could be commended on making this brave, if unpopular, move in order to shake things up. Perhaps their message came out just a bit more subtle than "one home defeat and you're out"!

For a couple of men the message was "you're in" when Heath visited Leicester Fosse the following weekend. William Dunn was back in the front line at the expense of Gillespie, only he was ushered to the left wing with Joe Cassidy stepping inside. Also, a lad named Frank Wedge was called up from the reserves where he had given a fine showing in a 7-1 slaughtering of Blackburn Park Road. He had been signed the year before from local club Talbot F.C. and he celebrated his debut by turning in Heath's goal in a 1-1 draw. The celebrations continued a week later as another goal in a 2-1 victory over Grimsby Town allowed Heath to leapfrog them into fifth. Two games, two goals, too much celebration for the directors' liking. They proceeded to thank Frank and send him back to the reserves for they had another stop-gap chap in mind.

James Carman did not command any large fee. On the contrary, Newton Heath picked him just when his previous club Oldham County went bankrupt. Heath's new good luck charm was a local lad from Salford of Irish descent, now instructed to fill Bob Donaldson's smelly boots. He was unwrapped on Christmas Day in front of 16,000 spectators at Hyde Road where highflying Manchester City remained unbeaten so far. Barrett was in goal, supported by Stafford and Erentz. This trio formed a fortress so mean that they wouldn't open the drawbridge to let their grandma in were she being chased by a pack of hounds. Billy Draycott had taken over from Jenkyns in the half-back line where he teamed up with McNaught and Cartwright while the strike force consisted of Bryant, Carman, Boyd, Cassidy, and Dunn. But only one of them

LANCASHIRE CUP WINNERS, 1898.
The biggest trophy Newton Heath ever won: the Lancashire Senior Cup,
in 1898. Back row, left to right: A. Norris (trainer), Harry Erentz, Fred
Erentz, Harry Stafford, Frank Barrett, Billy Draycott, James McNaught, &
Billy Morgan. Front row: Walter Cartwright, Jimmy Collinson, Henry Boyd,
Matthew Gillespie, Willie Bryant, and Joe Cassidy. Heath appear to be wearing
a one-off striped kit the colour of which has not been passed on.

was required to strike, Cassidy's goal simultaneously securing the
bragging rights as well as ruining City's home record.

After going down 1-2 at Gainsborough Trinity, the Heathens
welcomed in 1898 with a 4-0 demolition of Burton Swifts. It was
typical of James Carman's bad luck that soon after breaking his duck
for his new club, he broke his ankle as well. It was a bad injury,
his entire season over. It's very probable that when the unfortunate
lad got home that night, he discovered that his pet goldfish, Sushi,
had drowned.

Carman was representative of the current fashion for getting in
Newton Heath's first team before being ousted at the first chance
possible. Billy Morgan made a return or three. William Dunn
knacked his knee then, to the horror of the Bank Street masses,
Matthew Gillespie was back in! Harry Erentz made his debut on
January 8th at Woolwich Arsenal, partnering his brother at full-
back. Fred felt secure enough with one Erentz at the back to saunter
forward and shake the net for the first time in three years. Arsenal
took advantage and scored five. The Todd brothers, Edward and
Albert, attempted to replicate the Erentz's achievement, but only

Edward broke through. Just the once. For Fred's benefit match. Signed from Broadheath, he quickly realised it was safer to join the Army than solve Heath's injury crisis.

The rest of the forward line was functioning well, especially in consecutive league wins against Blackpool (4-0) and Woolwich Arsenal (5-1). Most thrilled by that last victory was goalie Frank Barrett, considering he had let in five in the earlier away encounter. He took to selflessly entertaining the crowd by executing eccentric sorties with the ball in a manner that would have been approved of by a future clown in goal with the same initials, Fabien Barthez. Disapproving of his tricks, coincidently, were the management on the sidelines, and they promptly ordered him to cease when Arsenal's White nearly punished him.

Those two victories, however, were six weeks apart. Newton Heath had been occupied with the annual New Year cup frenzy. The FA Cup Second Round had pitted the Mancunians against their future arch enemies Liverpool. Missing the leadership of Stafford, and forced to end the game with 10 men after one Heathen dropped out injured, the Mancunians failed to capitalize on their home advantage in a goalless draw. In the replay, Heath led 1-0 at half-time courtesy of a goal by Jimmy Collinson, the local lad who had broken into the team in 1895-96. He had just broken in again for the first time since that initial season to give the inside-right berth a crack. After the interval, though, Division One Liverpool piled on the pressure and equalised. With five minutes to go, they got the winner.

The Manchester Cup adventure lasted a month longer, thanks to Henry Boyd maintaining his early season form. His hat-trick at Bury helped overcome the top flight outfit 3-2 taking his tally to 18 goals so far. Yet disappointment was around the corner, and it came in a triple dose. Neighbours City won the Manchester Cup semi-final replay 2-1 and left the Heathens, possibly for the first time in their existence, wishing they had been in Luton instead. They had been scheduled to fulfil a league fixture there but cancelled it when the replay emerged. The understanding authorities fined them £63 4s, i.e. a Jenkyns and a half. Finally, Division Two leaders Burnley showed their pedigree with an epic 6-3 victory. It was a typical league match at Turf Moor that season, for Burnley had won all their previous 12 games and averaged four goals in each. The surprise was that Heath had obtained three themselves, considering Burnley had previously allowed just six at home all season. Bryant was responsible for two while Collinson netted his sixth goal in six matches. But Heath were back in seventh spot now, and their chances of promotion were gradually fading. Burnley were unattainable at 18 points away, and Heath trailed second-placed Newcastle by 10 points, but with a game in hand.

LANCASHIRE LIONS

MARCH 26TH, 1898: Newton Heath had a cup game. Being so far into the season, this contrasted with the club's recent policy of of exiting all knockout competitions at an early stage. But this time Heath made an exception. For this wasn't any old cup game. It was the final of the Lancashire Senior Cup. Sure, Heath had proven themselves to be the masters of their city on several occasions, but now they played to be top dogs of a whole county. When one considers the other teams who entered this competition: superpowers such as Preston, Everton and Blackburn, you could claim this was Newton Heath's Holy Grail, but back then you could equally say that about everything else, except the Manchester Cup. For their best showing up to now was going in level at half-time in the Second Round. So this was both a great achievement as well as a prestigious moment for the plucky Division Two club.

The Lancashire Cup journey had begun way back in early December when the Heathens thanked their lucky stars for granting them an easy home tie against Wigan County. They even felt confident enough to play Billy Morgan at inside-right. He gave a glimpse of his potential by notching three goals. The Heathens built the lead up to 6-0 when, bored with Wigan's incompetence, the sun set. In near darkness, the referee stopped the game with 80 minutes gone. Wigan immediately lodged a protest to get the match overturned. Their argument, apparently, was that they could surely have scored six goals in the last 10 minutes to force a replay. It took till the following Wednesday for the Lancashire FA to stop laughing and declare that the result stood.

From then on the competition evolved into the Jimmy Collinson show. Fifteen thousand saw him score the only goal of the Second Round tie against Manchester City. Then he got two in the semis as top tier Bolton were demolished 4-1 in front of 13,000 at neutral Hyde Road. He may have made his initial mark as a full-back, but Collinson had now morphed into a selfish, sharp shooting inside-right.

The omens did not look too promising for the final. The chosen venue was Everton's Goodison Park where Newton Heath had let in 22 goals in their last four visits! And awaiting them there were Blackburn Rovers whose typical response to facing the Heathens was to score four goals or more. But only two or three Heathens still had nightmares about those days. The rest of the players were new and, thus, hadn't developed an inferiority complex to First Division giants yet. Captain Harry Stafford would have led the team out, but he was injured. This gave the chance for brothers Fred and Harry to form an all-Erentz full-back line, 101 years before the Neville brothers repeated the act in the 1999 FA Cup final. The team in full read: Barrett; H. Erentz, F. Erentz; Draycott, McNaught, Cartwright; Bryant, Collinson, Boyd, Cassidy, and Gillespie.

From the off the Heathens seemed hungrier for success. They peppered the Rovers' goal with shots, including one from Bryant that scraped the woodwork. Fourteen minutes in, Heath went ahead when Jimmy Collinson, the Lancashire Cup goal king, fired a rocket home from far out. In the 14th minute, Heath went 1-0 up when Henry Boyd pounced on Killean's poor clearance and shot through. Confused? You would have been if you picked up more than one newspaper the day after the game. *The Umpire* journalist seems to have been in the minority advocating a Boyd goal. Bemused, the Dubious Goals Committee simply passed the matter on to its Dubious Reporting counterpart. A few minutes later, Blackburn equalised through Proudfoot and the game became disjointed. Barrett excelled in goal for Heath while Cassidy

JAMES McNAUGHT & HARRY ERENTZ
James McNaught and Harry Erentz defected to Tottenham in the summer of 1898, tempted by higher wages and a better chance of getting their mugs on trading cards.

was his usual menacing self up front. In the second half, Boyd was again deprived of scribing his name onto the score sheet, the referee's offside call interfering this time rather than accurate reporting. There was no confusion, however, over the identity of the next scorer: Collinson (who else?), receiving a decent pass from Gillespie, beautifully converted the winning goal. It was his fifth in the competition and guaranteed a deserved victory for the club, making them the first Division Two side to achieve this.

Newton Heath celebrated their biggest success with a smoking dinner at the Spread Eagle Hotel in Manchester, the 'smoking' part being literal in this case. Puffing away, gold medals around their necks, the Heathens sang late into the night.

They even had a team photo taken with the actual cup. The photo has stood the test of time and shows the Heathens wearing a coloured shirt with vertical stripes. It might have been a commemorative kit to mark the Lancashire Cup triumph, but chances are it was Heath's away strip for those matches against other white-clad teams. I have yet to meet a person who knows the exact colours of this kit. From the black and white photo, the shirt looks gray. According to Sir Alex Ferguson's "Great Book of Excuses", it could justify why, with players blending into the background, the Umpire hack could have had trouble picking a Boyd from a Collinson.

JEST MATCHES

IT WAS ONLY suitable that the Lancashire Cup triumph gave Newton Heath something to celebrate. For, on the same day, Newcastle thumped Grimsby Town 4-0 to end Heath's hopes of reaching second place in the table, even though the Mancunians still had six games to play! For only the second time since joining the League in 1892, Heath would not sample the end-of-season test matches.

That was a shame because victory in the Lancashire Cup gave Heath a cataclysmic surge in confidence. Top dogs in the county now, they strutted their stuff in the run-in at top gear. In the very next match, they thrashed Loughborough 5-1. That was actually a big improvement on Loughborough's part. The previous day they had lost 3-9 to Burnley! Boyd claimed yet another hat-trick while Cassidy got the other two. Then goalie Barrett saved two penalties at Grimsby, but he was unable to cause much damage at the other end. It was left to Boyd and Cassidy (2) to secure a 3-1 win, the latter converting a penalty kick of his own. Next Gainsborough Trinity were beaten 1-0, Cassidy again being the hero. He was now scoring goals like there was no tomorrow, which made one wonder, was there? Reassuringly, there was, and Heath capitalised by beating Small Heath 3-1. With one match left, fifth-placed Heath trailed Woolwich Arsenal by a point. A 3-2 win against Darwen pushed Heath up to fourth on 38 points and ensured that their superiority over all London clubs continued. They missed the chance to do likewise in Manchester by one point. The Heathens' eight-game unbeaten end to the season allowed them to also slash the gap to Newcastle in second place from 13 points to just seven. With the Geordies having done the double over Heath in 1897-98, it is galling to think that a reversal of scores in those two matches would have sent the Mancunians to the playoffs instead.

As Burnley and Newcastle went off to contest the dreaded test matches, Newton Heath busied themselves with defending the second annual Healey Cup. They didn't even bother with the formalities of a semi-final, entertaining Manchester City in the tie that counts: the final, on April 27th. A 2-4 defeat limited Heath to the one cup in the bulge-less trophy cabinet. However, interesting news from the test matches soon overshadowed all other matters. On the last match day of the series, Stoke and Burnley realised they only needed a draw from their meeting to finish ahead of Newcastle and Blackburn and gain entry to the First Division. Duly, a mundane goalless draw followed. But soon controversy raged over the fixed result. Poor Newcastle! They had flattened Blackburn 4-0 and any other result but a draw would have earned them promotion.

The authorities found themselves in a tight spot and, though they enjoyed it, they had to do something about all this. They eventually decided to allow Stoke and Burnley into the top flight, but they also expanded the division by two spaces. The two open slots were not only available to Newcastle and Blackburn, but also to the next four highest-placed teams in Division Two. Newton Heath were back in contention for promotion, along with City, Arsenal, and Small Heath.

With the players having put their feet up for the summer,

Newton Heath still participated in the playoffs, the contest taking place in the shape of a vote at the boardroom level of all 32 clubs. Of a possible 31 votes, Heath got three! The story was disappointingly similar to the Football Alliance days. Blackburn, with 27 votes, and Newcastle, with 18, were the winners in the Fantasy Test Matches. But a lesson was learned by our beloved club. In a short 17 years' time, Manchester United would fix a match of their own to guarantee First Division survival. At least some good news emanated from all the commotion. The Football League scraped the playoffs altogether, instating automatic promotion and relegation instead. The cheers in Clayton were louder than if Heath had won promotion itself.

Newton Heath's biggest success of the season was Boyd and Cassidy's lethal partnership in attack. Both were ever-present as the club racked up 64 goals in 30 league matches. Boyd selflessly contributed 22 himself, and that was good enough to make him top scorer of the division. In the process, he became the first Heathen to break the 20-goal barrier in the league. His total would be surpassed just once in the half-century that followed. Overall, Boyd got 27 of the 86 goals in all competitions. Cassidy was responsible for 18, while Bryant and young Collinson got to double figures and stopped.

Sadly, another ever-present player was leaving the club. James McNaught, the 'Little Wonder", had been ever-present, in fact, since February 8th, 1896. He had been such a splendid star the little wonder was how Heath had been able to hold on to him for so long. Just two months before the Lancashire Cup party at the Spread Eagle Hotel, McNaught had visited the same building for a different kind of gathering. A group of 250 professional footballers had met to form the Association Footballers' Union (AFU). McNaught, an intelligent and well-respected gentleman, was one of the prominent members of this body, which was the forerunner of the PFA. It was a big step forward for players' rights and it set the scene for the crucial intervention of future Manchester United icons Billy Meredith and Charlie Roberts a decade later.

But McNaught and one or two other leading lights of the AFU soon became a target for an emerging southern dominion. Tottenham Hotspur were out looking for talent. Since they belonged to the Southern League, they were not required to pay transfer fees to Football League clubs. So, they used the allotted dosh instead to induce star players directly. McNaught saw the £50 down and £4 per week terms and signed in one go. After the lean years at Clayton, this was too good to miss out on. Heath were eternally grateful for his five-year service. In 220 appearances he etched his name as arguably the club's most majestic footballer.

Spurs' bribery bandwagon did not stop there. On they went to the Erentz house trying to get Fred to jump on. A huge wad was waved too, but, already happily married to a Manchester girl, he refused, preferring instead to continue being Newton Heath's longest servant. However, the persistent Spurs would not leave without an Erentz, so Harry was enticed instead. In his first season at Bank Street, one weekend he would be right-back, the next he would be left back in the dressing room. So, he snatched the £30 down and decided he could live on £3/15 each week. He would prosper on the field too, for in 1901 he helped his new club become the only ever non-League winners of the FA Cup.

While Harry's tale had a happy ending, the rest of 1897-98's new signings were not so fortunate. James Carman, William Dunn, and Frank Wedge received no bribes from Southern League clubs. They didn't even receive new contracts from their current club. The only thing that called for them was the dark path to obscurity.

1898-99

CHORLEY AND CURLY

It is common knowledge, of course, that Manchester United's story got really worse before it got any better. In a few short years Newton Heath would plunge into the mouth of extinction and the club would dabble with the idea of bankruptcy again in the 1930s. Only then would United rise and rise, attaining new status and glory until the moment of absolute elation when Becks swung, Teddy flicked, and Ole toe-poked. That was the great season of 1998-99. Not only was 1898-99 a century behind, but it was an entire universe away. There was no chasing of trebles, except perhaps at the pub, as Henry Boyd would kindly demonstrate shortly. There was no worldwide fan base, although the diehards of Clayton still followed the Shirts through thin and thinner. And there definitely were no multi-million pound deals to buy a star or two. If anything, there was a pound or two to buy multi-million players.

Perhaps the one concept from the future that Newton Heath introduced for the 1898-99 campaign was a revolving door at Bank Street with a sign above it that read 'New Players'. Men were coming and going so often Mr. Albut had to have the door oiled on a weekly basis. It was customary for Heathen fans to congregate at the railway station to excitedly welcome the arrival of a new player. Yet they were at the junction so many times this season passengers thought they worked there. At least one did. The dignified Mr. Sedgwick ran Victoria Station and was such a big Newton Heath follower that he frequently reserved carriages for the players on away days.

The problem for Heath was that they were gradually losing their top players without managing to adequately replace them. Throughout this new season, the team consisted of a basic framework of eight to nine players plus a host of non-meritorious journeymen who only sought to scribble their names faintly into the illustrious history of Manchester United. I might as well get the list over and done with now, so bear with me for, apart from being a comprehensive one, it has no other adjectives.

First off is William Brooks, for he distinguished himself from the others by actually scoring for his new club. He had in fact spent some time on Heath's books once before in 1896, but in this second spell he got off the books and onto the field on three occasions. The first time, as it is in life generally, was the best time: he scored twice in a 6-1 violation of Loughborough. He struck again in his second match but then found himself the scapegoat at the end of a dismal derby defeat. Despite a goal per game ratio, Brooks was sent back to whence he came - Stalybridge Rovers.

James Cairns arrived from Lincoln City and, like his namesake full-back from 1894-95, made a solitary first-team appearance. His impressive form in the reserves portrayed him as magician, but his favourite trick was disappearing during matches. One month on, his act went on display at Berry's Association.

The Scot James Connachan joined from Airdrie in October and spread his four outings across four different positions. None worked out. The papers stated that dash was his principal quality, and that it was also his only one. A man of a dozen clubs, he was quickly sampling a new one. Glossop North End had just joined the Second Division and, despite Connachan's purchase, they won promotion come the season's end.

Then there were the Turners, John and Robert, unrelated, except in their negligible contribution to the Heath cause. John was dubbed 'Turner of Gravesend' for that was his previous club. In his three matches he convincingly demonstrated he was no James McNaught and disappeared. With no previous club, the other Turner turned out simply as Bob in defence. Two matches later he was sold to Brighton United.

The Joneses also came in pairs that season: Chorley and Curly! Owen John Jones was signed from Chorley and hence his distinguishing nomenclature. While in the absence of a team called Curly from contemporary scrolls, it can only be assumed Robert Jones' nickname referred to his hirsute features. Their moment in the sun occurred on the first day of September in a friendly match.

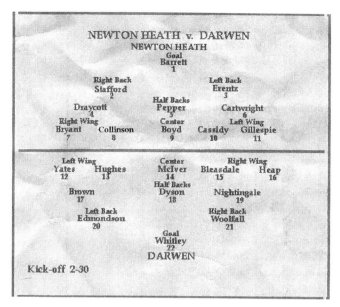

NEWTON HEATH v. DARWEN
NEWTON HEATH
Goal
Barrett
1

Right Back   Left Back
Stafford   Erentz
2   3
Half Backs
Draycott   Pepper   Cartwright
4   5   6
Right Wing   Center   Left Wing
Bryant   Collinson   Boyd   Cassidy   Gillespie
7   8   9   10   11

Left Wing   Center   Right Wing
Yates   Hughes   McIver   Bleasdale   Heap
12   13   14   15   16
Half Backs
Brown   Dyson   Nightingale
17   18   19
Left Back   Right Back
Edmondson   Woolfall
20   21
Goal
Whitley
22
DARWEN

Kick-off 2-30

DARWEN PROGRAMME, 1898.
This rare programme is of a Newton Heath league match against Darwen on December 24th, 1898. Result? A 9-0 victory for Heath!

Curly put in his one and only first-team appearance while Chorley scored the game's only goal against the club that lent him his name. He was then allowed three league attempts to justify being the new Bob Donaldson, but the only similarity was that his spell also ended with a suspension. He did not obey the directors' orders! He returned to his first club Bangor and compensated with two full Welsh caps.

In the one appearance Manchester-born James Hopkins made for Heath – an important meeting with New Brighton Tower – the fans rioted! Fortunately it had nothing to do with the ex-Berry Association inside-right's lack of pace and craft. Right winger Owen also played one league match, helping Heath to a 1-4 loss at Small Heath. The former Holywell F.C. player was prolific at reserve level, and did enlighten Fred Erentz's benefit match six months earlier. Yet his legacy at Clayton was confined to a 'W', the initial of his untraced first name.

We're only halfway there, but I'll try to squeeze in a few more terrace idols. Another three competed for McNaught's centre-half

ACTION V MAN CITY, 1898.
On Boxing Day, 1898, 25,000 spectators attended the top-of-the-table clash between Manchester City and Newton Heath. Here, Billy Gillespie (left) prepares to shoot as Heath's own Billy, Draycott, chases back. Heath lost 0-4.

position but were no little wonders. Twenty-three-year-old Frank Pepper was plucked from Sheffield United's reserves and tossed into the line-up to spice things up. Although efficient defensively, he suffered when compared to his illustrious predecessor's constructive play. After playing seven matches, Pepper was passed on to Barnsley. In the next two matches a trialist named Robert Walker took Pepper's shirt. He was tall, good in the air, and had a second touch to kill for... and a second match to forget. The directors picked yet another centre-half in the next match, then never again. That was the fate of John Gourlay, Annbank's latest export. And with barely enough space left for one more name, here's George Ratcliffe. Outside-right; one match; no goals.

A FEW GOOD MEN

WITH SUCH AN array of stopgaps that would have had Fergie drooling at the tinkering possibilities, it wouldn't have been a big surprise had Newton Heath imploded from the instability. Yet from the first four league matches of the season Heath collected all eight points. The surprise was that they weren't top. Burslem Port Vale, recently re-elected back into the League, had played five games and won them all. The thing is, Heath's starting eleven still had a core of decent footballers that were then supplemented (or hamstrung) by the talentless masses. They would have made a cracking eight-a-side outfit. The directors were taking a gamble on these few good men staying fit long enough to secure a much-needed promotion. The management should obviously be complimented on patching the side up and keeping the promotion hopes alive despite the ever-deteriorating financial health. The preferred line-up at the onset of the campaign consisted of: Barrett; Stafford, Erentz; Draycott, Morgan, Cartwright; Bryant, Collinson, Boyd, Cassidy, and Gillespie. Most were experienced remnants of previous seasons, while the likes of Collinson and Morgan were now establishing a permanent starting spot.

The highlight of the opening month was the 3-0 spanking of Manchester City, Cassidy (2) and Boyd as ever having first option on the goals. This guaranteed Heath were still Top Dogs in derby clashes. Out of nine league meetings since 1894, they had won five and lost just the once. The first blip coincided with the arrival of October when the Mancunians inexplicably crashed 1-5 at Burton Swifts. But a five-figure crowd still gathered at Bank Street the following weekend. The guests were Burslem yet Heath showed no hospitality, edging ahead 2-1 to end the leader's six-game winning streak. William Bryant was the hero with a brilliant solo goal, à la Giggs and the hairy chest occasion. Heath were back in second and the directors' anorexic plan was working to perfection.

It was now that Henry Boyd thought it appropriate to demonstrate that he was a Heathen not only in name but in nature. Fate always had a mysterious way of stepping in during Newton Heath's happiest moments, and this time misery came in return of the 'Curse of the Top Scorer'. Both Bob Donaldson and Dick Smith had eventually lost the map to the opposition goal after outstanding initial seasons. Boyd now misplaced the directions to the ground and missed training one day. It might have been due to a serious personal reason but the directors did not bother to check. Not when a juicy opportunity arose to sadistically impose their automatic suspension: banned for seven days! Did Boyd bow to the enforced discipline? No, he offed to Glasgow in a strop and, days later, sent a telegram to Mr. Albut asking for a leave of absence. His reaction obviously proved that he did perhaps have mitigating circumstances and, thus, felt a sense of injustice emanating from the club's stance. The directors' response? Banned for 14 days! And put on the transfer list.

Obviously Newton Heath felt they didn't need their leading

SPURS V HEATH, FA CUP, JANUARY 1899.
*(Top) Heath's captain, Harry Stafford (white shirt), contests
the coin toss at kick-off. (Bottom) Heath's Willie Bryant
(white shirts) hares down the wing against Spurs.*

marksman from last season. Not when Bryant was in such stunning
form – he replicated his Burslem goal with another mazy dribble
and winner against Lincoln City; and not when Joe Cassidy was
back to his brilliant best with eight goals in the first eight games;
and Matthew Gillespie's one goal helped too.

At first Heath made do with the likes of Brooks and Owen,
but then they decided to bring in a half-decent replacement. John
Cunningham's CV made for impressive reading – mainly due to
its considerable length. He had played for a host of Scottish clubs,
including Celtic, Rangers, and Hearts, but alas no Dundee! But he
had also done the English circuit with stints at Preston, Aston Villa,
and Sheffield United, where he had just won the title the previous
April. And he was still in his mid-twenties! Heath could do with a
First Division striker, even though he resembled a latter-day Bob

Donaldson, both in physical appearance and goal record.

The Bank Street faithful didn't have to wait long for Cunningham's first big contribution. In his third match Heath visited New Brighton Tower, one of the four newly-admitted teams to the expanded Division Two (along with Burslem Port Vale, Glossop North End, and Barnsley). New Brighton were an expensively-assembled outfit who had started well and had not yet lost at home in five matches. Heath joyfully took it upon themselves to put an end to that run with a three-goal drubbing. Cunningham's first goal for the club added to a double from Collinson. Even better, this took Newton Heath to the top of the table for the first time in over two years. They stayed there for two weeks but then lost 1-5 at Woolwich Arsenal for the second year running. It may have been a heavy defeat for a table-topping team, but this was not uncommon for Heath this season. When they lost, they really stank. This was their third defeat of the campaign, and on each occasion they let in four goals or more. Not to undermine their consistency, their exits would be just as porous in all three cup competitions as well.

Newton Heath had 19 points from 13 matches, but Manchester City had nudged ahead in the standings on account of a superior goal average. But pride and excitement were swelling in Manchester as the city's two clubs jointly stood at the top of the table.

ERENTZ V ERENTZ

A WEEK BEFORE Christmas there was a knock on the door at Bank Street. It was Henry Boyd! He had sorted out his demons during his self-imposed leave of absence and was now ready to beg for forgiveness. The directors mulled about it, reminisced over Cairns, Connachan and the likes, and came to an agreement: A Boyd in the hand is better than two months on the transfer list. All was forgiven... for the time being. After all, Boyd had brought with him an early yuletide present: a sackful of goals. Not for him, but rather selflessly for the rest of his team-mates. Most pleased was wide-eyed Willie Bryant who opened the bag and picked out a hat-trick for the 5-0 victory over Darwen as Newton Heath began their defence of the Lancashire Senior Cup. Cassidy converted a penalty while a new lad claimed the last goal. His name was

W.A. Roberts but his team-mates called him "Bogie" and so shall I. Bogie was a scrawny little wingman with speed to burn. Soon he would break into the league side and tally up a few appearances over two seasons.

As luck would have it, Darwen were due at Bank Street again a few days later for a Division Two clash. As even better luck would have it, they turned up two players short. Newton Heath grasped the opportunity to demonstrate how lethal they are when faced with just nine men by racking up a 9-0 hammering. That's 14 goals past Darwen in six days for the one mathematician reading this. The consistent Bryant maintained his three-goal quota while Cassidy matched him at that. The returning Boyd surprisingly failed to net any at all, probably from the shock of seeing Gillespie score twice! It was Bank Street's record score and the club's second biggest league victory ever after the 10-1 mauling of Wolverhampton in 1892. The best Manchester United could do was equal it in 1995 when Ipswich Town were ravaged by Andy Cole.

This set the scene for arguably the most eagerly awaited pre-war Manchester derby. With both teams battling neck and neck at the top of the standings, and the Hyde Road fixture falling on Boxing Day, as many as 25,000 fans showed up. It was easily the largest crowd ever to watch Newton Heath. It was also the largest gathering to laugh at the club. The programme may have advertised the appearance of Barrett, Stafford, Erentz, Draycott, Pepper, Cartwright, Bryant, Collinson, Cassidy, Brooks, and Gillespie, but effectively none of them turned up. Lifted by the ever-expanding influence of Billy Meredith, City sauntered to a 4-0 victory. True, when Heath lost in 1898-99, they tended to lose big, but this defeat had far-reaching significance. It was the first time they had surrendered so meekly to their neighbours, and this betrayed a tangible shift in the balance of power. For the first time City could claim the upper hand in Manchester football. They would enjoy their status for a few years until United gazumped them with the raid that took Meredith to Clayton. City would then tilt the balance in their favour again by luring United's first great manager Ernest Mangnall across town in 1912. It would take a long while for United to reclaim their superiority, eventually achieving it by acquiring City's former star Matt Busby as manager. From then on, apart for a brief period in the early Seventies, Manchester would be United's.

Meanwhile, the Boxing Day knockout at Hyde Road was such a slap in Heath's face their damaged pride turned into anger. They immediately went out and grabbed the first Gainsborough Trinity they saw and gave them a 6-1 shaking. Burton Swifts saved their skin with a 2-2 draw but Glossop were not so lucky. They received a 3-0 whipping. In three matches, Heath had released their rage with 11 goals that came from nine different scorers, including even Gillespie.

Suddenly Newton Heath stepped into a surreal alternate universe where, it wasn't that they were the worst team around, it was just that everybody else was better than them. In one month of mediocrity, they lost both league matches and got knocked out of all three cup competitions. Yes, that included letting go of the Lancashire Cup, and they did so without the inconvenience of a fight. The draw had sent them to last year's beaten finalists, Blackburn Rovers, who were flying high in the First Division and looking to put the record straight against Heath. In terrible conditions at Ewood Park, Heath's defence of the cup washed away with the heavy rain and an equally heavy 1-6 wipe-out.

The story was similar in the Manchester Cup. Newton Heath welcomed top flight Bury but only 300 or so fans were interested enough to show up. At least that limited Joe Cassidy's embarrassment when he missed a penalty at 0-0. Jimmy Collinson gave Heath the lead, but Bury responded with four of their own, including one from Charlie Sagar, who would become in 1905 the only man before Wayne Rooney to score a hat-trick on his Manchester United debut.

Which leaves us with the FA Cup and an epic battle with Tottenham Hotspur. It just had to be Tottenham, the Southern League team who had raided Clayton for players in the summer just gone. Manchester United and Tottenham are, of course, the FA Cup's most successful teams yet surprisingly they've never met in a final. In this season they produced a tie worthy of one when they squared up, first at Tottenham's then home, Northumberland Park, and later in a replay at Bank Street. Heath suffered a double blow just before the first game when Boyd and Cartwright screamed "ouch" at the last minute, and they took to the field with this line-up: Barrett; Stafford, Erentz; Draycott, Pepper, Morgan; Bryant,

Collinson, Cassidy, Cunningham, and Gillespie.

And so it was Erentz v. Erentz, and McNaught v. his ex-team-mates, but it was Cassidy who stole the thunder with a typically unstoppable shot. Barrett was in fine form too, earning the applause of the opponents' fans at one point. He remained unbeaten until literally the very last lucky swing of the boot in the match. Centre-forward Joyce was Tottenham's saviour.

Cartwright was deemed the missing ingredient when he replaced Pepper for the replay when some 6,000 fans marvelled at William Bryant's exploits. For the third time this season he turned in a hat-trick from the right wing to give Heath a 3-1 half-time lead. However, he didn't save any goals for the second half and the Bank Street faithful must have wished they still had McNaught in their ranks. He performed as splendidly as he always did in these parts and even scored to level the scores at 3-3. Then Fred Erentz had to leave the match having dislocated his arm. Goalie Barrett picked up an injury too but soldiered on, and a disappointing second half ended with Spurs winning by five goals to three. FA Cup success would have to wait another 10 years.

ALBUT'S ARMY

In early March, Newton Heath were invited to Springfield Park for a friendly against Wigan County. They refused point blank. It was only last season that Wigan had protested to have the Lancashire Cup tie replayed when it was stopped on 80 minutes with Heath leading 6-0. Thanks, but no thanks was Heath's polite reply. Somehow, Heath didn't have any moral issues when arranging a friendly with West Bromwich Albion instead. The last time the two teams met, if you can recall, Albion protested so loudly that the outcome was an infamous court case that rendered Heath a financial cripple for the rest of the decade. Five years later, though, Heath had apparently forgotten about that. So the two clubs met at Bank Street where Bryant settled the issue with two late goals.

However, there was something strange about Heath's forward line. There was no Boyd; no Cunningham; no Gillespie. No, they weren't rested out of the trivial friendly. Instead they were axed, or to use the directors' favourite word, suspended, and placed on the transfer list for the most heinous of crimes. Did Cunningham forget to report for a routine drug test? Did Boyd leap feet-first into an abusive crowd? Perhaps Gillespie had published major no-noes in his autobiography? None of the above, actually. The truth, though never officially disclosed, was believed to be that the three Heathens had been out drinking! "What disgrace", Norman Whiteside was heard to have said as Paul McGrath's face widened in disbelief! The trio of drunks had appeared worse for wear and, with the ethical culture of that day and age in mind, the righteous directors couldn't wield the axe fast enough. Even the papers agreed and blatantly disregarded any possible excuse for such behaviour.

Maybe Henry Boyd's personal issues were still ongoing and he had sought the comradeship of fellow Scots Cunningham and Gillespie in a time of need. Perhaps then he should have asked the other Tartan Terror in the forward line to come along. There is no way the management would have sacked Joe Cassidy and his mates for one evening of over-indulgence. But alone the three culprits stood no chance. Cunningham's spell at Clayton was short and insignificant. Gillespie, at 29 years of age, had years beyond his wisdom. And Boyd, though a smashing marksman with a goal ratio bettered by just two players in Manchester United's history, was too much trouble for the club's liking.

In no time Gillespie was slithering his way into the manager's shack pathetically wailing and begging for forgiveness. Yes, he's been suspended before and now he's got himself in trouble once more. But he promises he won't do it again, and this time he really, really means it. What's more, he unselfishly vows to add one more goal to his yearly tally. Don't laugh, that could be a 25 to 30% increase in goal return. Amazingly, that was good enough for the management and Gillespie was reinstated. Again. Cunningham and Boyd, meanwhile, were swiftly ushered out of Bank Street, to Wigan County and Falkirk respectively. While Cunningham had not even been at the club five minutes to cry over, the sad end of Boyd's prolific spell brought a tear to the eye during allergy season.

Just one week later, there was further trouble at Bank Street but this time the perpetrators were not the type the directors could suspend. And how they would have loved to, considering New Brighton Tower had handed Heath their first home league reverse in 16 months. Typically the directors' spontaneous reaction would have seen them stir up a bigger fuss than Fergie turning up at a Lee

Sharpe party. On this occasion, however, they found themselves playing peacekeepers when they were beaten to the fuss by the common man in the stand. The Heathen masses, or at least a fraction of the 20,000-strong crowd, invaded the pitch at the final whistle and went after the referee. By all accounts, he had made several poor decisions, even disregarding his linesman's input during one crucial incident. In no time he found himself 'jeered and booed' by a 'mob of hot-headed youths', several of which were identified as some of the Doc's Army members' great grandfathers. All they wanted to do was unify the ref and his whistle without the need of a pocket, but quickly the directors and a few policemen jumped in to help the poor, incompetent soul and drag him to safety.

The papers were appalled by this act of hooliganism though one could understand the fans' frustration. Not only did the dodgy refereeing end Heath's 22-match unbeaten run at home, but the defeat was also a kick in the soft, painful region for the club's promotion chances. While Brighton had leapt to joint top on 39 points, Heath had fallen all the way to ninth with 32 points. They may have had two games in hand on the top teams, but the promotion window was slowly shutting. The season would be climaxing soon and only then would the damage caused by this loss become apparent.

GLOSSOP WHO?

It was obvious to the management now that Newton Heath needed a lift to mount any sort of final push for a top two spot. A centre-half was desperately needed, as well as a centre-forward for which they decided to promote from within. Already there had been Chorley, Curly, and Bogie at Bank Street this season; now 'Neddy' was added to that exotic list. This was the preferred nickname for Edwin Lee. 'Neddy' had transferred the previous summer from Hurst Ramblers and was leading the scoring charts for the reserve team. It was decided that now was the time to make him the eighth centre-forward of the season.

A similar number of candidates had given the centre-half position a try already, but the directors were still looking for the right one. He didn't even need to have an exotic name. As long as he was fully loaded. That is, he had to be capable of filling McNaught's boots; had to be speedy; possess a powerful shot; and perhaps be a frequent goal scorer as well! The marvel wasn't whether such a player existed, but that he was found around the corner making shoe polish. Billy Griffiths worked for the polish manufacturers Berry's Association all day and starred in their football team on weekends. That was the same outfit to whom Heath had recently sold James Cairns but there was no hint of a qualm about who got off with the best deal. While Neddy Lee's success was more short-term and similarly short-lived, Griffiths would give the club years of sterling service. He would end the search for McNaught's replacement, see through the transition to Manchester United, and even finish as joint top scorer in 1903-04. It would require the purchase of arguably the greatest centre-half in the club's history – Charlie Roberts – to finally halt his Clayton career.

The first time both new recruits were picked together was at Blackpool on April 3rd. There were still six matches left and, apart from one minor change, the starting eleven was settled upon thereafter. Barrett, Stafford, and Erentz formed the rearguard as usual; Draycott and Cartwright flanked Griffiths in midfield; and a reshuffled front line now read Bryant, Morgan, Lee, Gillespie, and Cassidy. The latter got the only goal of the game at Blackpool. The next day trigger-happy Lee notched both strikes in a 2-0 win at Barnsley. And on the weekend he claimed the match's solitary goal at Luton. He was on the score sheet again in the Luton return though four other team-mates joined him. Four wins out of four and suddenly Newton Heath were third. They had amazingly caught up with New Brighton Tower on 41 points!

Manchester City had already secured promotion – and the Division Two title – but the real surprise was the team in second place. While one newcomer (New Brighton) had challenged all season, it was another that had hoodwinked everybody else at the final stretch. Glossop North End emerged as the dark horses, even though Heath had tamed them home and away. They had won seven out of the last eight matches to reach 43 points. There were now two games left. Heath's next match was against Leicester Fosse, also on 41 points. Both teams battled fiercely for the win but a 2-all draw was a result neither wanted. Although Glossop were held to a 1-1 draw at Small Heath Alliance, they boasted a greatly superior goal average.

The Heathens still had a small chance. If Glossop were to lose their last match, Heath would finish second if they won theirs by a 12-0 score line! Possible? Of course, for their final opponents were Darwen, the team they beat 9-0 in December. Not only that, but the division's bottom club had let in eight goals or more on six occasions so far that season. They had already been relegated from the League and, though no one knew it then, this was to be their last ever Football League fixture. They had even sold their club captain the previous afternoon to pay off the players' wages.

Though everything seemed set for a massive win, Newton Heath sadly failed to capitalize. The fact that Glossop were entertaining second-from-bottom Loughborough did not inspire much confidence. And over at Barley Bank, the Darwen men played out of their skins in their farewell match. They even took the lead against the run of play. Though Heath equalised in the second half, the home team's extraordinary effort allowed them to achieve an honourable 1-1 draw. Meanwhile, Glossop sealed their promotion with a 4-0 victory while Leicester Fosse also won to knock Heath down to fourth for the second year in a row.

So, another long season ended in disappointment for Newton Heath. The only highlights were the scoring returns of Cassidy (21) and Bryant (16). The low point obviously was that Manchester City had brushed Heath aside to join the elite and beaten them 2-1 in the Healey Cup for good measure. And seeing newcomers Glossop cut in front of them in line to get into the First Division didn't sit well. Especially as the minnows were bounced right back out at the first attempt with a worse record than when the Mancunians were last in the top tier.

If anything, Darwen's conclusion proved that only the fittest could survive. And Newton Heath's Division Two diet was leaving them weaker by the year. Another of the prominent servants was on his way out of the club – Billy Draycott joining Bedminster. There were some stars left but would they be enough to secure the club promotion? Or would extinction be reached first?

1899–00

WE ALL FOLLOW

IT IS TEMPTING to imagine a scene in Manchester on the opening day of this new season. It was still the nineteenth century but only for a few more months. Photographs of the time invariably depict an overcast, empty street; houses symmetrically organised; their rigid structure exemplifying the general mood of the day. Over at Clayton, an incredible zest for life can easily be detected. Try to visualise a sequence of events inside Bank Street, where the soul of the city had congregated. The grass is still green for the time being; a shred of sunlight stealing in here and there, with the noxious smell and foggy atmosphere as always filling the air. There's a melee around the centre circle, then Walter Cartwright comes out with the ball and smuggles it out to Willie Bryant on the right wing. Bryant, in his clean white top and baggy dark blue shorts, takes a couple of strides straight ahead. He cuts inside his Gainsborough Trinity marker, but he quickly flicks the ball back out. He sprints down the touchline barely gaining a step on the full-back. It's enough to thump in a low, square centre. The ball ricochets once or twice before breaking. In an instant Joe Cassidy pounces to smack it goalwards. You can't go wrong with envisaging Cassidy scoring. That year he netted in every home league match from March through October. The ball skips past the keeper and nestles in the net. At once, 8,000 fans in the stands leap into the air disturbing the serenity of the stench. Though immaculately dressed in the acceptable formal wear of the times, they are lost in the delirium of the moment.

These were the original Reds; the die-hards who started the obsession of following the club and passed it down generation after generation. Do you think they loved Newton Heath more than we now love Manchester United? This was 'their' club and they followed it from North Road to Bank Street and later on to Old Trafford. They cheered on when the Shirts played Loughborough, Burton, Bootle, South Shore, and so on. We now come from all over the place to worship. They sacrificed the healthy state of their lungs to stand on the terraces and cheer. We spill our blood at places like Anfield, Elland Road, Porto, and Rome. They injected more life into the club by feeding the "bucket brigade" that went around the stadium pleading for donations. We still feed the bucket brigade too, only it's now called MUTV, the Museum, the Stadium Tour...

The club may have been stuck in the Second Division but the fans were always there. They were the soul of the club. And if the centuries have altered life beyond recognition since then, one thing has rebuffed all change. We like to think that we are still the soul of this club.

There were some individuals whose loyalty and affection for Newton Heath were so strong their names have been passed down the generations and are legendary today. George Lawton was an accountant who worked for JH Davies, the man who would save the club from extinction in 1902. On Saturdays George would make his Tour de France contestant impression as he frantically cycled to Bank Street to watch the Heathens. He became close friends with captain Harry Stafford and would occasionally help out in club matters. He hung around so much they finally made him director. Another close fan was 'Father' Bird. A priest he was not, but he could exorcise your chimney, for he made a living out of sweeping them. His thick beard must have come in handy. However, 'father' was how Heath's players affectionately called him. And some of them probably wished he was their real father for he frequently stuffed their mouths with his famous potato pie and hot-pot. It must have been really yummy since they sometimes let him in the team photo! Which makes it tempting to let Wayne Rooney feast on my special Steak and Kidney Pudding recipe.

There were numerous others who were on first-name basis with the Heathens. Back then, the players and the fans socializing was the norm, as demonstrated by Mr. Albut's billiards hall. At such times supporters could really claim to be a part of the club. Chumminess built loyalty and the fans still showed up in their thousands to Bank Street. The latest statistics, for instance, revealed that, despite continuing to dwell in the bottom division, Newton Heath still enjoyed the 14th largest support out of the 36 teams in the Football League.

However, it is certain these die-hards did not enjoy the start of the new season as Heath could only provide them with one victory in September. In 1898-99, there had been no relegated teams from Division One following the expansion and the playoffs scandal of the previous year. The Heathens wished there weren't any relegated teams this season either. The dropping duo, Bolton Wanderers and Sheffield Wednesday, both handed Heath defeats in the first five matches and were cementing a place at the top end of the table. Newton Heath, meanwhile, were stranded in 10th already five points adrift of the promotion zone. The team seemed shorn of sufficient stars. Oh, and the financial situation was getting even worse. Welcome to another season in the Second Division.

DUNDEE DONE

AROUND THIS TIME Newton Heath's economic crisis really started to bite. Especially more so now that they decided to take one last, desperate splash into the transfer market. And they used both their coins as well. The plum purchase was William Jackson who came with his freshly-knit Welsh cap from the fearfully-named St. Helens Recreation. He was a 23-year-old inside-forward born in Flint, had three separate spells with Flint, and eventually passed away an old man in Flint. In playing style our man from Flint was a cross between Henry Boyd and Matthew Gillespie in that, though a decent linkman with a precise shot, he tended to expend more energy on hard toil than on actual scoring.

James Bain and Joe Clark had the honour of being the last of the Dundonians – Heath's final impulse buys from the Dundee store. It had been a while since Albut and co last dabbled in that club's products, but they couldn't resist the temptation of the 'Everything Must Go' sale. Dundee sold all their players in the summer of 1899 (except, curiously, for one) then moved away to the new location of Dens Park, just in case some of them decided to return. Why Heath would consequently bother with Dundee's rejects was a worrying thought that was soon justified. Bain and Clark failed in their expedition to find the solution to Heath's forward line troubles. Bain scored on his debut as Loughborough were beaten 4-0 but he was only able to add one more first-team appearance before his first-team disappearance. Clark enjoyed a relatively longer run of nine matches until injury ended his season. He may have received decent reviews but he gave no goals in return.

A familiar face appeared in Heath's ranks on the opening day of the season. Fitzsimmons was back, not Tommy of 1893 but thankfully his younger brother David of the 1896 vintage. He had done the rounds with teams in the area, but it was soon apparent that his deterioration rate far exceeded that of Newton Heath. He sought a second opinion a month later; the verdict was unchanged. Mancunian Alfred Ambler was similarly deemed not good enough after playing in the season's first two games, despite netting one goal. Not much money could have been spent when signing the left winger from Hyde United, but luckily for him, injuries to the half-back line in the season's run-in provided him with another first-team spell.

As in 1898-99, a host of short-term possibilities kept popping up during this new campaign. The team ached for the stability of two or three years ago. There was still a solid backbone of about eight or nine first-team fixtures. The rest of the body, though, kept rejecting the new implants. On October 14th, for instance, Newton Heath had to visit highflying Small Heath with a debutant on the right wing. Willie Bryant was injured after scoring at Sheffield Wednesday a fortnight earlier when 10-man Heath lost 1-2, and a new debutant, Thomas Sawyer, was now asked to fill in. Though Collinson and Gillespie also appeared up front, they were no longer considered regulars. With a blunted forward line, Heath (Newton, that is) lost 0-1 to remain tenth while the Brummies climbed to the top of the standings.

Bryant was back for the next match against New Brighton Tower but now Walter Cartwright was missing due to illness. A 20-year-old local lad named Peter Blackmore came in at centre-forward in a reshuffled line-up. Fortunately for Newton Heath, Joe Cassidy was at his healthy best. He scored very early in each half to secure a 2-1 win. At least he was as sharp as ever, as well as an early riser. He had now notched five goals out of the team's eleven in eight matches. A fortnight later it was Bogie Roberts who shouldered the responsibility of scoring inside three minutes.

Then international man William Jackson decided this was the right time to finally break his scoring duck in the league. Woolwich Arsenal couldn't pick up the pieces and duly lost 0-2.

In between those two victories Newton Heath had an early FA Cup tie. It is hard to decide what was more embarrassing: having to shamefully participate in a qualifying round or being humiliated 1-3 by the might of South Shore? All this having taken the lead through internationalist Jackson! If it were any consolation, the Heathens at least got the old cup out of the way early on this season. This hiccup aside, Heath's league form was improving. A nil-nil draw at Barnsley was the only game they failed to win out of six. It was still a special day at the office for a couple of employees. Happy chappy number one was Fred Erentz as this was his landmark 200th league match for the club. Erentz was one ex-Dundonian Heath never wanted to return for a refund. His consistency and efficiency were a bit Irwinesque, you could say. As was his icy temperament. And his accurately-dispatched penalty kicks. The other chap with reasons to fondly remember this stalemate in Yorkshire was debutant Robert Parkinson. Just signed from Nottingham Forest, the newcomer looked to have finally enabled Mr. Albut to take down the 'Centre-Forward Wanted' sign. His introduction coincided with Heath's revival, and by mid-December, they had risen to fifth. They had collected 17 points from 13 matches as the promotion candidates began to peel away. From now until the end of the season the same five teams (Newton Heath, Bolton, Leicester Fosse, Sheffield Wednesday, and Small Heath) would exclusively occupy the top five slots while continuously swapping order.

A NIGHT OUT

ON NOVEMBER 29TH, 1899, Newton Heath put aside the rigours of the league race to honour one of their most faithful players. The lovable Walter Cartwright had been around for five years now and he was due a benefit match. The directors made all the right noises to guarantee him a fitting tribute. Top division Manchester City were invited for a friendly at Clayton along with their crowd-magnet Billy Meredith. The match was hyped in the local press. Even the 'Bucket Brigade' was enlisted to work the masses. All proceeds will proceed to Cartwright's pocket, it was assured. The only problem was that Heath's finances were in such a dire state that the Official Receiver was practically waiting at the door on a daily basis to make sure the debts were serviced. After the match ended, the nice bailiff grabbed the collection bag, poured the pickings into his pocket, and departed a mildly-satisfied man. A few coins rustled in the bag and were joyfully handed to Cartwright. The sum? £1.30p! Contrary to general advice, he spent it all in one go – a night out on the town – as he made his way back home to Crewe.

It is interesting to note the contrast in the club's fortunes of 1899 with that of a century later. Exactly a hundred years on, give or take a few hours from Tokyo time, Manchester United defeated Brazilian outfit Palmeiras to officially become the top team in the world. With one simple digit in mind, it is a shame Cartwright picked the wrong '99 to ask for a benefit. But with a midfield consisting of Beckham, Keane, Scholes, and Giggs, it is doubtful Cartwright would have even had a look-in. Then again, in his prime it was once claimed that "a team of Cartwrights would lick creation". My first thought was "eeow"! But then if Jonathan Greening could find a squad place in the 'Best Team in the World' then so can Cartwright.

Robert Parkinson was starting to justify the claims that he could become the permanent leader of the attack. The first hint came just after Newton Heath had fallen behind at Bolton in the Lancashire Cup First Round. Parkinson reportedly picked the ball up fully 40 yards out and fired home such a scorcher no camera caught it. A Cassidy brace ensured a 3-2 victory. Soon Parkinson was scoring in game after game until he reached a club record haul of five consecutive league matches. The run began with another club record when Heath visited Grimsby Town on Boxing Day. The pitch was covered with snow but that wasn't as bad as the fog which rendered the goalposts invisible from the halfway line. But that was no excuse for the Grimsby goalkeeper for the Heath forwards were not that far out when they rattled three goals in the first quarter hour. Four more followed to secure a record away win of 7-0. It stood for a full one hundred years until Manchester United took liberties with Nottingham Forest's hospitality in an 8-1 demolition in 1999. That year again!

Parkinson had scored Heath's last goal of the 19th century, so it was only appropriate he should also claim the first of the 20th. That came in an epic tussle with Bolton who came to Clayton three points ahead of Heath. It was the type of four-pointer the Heathens knew they had to collect. The crowd knew it too but excessive rain limited the gate to 5,000. Heath lined up as follows: Barrett; Stafford, Erentz; Morgan, Griffiths, Cartwright; Bryant, Clark, Parkinson, Jackson, and Cassidy. The match began terribly for the Mancunians when creation-licker Cartwright had to trudge off injured inside a couple of minutes. By the time he had licked his wounds and re-entered the fray, the Wanderers were ahead. From then on Heath switched to their customary Bank Street blitzkrieg mode and dominated both air and ground. The only problem was that they encountered Bolton's custodian Sutcliffe at his England best. Parkinson got the equalizer with a header but numerous other shots were diverted off course by Sutcliffe, of course. With time running out Heath's own keeper Barrett decided to show his forwards how it was done when he carelessly let in the softest of goals. Time was up. Barrett's howler had saddled Heath with their only home defeat of the season as well as preventing them from catching up with their opponents.

Amends had to be made. Loughborough were defeated 2-0. Then Matthew Gillespie wastefully used up half a year's allocation of goals by squandering a hat-trick on Burton Swifts. Another promotion rival was up next at Bank Street: second-placed Sheffield Wednesday. Trying to kick the ball in obviously didn't work against Bolton. A different strategy of kicking the shin instead was now implemented. But the Heathens were not the sole culprits. Wednesday responded with equivalent roughness and an ill-tempered battle ensued, much to the jubilation of the 10,000-strong crowd. It ought to have been a much stronger crowd, heaven – and the creditors – knew how badly Heath needed that. The weather, however, again conspired against them, this time in the form of a toe-freezing, manhood-shrivelling cold front. Yet they were able to return home with warmness in their hearts after Willie Bryant took a bit of time off the hacking free-for-all to grab the game's only goal. Three consecutive wins had taken Heath back to within touching distance of the promotion zone.

HEATHENS AT WAR

THE NEXT THING Newton Heath did was rid themselves of two unnecessary cup distractions. At least that was how they justified exiting the Lancashire Cup with a gentle 0-1 embarrassment at some team called Southport Central, and getting kicked out of the Manchester Cup with a 0-5 stomping at Bury. Now they could solely focus on the league programme but there are other ways the season could be gripped by uncertainty. Heath were still losing too many games for their liking and it probably had a lot to do with the instability of an ever-changing line-up. The players would show up to training and encounter a new face every week. And one old face as well. One of the new ones was Joe Heathcote who followed Billy Griffiths from Berry's Association. Born in Manchester around the same time as his new club, the inside-forward impressed his audience with some fancy dribbling in one first-team match. That was good enough for now and he was subsequently put on the shelf for a year or so. Despite having the flu, New Brighton Tower's Tom Leigh passed Heath's stern medical. He had twice previously been top scorer at Burton Swifts and the Heathens were willing to wait out the virus. What's more, he had certain Maradonesque qualities, but that had more to do with his tendency to fist the ball than with half-field dribbles.

Former favourite Bob Donaldson was soon on the line. Of course he had been banned out of Bank Street last time around, but the directors had since regretted their foolish decision. They would have loved to have had Bob back; however, he was only calling to recommend a couple of forwards from his current club, Ashford F.C.: Gilbert Godsmark and George Foley were duly snapped up. Godsmark was a 23-year-old Derby lad who could form an entire team from his siblings. Plus one sub. He immediately made the inside-right spot his own. Meanwhile, Foley, who lacked both league experience and enough siblings for a family team, had to bide his time in the reserves for now.

While the management wasn't able to get Donaldson back in their attack, they gladly brought back another old face they had ushered out around the same time. The old face in question? Dick Smith, the club clearly unfazed by David Fitzsimmons' sparkless return earlier in the season. Smith had spent the last two years on a personal crusade, visiting various clubs and exchanging speed for experience. The Heath management, though, still saw him as a Dick-of-all-trades. Despite initially forming the snappily-named "Wigan County Wing" with ex-team-mate William Jackson, he ended up filling six different positions in his twelve appearances during the remainder of the campaign.

Godsmark first got off the mark for his new club in a crucial 3-2 defeat of Small Heath. He scored again the following week in a 4-1 drubbing of New Brighton Tower. That was Dick Smith's comeback match and he celebrated with a goal. Smith then claimed the only goal as the Heathens beat Grimsby 1-0. So far, so great. Despite a minor blip at Woolwich, the goals were coming from everywhere. However, Newton Heath could always find a way to wreck a perfectly good promotion drive, whether it was in an evenly-balanced test match or a crucial run-in encounter. This time they opted for the old board favourite, Sack the Forward Line, with a more serious disruption halfway around the world as a fallback measure.

On a gloomy morning in mid-March, Willie Bryant and Robert Parkinson were summoned to the Bank Street offices. The two were being suspended from the club. Effective: immediately! Were they caught out drinking? Were they to blame for some defeat? No one knows as no explanation was ever given. The dictators, er, directors' word was final. Dick Smith was all too familiar with this as he nodded knowingly. It mattered not that Bryant had been a constant star on the wing for four years. Nor that Parkinson had scored seven goals in 15 consecutive appearances to make the centre-forward position his own. Both would never play for the club again. In fact, Parkinson would never play for any other club again, as far as our trusted historians claim. Perhaps he was disenchanted with football following this treatment and no longer cared to continue. Or was his crime so grave no other club would touch him? Bryant did not face such a denouement. After scoring 33 goals in 127 league and cup matches, he was sold to Blackburn Rovers for a sizeable £50 fee. Picked up by First Division giants? Bryant's fortunes could not have contrasted more with those of Parkinson.

Yet Parkinson's predicament paled into utter insignificance when compared with that of Gilbert Godsmark and Joe Clark. Just the previous October, fighting had broken out at the bottom of the globe in southern Africa. The Boer War had begun. British soldiers were dying by the thousands and new enlistees were urgently needed. Both Godsmark and Clark were called up to represent their country. Clark had been absent lately with an injury but Godsmark had settled well and scored four goals in nine games. Unfortunately, neither was to play for Newton Heath again. They exchanged Heath's front line for the real front lines in Africa. While nothing further was heard of Clark, in February of the following year, the club was sadly informed that Godsmark had been killed in action.

It was certainly a tragic end to a likeable fellow with a promising career ahead of him. Several Manchester United players would perish down the years, be it in wars, accidents, or at Munich, of course; but Gilbert Godsmark was United's first fatality.

Incidentally, Godsmark's previous club, Ashford, was still owed half of the original £40 transfer fee. Heath were now reluctant to pay it off, but found the motivation once Ashford issued a writ. Heath almost paid a much heavier price actually. While Godsmark and Clark were lost to the war, it could so easily have been Harry Stafford too. He was on 24-hour notice but fortunately was never called up. In view of his future role in the creation of Manchester United, the club itself could very easily have been one of the casualties of the Boer War.

THE LAST PROMOTION DRIVE

IN HIS LAST match Gilbert Godsmark made sure he left behind a farewell brace for the fans to remember him by. Luton were the opponents and they were dispatched 5-0 just like the previous season. Earlier, Heath had won 1-0 at Luton just like last year too. Come to think of it, this is one team United have missed playing against in the Premier League. The other three goals in that victory were all provided by Joe Cassidy. While no one knew it then, this hat-trick was also a parting gift, for soon Joe would follow Godsmark out of Bank Street, his sacrifice reluctantly made to save his own club.

Now was the time to give the new lads Tom Leigh and George Foley a run. They had made their bow in mid-March against

Barnsley. The management had been waiting till Leigh completely got over the flu and, to make sure, they threw him on in a blizzard. He coughed up a goal in a 3-0 win. However, a 0-1 reverse at Burslem Port Vale knocked the wind out of Heath's promotion push. Sheffield Wednesday and Bolton were enjoying unbeaten runs and were beginning to peel away. This was Heath's first match after the call-ups and suspensions, and the front line was almost unrecognisable. With Bryant, Godsmark, and Parkinson no longer around, the forward line consisted of Foley, Smith, Leigh, Jackson, and Cassidy. Then Gillespie forced Smith back to half-back for the visit of promotion rivals Leicester. He scored, as did Jackson and Griffiths, to secure a 3-2 win. If Heath were not going up, at least neither were the Fosse. That's the Good Friday spirit!

The next day Cassidy kitted out for what would be his last match for Newton Heath. To show their appreciation, his team-mates took it upon themselves to score all the goals in a 5-0 thrashing of Walsall. Heath now had 41 points with three games to go. Wednesday, who won again, had already secured their return ticket to Division One. Bolton had one hand on theirs too, their 46 points leaving Heath with barely enough room for one tiny finger.

Bolton were nice enough to lose their next match, but the Heathens, despite facing Walsall again, could only muster a goalless draw. They were only hanging by one bitten fingernail now. In the penultimate game Heath made their visit to Middlesbrough and their then home, the Archery Ground. Considering the way events unfolded for them in the following two seasons, this proved to be the Heathens' last match of any real importance. It is bewildering then that as the day of the encounter approached, they were busy looking for a forward to play outside-left. Eventually, Tom Leigh's presence reminded the management of a striker with a similar-sounding name. Neddy Lee, the breakout star of last season's run-in, had been reserved for the reserves since the opening day of this campaign, where his goals had reached into double figures. He was called up to fit in with the following assortment: Barrett; Stafford, Erentz; Smith, Griffiths, Ambler; Foley, Gillespie, Leigh, Jackson, and Lee.

Their task was straightforward: win their last two matches and pray that Bolton lose theirs and the extra one they had in hand too. Straightforward and inconceivable, then. Newton Heath proceeded to falter 0-2 at Middlesbrough while Bolton strolled to three straight victories to disappear over the promotion hill. About the only thing that went Heath's way was that they won their final match against Chesterfield. And they required the help of yet another two new strikers to do so. Edward Holt, previously at Newton Heath Athletic, dropped the 'Athletic' suffix and filled in on the right wing; while John Grundy, signed from Halliwell Rovers, marauded on the left. Although both scored in a 2-1 triumph, only John was asked to return after the summer break. The significance of the last day win was that Newton Heath leapfrogged Leicester Fosse to finish fourth for the third year in a row. Teams came down and others went up, but one thing you could say about Heath was that they knew their place. And that was right next to Leicester Fosse. In six of their eight seasons in Division Two, Heath finished just one place either above or below Fosse.

THE GREATEST HEATHENS

NOT GOING UP was harsh on Newton Heath. They had won 15 of the 17 home matches losing only once. The 44 points collected was their highest total ever. But Sheffield Wednesday and Bolton had raised the bar, and that made it easier for their wayward shots to sneak under it. True, the Mancunians trailed Bolton by eight points, but had they beaten them in the head-to-head games, especially at home where Barrett dropped his famous clanger, Heath would have pipped Wanderers on goal average. As it was, Heath had to wise up to another year in Second Division hell. Only now it was getting suffocating in the fire and the Heathens would have to sell their soul to the devil were they to earn an extension on their breathing rights.

Joseph Cassidy was the scorer-in-chief again. By a distance. He got 16 league goals while the next name wasn't even on the same page. William Jackson barely tallied half Cassidy's haul while Parkinson came third with seven. In total, a Manchester United record 18 different players contributed league goals, instability rather than collective effort being the driving force. There would come a time when United could replenish a Van Nistelrooy with a Rooney then replace him with a Tevez. But back during those dark, grim days, Heath definitely fitted a selling club's description, and Cassidy was the prized asset. He had scored 100 goals in 174 competitive matches, in the process becoming the club's first centurion. He was now to be the first saviour. Willie Bryant had fetched £50 from Blackburn, but that figure was but a spit in the bucket marked "Newton Heath's Enormous Debts". To the regret of the board of directors, and the chagrin of the Bank Street faithful, the favourite star was sold to the evil entity down the street, namely Manchester City. In return, a gigantic fee of £250 was handed over to guarantee Heath's existence for a while longer. Cassidy's sacrifice was for a greater cause, but the regret was always there, deep in the soul of Heathen fans. Considered Heath's greatest ever striker, Cassidy would go on to finish as City's top scorer with 15 goals in 1900-01. He would then move on to Middlesbrough, score another 15 to win them promotion, and then lead their scoring charts in their first two seasons in Division One. Thousands dreamt this could have taken place at Bank Street instead.

Despite flogging their greatest striker for dough, Heath were still skint. The club's problems far exceeded what could be resolved by the simple use of an old-fashioned plunger. The next viable solution involved offloading their greatest custodian as well. It was time to cash in on Frank Barrett's eccentricity. The keeper, who hadn't missed a match in over two years, was no longer a keeper. Not when big-spending New Brighton Tower came over waving a large cheque. In a flash, Newton Heath's only internationally-recognised goalie was gone. He had represented the club on 136 occasions and conceded 148 goals at a very decent 1.09 goals per game average. This final season had been his best yet as he let in just 27 goals in 34 league matches. Barrett would subsequently play for several other clubs as well before sadly passing away at 35, just seven years after his Bank Street exit.

The loss of Cassidy, Barrett, and Bryant in one go can in no way be downplayed. The first two can easily walk into a Newton Heath Greatest XI while the last would eagerly look on from the subs' bench. Come to think of it, now would be an appropriate time to choose the names that would make up such a side. Although a further two years remain of the Newton Heath story, rest assured you have already met all the possible candidates. So, while the departing Barrett easily claims to be the number one number one, he leaves behind the club's greatest full-back pair: Harry Stafford and Fred Erentz. While Stafford could never match 1880s right-back Jack Powell's collection of caps were he to scour every hat shop in town, there is no denying him his rightful place as leader of this chosen eleven. This is one instance where the greater picture takes precedence over any other footballing merits. In his 1960 book, 'Manchester United', Percy Young tells a revealing story that was passed down by an actual eyewitness. Not too impressed by Stafford's constructive play, or lack of, one terrace pedant taunted him by saying: "Harry, you can't play football". Stafford instantly quipped: "No, but I can stop those that can!" Ironically, it was Stafford's superhuman efforts that allowed hundreds of future Manchester United footballers to play.

Erentz, on the other hand, is a shoe-in at left-back, and not just because you have to take the train back to North Road to locate the previous incumbent. His consistent performances in nearly 400 first-team games see to that. There are various strong candidates for the half-back line with special mentions afforded to the likes of Tom Burke, Joe Davies, John Owen, Will Davidson, and Caesar Jenkyns. But the crème de la crème would have to be a McNaught-Stewart-Cartwright axis that provides the perfect blend of creativity, power, and guile. All three were great long-term servants for the club as well.

Though Bryant is a very strong contender for the right wing, it is Alf Farman who succeeds as the original great number seven in a long line of outstanding Manchester United stars. His First Division exploits give him the edge over Bryant. The free-scoring heroes Jack Doughty, Bob Donaldson, and Joe Cassidy are each guaranteed a spot up front. Their records speak for them. That leaves one vacant slot for the rest to fight over. Henry Boyd merits a mention though his relatively short stint does not back him up. The mercurial Jack Peden is an obvious possibility at outside-left, but his stint was even shorter. The best solution would be to shift Cassidy out to the left wing where he spent half his time, and to put Roger Doughty in alongside his brother, on account of his excellent pre-League deeds. So, the Newton Heath Hall of Fame would line up as follows:

BARRETT

STAFFORD ERENTZ

McNAUGHT   STEWART   CARTWRIGHT

FARMAN   DONALDSON   J. DOUGHTY   R. DOUGHTY   CASSIDY

The selection is purely subjective so, please, feel free to agree with it. After spending time with such exalted company, it is best to quickly discard the residue of 1899-00's bottom of the barrel. Bogie Roberts and George Foley were no longer to be seen near Newton Heath's first team; Neddy Lee found his level at Hyde St. George; and Matthew Gillespie, miffed at being overlooked for the Greatest XI squad, never played for the first team again. His goals, as always, would be missed.

1900–01

OVERDUE RECOGNITION

ZERO IS GENERALLY where everything begins. In a sense, 1900 was a beginning for Newton Heath; the beginning of the end, to be precise. For six years they had circled the Division One castle and knocked on the gate at each turn. But it was never opened. Now the big, bad bailiff had caught up with them. Stripped of their Bryants, their Barretts, and especially their Cassidys, Heath would be practicing a form of extreme football management from now on. Their main act? Bungee-jumping without a cord.

Mr. Albut had all but used up his stunts. For a decade he had performed every trick from the Houdini Book of Great Escapes and he had had enough. Newton Heath thanked him for his decade of service and turned their attention to finding a new fall guy. They did check to see whether someone had broken the Old Firm duopoly up in Scotland only to discover Aberdeen hadn't been formed yet. Subsequently, they set their sights lower (or were their heads bowed from desperation?) and settled on the master-manager who in three years had taken Lincoln City from the very bottom of the Second Division to the heights of mid-table mediocrity. The messiah in question? Mr. James West, the first manager of Manchester United. With such an accolade you would think the Old Trafford hierarchy would care to laud him these days. Instead, he barely gets a mention in official United histories. Alright, he did go by the sobriquet 'secretary' back then but this title never shielded his more successful successor Ernest Mangnall from the lavish praise bestowed upon him. West, after all, saw through the intricate transition from Newton Heath to Manchester United during an understandably chaotic period in the club's history. He was a good man who, like Albut, worked tirelessly during Heath's last couple of years to keep the heart pumping. In fact, so honourable was he that he personally stepped down from his post in September 1903 when he felt accountable for the inability of the new Manchester

United outfit to gain promotion at the first attempt. James West deserves his due whenever this great club's story is told.

Not much has been traced, mind, about this gentleman from Lincoln. Prior to taking charge of his hometown club in 1897, he was a respected referee. His claim to fame, oddly enough, was that he once caused a full scale riot at Everton's Goodison Park. His 15 minutes in the sun, or 37 to be exact, happened in December 1895. That many minutes had elapsed from Small Heath's visit to Goodison when Mr. West abandoned the match due to the waterlogged pitch. All was routine so far. But then, persuaded by an insistent management, he decided the game should resume. The problem was that most of the players had already bathed, moisturised, and changed into their civvies. West had no alternative but to call the match off again. Peeved by the indecision, a terrace mob invaded the pitch pelting the staff with stones and demanding their money back, regardless of having a receipt or not. It took the intervention of Merseyside's finest, oxymoron not intended, to stifle the hooligans.

James West's case is not unique in the Manchester United narrative. Another man is criminally overlooked in most official publications. Here's a trivia question: Who acted as Manchester United manager during World War II? You won't find the answer in any of the club's numerous quiz books. Walter Crickmer is frequently listed as being in charge, and he was – in a secretarial capacity. But the man who took charge of the players on a day to day basis was a chap called Jimmy Porter. He had most power of team affairs during the final pre-war season of 1938-39 and then throughout the conflict until March 1944. It was his training that helped put together Sir Matt Busby's first great team, the one he 'inherited', at least according to the likes of Johnny Morris and John Anderson, stars of United's 1948 cup-winning team. Perhaps Sir Matt's incredible tenure blanked his predecessor from most people's memories, so, despite this being a departure from Newton Heath's tale, it is time the record was put straight.

James Porter was born during James West's three-year spell at Bank Street but, considering the birthplace was in Hamilton, Scotland, this most probably had nothing to do with him. Porter grew into a 5'11' right-half who made over 400 appearances for Bury from 1922 until retirement in 1935. After coaching at

Leicester and scouting for Bury, he moved to Old Trafford in 1938 where he helped mould such legends as Jack Rowley and Charlie Mitten. In March 1944, he returned to Bury but as manager this time. Finally, he was the gaffer at Accrington Stanley from 1949 to 1951. Impressive? Hardly. But this story is not about glory. It is about common heroes like James West and James Porter whose tireless contribution to Manchester United's history should never be forgotten.

FORWARD PUZZLE

NEWTON HEATH HAD a simple template at the beginning of 1900-01: win the home games 4-0 and lose the away ones 0-1. It wasn't a template that would win them promotion but it got them through the first month of the season. Problem was Plan B consisted of them embarking on a six-game winless streak so that after 13 matches they were 15th in the table. Out of 18 teams!

Funny thing was that, for the first time in years, they were able to field a stable selection. On the opening day, for instance, Heath lined up thus: Garvey; Stafford, Erentz; Morgan, Griffiths, Cartwright; Schofield, Lawson, Leigh, Jackson, and Grundy. Garvey? Schofield? Lawson? It's time for some introductions. Frank Barrett had not missed a match for so long the directors lost all contact information of his last understudy Joe Ridgway. It was now time to replace him. Yet Barrett had been so good Heath decided to sign not one but two keepers to make up for his departure. Obviously the two wouldn't be fielded simultaneously, unless the first-team and reserves fixtures overlapped. Born in Manchester in 1878, James Garvey was brought back to his hometown after making the breakthrough at Wigan County. Five years Garvey's senior, Jimmy Whitehouse boasted a lot more experience when signed from Grimsby Town. One of his previous clubs was Aston Villa, where he won the league and cup double in 1897. Garvey played in the first two matches of the season and distinguished himself by proving to be the inferior of the two Jimmys. He duly became Whitehouse's sidekick and would fill in every now and then throughout the campaign.

Alf Schofield was good enough for Everton Reserves and now Newton Heath's first team. The Scouser found his best form

BAZAAR POSTER (*left*) AND PROGRAMME (*right*).
Of Heath's infamous Grand Bazaar of 1901.

at Bank Street and proved to be an equivalent replacement for Willie Bryant on the right wing. Schofield would actually go on to represent Manchester United for years to come, including a spell in the First Division. Eventually, he would pass on the torch, and a pack of toothpicks, to a certain Billy Meredith. Interestingly, Schofield enjoyed a couple of similarities with the occupant of the right wing of a century later, David Beckham. And good looks were vehemently not one of them. Rather, he was a great crosser of the ball who would provide numerous assists down the years. Also, he had his own business and at times allowed his off-field activities to interfere with his training. It's not known, though, whether he received a boot in the eyebrow for his extra-curricular distractions.

Lawson was a clever footballer, for he attended Cheshire College. His full name was Reginald Openshaw Lawson and, by the time he stated it all, his Heath career was over. After only three games he decided to listen to several self-appointed terrace counsellors who advised him to continue his education. The streetwise Dick Smith was given his spot instead. One month and as many goals later, Dick opted to leave before he got suspended again. He packed his bags once more and departed to Bolton. And this time it was for good. He had made exactly 100 league and cup appearances in his two spells at Clayton and scored a respectable total of 35 goals, the bulk of which came in one voided game against Walsall in 1895.

The only other member of the opening day team to lose his place this season was left-winger John Grundy. After a bright start his inclusion became synonymous with defeats. He was soon given the same map to Burnden Park as Smith. With two Newton Heath rejects in their front line, is it any surprise Bolton enjoyed the third worst strike rate in Division One in 1900-01?

These departures meant there were vacancies now at inside-right and outside-left. Two newcomers would soon come in as the final pieces in the jigsaw puzzle. It wasn't a top puzzle by any stretch of the imagination. However, it would be most often on display for the rest of the season, barring a few touch-ups along the way. The first player was the cream of the crop, the crop in question being four men signed by Heath in the space of eight October days. Named James Fisher but known as 'Cud', he was born in Denny, Scotland. Cud was a "pacey wingman who couldn't cross", at least according to the witty judges at his previous club, Glasgow Celtic. Yet that didn't stop them signing him twice. Eventually, they sold him to King's Park and that's when Heath pounced. It was a good thing they did for 'Cud' soon excelled on the left flank. In no time he became "the wingman who crossed very well... but couldn't score!" Despite appearing in 25 matches this season, he only bothered the scorekeepers in a 2-3 home defeat to Leicester Fosse. Ironically that came on a muddy afternoon when it would have been more sensible to just cross the ball. His best display came in another home defeat, mind. He Ronaldo-ed the Burnley full-back and provided more crosses than a Vatican mass, only for the other forwards to miraculously conjure a 0-1 defeat.

The final piece in the jigsaw answered to the name Hugh Morgan. He fitted in just in front of his namesake Billy at inside-right. He was a wee Scot who buzzed around and bristled with experience. After aiding Sunderland to second spot in the League in 1898, he had starred as Bolton pipped Newton Heath to promotion the previous season. The Mancunians hoped Morgan would now replicate his deeds for a second year running.

TO SCORE A GOAL

HUGH MORGAN MADE his Newton Heath bow on December 15th. The team was joint 15th with Burton United, only three points off the bottom. This may have been James West's neighbourhood but it was uncharted territory as far as his new club was concerned. Just a couple of months earlier Heath had been a win away from the promotion zone; now they were two months away from their last win. The defence was still keeping the score low, but the previously fearful attacking threat had whimpered off. The forwards were still trying to set Joe Cassidy up but his goal return had diminished alarmingly since he left; even though some of their wayward crosses had landed on his feet over at Hyde Road!

December 15th, however, was a big day; especially for Mr. James West, what with his old boys Lincoln City due in town. Luckily, Lincoln behaved as they generally did when West was stood on the touchline and they lost 1-4. Hugh the New scored one goal in his eagerness to make a good first impression. But the gathering was more impressed with Tom Leigh who grabbed the other three goals. Although a hiccup followed next at Chesterfield, Newton Heath set off on a mini-revival. The team was starting to take this shape: Whitehouse; Stafford, Erentz; B. Morgan, Griffiths, Cartwright; Schofield, H. Morgan, Leigh, Jackson, and Fisher. Blackpool received a black eye on Boxing Day when they were laid low 4-0 before Bank Street's first five-figure crowd of the season. Then Heath proceeded to wallop Glossop 3-0. Finally, on New Year's Day, Heath travelled to Middlesbrough and triumphed 2-1 in front of 12,000 weeping Teesiders. And voila, just like that, Newton Heath were up to 10th spot. Although a gap of 10 points still separated them from the promotion zone, surely if they continued in this recent rich form they should propel themselves towards the coveted second spot.

There was a simple flaw with this plan and that had most to do with Heath's New Year resolution to refrain from scoring any league goals. After Alf Schofield's brace at Middlesbrough on January 1st, the Heathens did not bolster their Division Two goals tally until February 25th. That consisted of an unwanted record run of four matches which eclipsed the previous record of three set on the other side of the mini-revival. It seemed all sorts of factors were collaborating to thwart the Heathens. True, the new forward line was clueless in front of goal but the barren run should never have exceeded two matches. On January 26th, James Fisher gave Heath the lead against Barnsley in wretched weather, only for the manly referee to call off the match after half an hour's play because he couldn't hack it in the worsening conditions. A week later, Newton Heath should have entertained Leicester Fosse, who already boasted eight defeats out of 12 away matches. Then

MAJOR THE DOG.
*Man(chester United)'s best friend, Major – the dog who saved
Newton Heath, with the collection box still attached to his back.*

Queen Victoria died. With the funeral falling on the Saturday, all sports were cancelled. The nation's mourning was tempered with amusement at Heath's ill fortune.

The management had to do something to end this draught. So, for the trip to Walsall, they decided to field two goalkeepers! Both Whitehouse and Garvey were included in the line-up. The joke wasn't that the management played both but that they had to. With Stafford, Griffiths, and Jackson missing, as well as their replacements Collinson and Heathcote, it was time for desperate measures. Fits-anywhere Walter Cartwright was asked to fit in at right-back; a young lad from Miles Platting named Vince Hayes was given his debut at centre-half; and John Whitney was selected at left-half. He wasn't another debutant for he had played a couple of matches just five years before in February 1896. He had since drifted into the non-League but the directors knew that holding on to his registration would come in handy in the following century. But their masterpiece in creative resourcefulness was recalling James Garvey to keep goal while moving Jimmy Whitehouse up to inside-left. It was just like the time in 1895-96 when Heath had outfield players in goal only this time in reverse. Funny thing is those were John Whitney's aforementioned two games. So, Heath's over-complicated line-up for the trip to Walsall was: Garvey; Cartwright, Erentz; B. Morgan, Hayes, Whitney; Schofield, H. Morgan, Leigh, Whitehouse, and Fisher. Not the most fearsome combination but it confused Walsall long enough for Billy Morgan to steal in and break Heath's New Year resolution. The star of the show by all accounts was Whitehouse. Not for pulling any great saves but for creating the goal and for some dazzling footwork and silky skills. Stepovers, dragbacks, you name it. He may or may not have even been credited with inventing the Whitehouse Turn. However, the experiment was not completely successful. Despite the simultaneous use of two goalies, Heath still let in a goal and had to settle for a draw.

FROM BIZARRE TO BAZAAR

BARREN RUNS. GOALIES in attack. An embarrassingly low league position. You would be forgiven for thinking that matters could not get any worse... but you would be wrong, as Burnley handed Newton Heath a record 7-1 FA Cup defeat. The winter of 1901 was proving to be a rather dismal time for the Heathens. The financial noose was tighter than ever. The club had no money to pay the players, let alone buy better ones or attempt to service the debt. The manner in which the players got their wages was uncomplicated in principle. The directors would add up the gate receipts, subtract enough to cover expenses, and divide what remained evenly among the players. A simple mathematics equation, really. Yet the story goes about one lazy Heathen whose injury-proneness was proportional to the total attendance. Before each game he would inquire about the size of the gate and, if it appeared to be small, would automatically declare himself unfit!

There is also the tale of one Heathen, paid three half crowns one week, who complained about not being able to go out that weekend. Not for his inability to pull a date, but because he had pawned his trendy outfit. The directors felt sorry enough for him to pay for the clothes, plus some additional "spending brass" for the social perks. And spare a thought for the poor Heathen who could only get his kids for Christmas a pack of batteries with a note attached that said: "Toy not included"!

Obviously, something had to be done. Heath needed to come up with enough dough, say £1,000, to buy some decent footballers and gain entry to the promised riches of Division One. Captain Harry Stafford was tasked with unearthing ideas ... as long as they were not like the one he had for his benefit match! Having been at

Clayton five years already, Harry was due a testimonial. Flamboyant as ever, he decided to stage the game at half past six in the evening. Floodlights not invented yet? Bah, special Wells' Lights would be used to illuminate the ground and dazzle the opponents, New Brighton Tower. After all, didn't the Heathens play Ardwick under a similar setup way back in 1889 and raise £140? As for the ball, it would be gilded to shine visibly. These were the sort of cutting-edge special effects that would have had a young Steven Spielberg scraping his jaw off the floor. Too bad Harry did not have a retractable roof installed, for the evening turned out to be a typically windy one. And that wasn't part of the special effects. As soon as the match kicked off, the wind blew off one light. The crew rushed to get it lit again. Suddenly another one blew on the other side. Off they scrabbled again to fix it. After enough relay racing to merit a gold medal at the Olympics, the exasperated workers chucked in the towel. There was only one light still flickering and the referee used it to find his whistle and prematurely blow for time. This was not the end of the farcical element, though. When the ref stepped back into the dressing rooms he discovered that several of the players had tiptoed off in the darkness and had been enjoying their hot bath for quite a while!

Although his big night was ruined, all that the honourable Stafford was worried about was the convenience of the paying fans. He decided to grant them free entry to the re-arranged benefit. This time, though, there would be some adjustments which included a portent of what would happen a year on. New Brighton were still the opponents but now they faced a combined selection from the city playing under the name 'Manchester United'. It was the first ever occasion that such a name existed but, despite guest appearances by the likes of Billy Meredith and Joe Cassidy from City, the team lost 2-4 and folded after one match.

Stafford's bigger concern, however, was the health of his own team. Again he did not disappoint. He gathered a few shakers inside the club as well as friends like George Lawton for a brainstorming session. Had ideas for a megastore been mooted they would have instantly been booted. After all, was there any mass appeal for plain white shirts? And there would only be two selections in the retro department. Instead, the best solution to the club crisis was to plan a bazaar. Yes, a bazaar run by the Newton Heath players and staff.

It would be a Grand Bazaar that would lure enough visitors to save the club.

A fancy programme was printed. 'Sunny Lands' was the name of the event. It would run for four days, Wednesday, February 27th, through Saturday, March 2nd, at St. James Hall on Oxford Street. Prices were posted for each day and time but you could nab yourself a four-day pass for three shillings and sixpence. One of the main attractions was the famous Besses-o'th-Barn brass band from nearby Bury. Also the Northern Military band was present both to play and possibly maintain order should trouble arise. The hall would display picturesque exhibits and an assortment of Oriental, Italian, Mediterranean, Indian, Riviera and Nile stalls. Paint a blue sky with white clouds on the ceiling and you get the Trafford Centre. The role of the players was unclear for it was not known whether a ball-juggling act would have been beneficial or detrimental to the size of the coffers.

Glitzy it may have been but the bazaar did not turn out to be the success it was hoped. The Heath directors had done their best, inviting Sir James Fergusson, MP for the city, to open the ceremony while dignitaries such as John Chapman donated a guinea. Even Manchester City forwarded £10, and United should never hesitate to repay the tenner were their neighbours to sink into financial strife in the future. But it was the city of Manchester's weather that did not collaborate. Rain, as always, came between Heath and its paying customers. It could be argued that February in Manchester was not the best time to hold such an event, but had the Heathens waited for a beautiful summer day there might not have been a club left to fight for. On top of that, at least five thousand possible visitors missed Saturday afternoon because they were over at Bank Street watching the Division Two exhibit featuring exotic Burton Swifts.

When the proceeds were tallied up and the expenses to book the hall were deducted, there was hardly any profit left. Indeed, for the next few months, the whole experience was deemed nothing but a unique diversion. However, a totally separate development had inadvertently sprouted out of the event. In a short time it would blossom to make the bazaar more successful than Heath could have hoped.

CONCEPTION

The Theatre of Dreams. Wembley '68. The Bouncing Busby Babes. Giggsy's semi-final dribble. One hundred and forty million worldwide followers (I counted them). The Holy Trinity of Charlton, Law, and Best. King Eric's upturned collar. The Treble. Every single cherished moment in Manchester United folklore owes its place to one dog! His name was Major and he was a St. Bernard who belonged to Harry Stafford. While there is no doubt about Stafford's role in the creation of United, Major's part should never be buried in the dirt. Some pets look like their owners; Major acted on his behalf. As far-fetched as the following story might sound, you would do well to keep in mind that it did indeed unfold and lead to the metamorphosis of Newton Heath into Manchester United.

Stafford had come up with an idea to bring in more money from the bazaar. He tied a collection box around Major's neck and sent him to wander around the hall to fetch donations. Late in the third evening of the event, the dog bumped into one of the stalls causing a ruckus. A security guard approached to check. Here is where little things began to happen in a certain way without which Manchester United would not have come into existence. A brave guard would have stood his ground when he saw two eyes glaring at him in the dark. Instead, he soiled himself, slipped, got up and ran away through a side door. Seconds later, Major used the same exit into the street and went chasing his destiny. There he was, a creature in the night trying to find his way to where creatures of the night usually go. He stumbled upon a pub, drawn by a divine scent – or was it beef stew? In retrospect, we have to be thankful he didn't stumble upon a lady of the night first.

The pub's licensee, a Mr. Thomas, found the dog and took him in, only until the establishment's owner dropped by. He instantly liked Major and decided to buy him as a gift for his daughter, Elsie, on her birthday. As luck would have it, the owner turned out to be a wealthy businessman who was in charge of Manchester Breweries, one of the city's leading beer companies. His name? John Henry Davies. A shrewd and successful man he may have been, but first and foremost Davies was an honourable person. When he came across a circular inquiring about a lost dog, he was not hesitant in contacting Major's owner. The scene set, that's when Harry met Davies. It was the meeting that would eventually change the shape of English football. When Stafford came over to pick Major up, he struck up conversation with his host. While explaining the chain of events that led to their encounter, Stafford disclosed all of Newton Heath's problems. Davies was fascinated. He may not have been a football man, but he had had a previous experience related to the club. Curiously, it involved Stafford's friend, George Lawton. A big Heath aficionado, Lawton in fact worked as an accountant for Davies. The story goes that on one occasion, Davies' carriage accidentally knocked over Lawton's bike while he was frantically cycling to make the Bank Street kick-off. Lawton's enthusiasm for Newton Heath had impressed Davies. Now he was completely taken in by Stafford's superhuman efforts. He saw Stafford as a trustworthy fellow and promised him that he would help the club were its desperate plight to continue.

Those were the words Stafford needed to hear. As he departed Davies' house, dog in tow, he realised the significance of that evening. It was a moment he had long been waiting for. It was the moment of conception. At long last it had happened. Stafford had thrown that four-day party and flogged Newton Heath to any potential suitors. The party bombed, but it was events after it that led to Stafford pimping his beloved club to the intrigued rich man. That night Davies and Newton Heath were matched together and a seed was planted. For one year after that, a pregnant Heath would stutter along until eventually giving birth to an extraordinary offspring.

THE LOWER HALF

With the players having so much fun partying and socialising, it should not be forgotten that Newton Heath were still a football club. And a pregnant one at that. The first signs were a couple of nauseating results such as a 2-3 home defeat to Leicester in a quagmire. Ex-Heath flop James Connachan displayed the form he ought to have shown earlier and scored twice to rub the Mancunian faces in the mud. This was Heath's third home loss of the season and the chink in Fortress Bank Street can only be attributed to the inclement conditions. For the adjacent chimneys were still as noxious as ever and there had not yet been any sightings of opponents wearing gas masks. If anything, next year's home record would be worse. Even the directors were becoming indifferent. Previously, a Clayton reverse would have had them tearing the line-up inside out, but in the current stricken state, any incomers would not be of the desired class. Take Wilson Greenwood, for instance, and keep him away. He was a tiny winger signed from Grimsby Town. Having spent his entire career trying to prove he was in the wrong business, it took him just three outings to decide he needed to go find the right one. There was no golden generation coming through the ranks either. The directors took one glance at the reserves table, spotted Heath at the very bottom below such institutions as Oswaldtwistle Rovers, Turton and Leyland, and opted to keep selections to a minimum. Sam Johnson, newly recruited from Tonge F.C., was supposedly one of the better ones. Yet his promotion simultaneously weakened the first team and the reserves. He managed a solitary game before moving on to Heywood. William Booth, meanwhile, had twice the impact, for he made two appearances. The Stockport-born left winger came from local club Edge Lane. Despite providing an assist as Heath won both matches, he drifted back permanently to the reserve scene.

The Leicester loss apart, Heath put on a decent run of victories to climb to ninth by the end of March. However, results elsewhere meant the Heathens had missed out on promotion with five games to spare. For the first time in years there would be no end-of-season fretting about claiming a top two spot. In fact, all the Heathens had to worry about was finishing the campaign in a respectable position. After all, they were currently just two points away from fifth spot. But did the players follow the instructions accurately? No. Instead they took the shortest route to 12th place with a trio of defeats that culminated with their worst league loss since 1895. Back then, an emerging Liverpool had put seven past them. Now, though, they received a humiliating 2-6 spanking at the hands of Barnsley. Yes, Barnsley! Bottom but two Barnsley – a team so bad their highest mark was getting formed. But for Newton Heath, it was the lowest point in a season of lows. They did manage to win the last two matches, one of which was against leaders Grimsby Town, to earn a top ten finish. However, that did not disguise how

HEATHENS OF THE 20TH CENTURY!
This team photo was snapped on September 21st, 1901, before Newton Heath defeated Bristol City 1-0. Left to right, back row: James West (secretary), Harry Stafford, Jimmy Whitehouse, and Fred Erentz, who had considerably filled up by now. Middle row: Alf Schofield, Bill Williams, Billy Morgan, Billy Griffiths, and Jack Banks. Front row: Steve Preston, Harry Lappin, and James 'Cud' Fisher.

far down they had fallen this season.

The odd statistic was that as many as nine Heathens appeared in 29 or more league matches throughout 1900-01. If anything, this proved that stability had nothing to do with performances. What mattered was the goals total and this was where the team failed. A meagre tally of 42 only confirmed what everybody already knew about the missing Joe Cassidy factor. In his absence only Tom Leigh cared to dabble in the mildly prolific. His 14 league goals far exceeded anybody else's. He could have stayed home throughout the New Year and still finished top. Wingman Alf Schofield came second with seven goals, but the real disappointment was international man Jackson and the top flight-tested Hugh Morgan who scored just 9 goals between them.

If that didn't impress you then neither did it the directors. They decided to scrap the whole central forward department, including, surprisingly, Tom Leigh. William Jackson worked hard but that hardly worked, so he was wheeled to Barrow. Meanwhile, Hugh Morgan never lived up to his earlier promise and was sent to Manchester City as an agent of doom. Within a year he would get them relegated. Yet what boggled the mind most was the management's incessant habit of letting their leading marksman go. First Boyd, then Cassidy, and now Leigh. It would make sense if you sold your top scorer to, say, Real Madrid for £80 million, but just how much could Heath have possibly milked out of non-league New Brompton? Thomas Sawyer and James Garvey were no strikers but they set out to sample the non-league scene too, at Chorley and Middleton respectively. Local hero Jimmy Collinson, meanwhile, disappeared into the great untraced.

It could be that the Heathens had perhaps saved their best form for a crack at some silverware. With promotion never a probability, and both Lancashire and FA Cups out of the way early on, Newton Heath made the Manchester Cup their prime target. Rochdale did not stand a chance in the first round as Heath recorded their biggest win in the competition since the 1880s. Jimmy Collinson scored twice in a 4-0 drubbing. This set up an exciting semi-final between Newton Heath and Glossop, or rather Glossop's keeper Birchenough. He alone held the Heathens at bay for ninety minutes and in the replay as well. It wasn't until extra-time, when he was probably promised Manchester United would sign him next year, that Billy Griffiths was able to beat him.

And so, after an eight-year break-up, Newton Heath were again courting the beloved Manchester Cup. Manchester City were the opposition and Manchester City's very own Hyde Road was deemed neutral enough for the tie! Five thousand Mancs gathered for the last game of the season as the following Heath eleven set out for glory: Whitehouse; Stafford, Erentz; B. Morgan, Griffiths, Cartwright; Schofield, H. Morgan, Leigh, Lappin, and Fisher. It was City, though, who took the lead. Heath thought they had equalised, but Leigh was harshly ruled offside. With home advantage and the ref in their pocket, City also used their top flight status to their benefit and romped to a 4-0 triumph. It was an appropriate ending to a dismal season for Heath, one in which they ceded their customary high finish and lost finals and pets in equal measure. The summer break beckoned and God knows they needed it, for when they returned in a few short months they would embark on their most monumental season yet.

1901-02

THE END BEGINS

WITH AN ASSIDUOUS captain, one productive wide man, and an admittedly multi-functional half-back line, Newton Heath set out to tackle the most decisive season in their history. Well, they did not have much else really. Their office was a wooden hut. It housed a swanky clock... which a gleeful bailiff would shortly seize. They had a bank balance that was a few grand in the negative. They had no top scorer, no internationals, and their one-time mascot had long since been cooked and devoured! Even their ground had lost its aura, if not its stench.

Nonetheless, the club strode into 1901-02 and what may come. A century later, in 2001-02, Manchester United also entered the new campaign with the uncertainty of Sir Alex Ferguson's future hovering in the air. The fears were dispelled, of course, when he decided to stay on as manager and lead United to happy times again. In 1901, only in their wildest dreams could Heath wish to have a happy conclusion to their season. They would, in the end, but the fear of extinction had loomed large for so long that the end seemed inevitable.

Nevertheless it was the dawn of a new campaign and, despite the financial restrictions, Heath, as usual, would be going out to earn the promotion that might yet save their skins. So, Mr. West and his staff embarked on an expansive recruitment drive in which quantity, not quality, was the overriding maxim. But were quality to rear its head, the scouts would not be averse to snapping it up. Obviously the management felt the team was lacking a Brummie twang, for they went out and bought three Midlanders. Jack Banks was lured in from West Bromwich Albion while team-mate Billy Richards would follow in a few months. Both men were experienced, mid-twenties reinforcements with the added pizzazz of FA Cup finalist medals from 1895 to their name. While their capture could be considered a coup for Heath, the fact that Albion had just been relegated meant the two would have been playing Second Division football irrespective of Heath's intervention. So, Banks added his nimble, cultured style to the midfield while Richards supplied the centre-forward position with the kind of form that got Albion demoted in the first place. The last Brummie was actually signed from Middlesbrough. His name was James Saunders and his principle role was to assist goalie Jimmy Whitehouse with the burden of picking balls out of the back of the net.

The Brummie quota satisfied, Mr. West turned his attention to the local allocation and endorsed the merits of one Harry Lappin. From contemporary team photos, he gives the impression that he required at least a couple of weeks of beauty sleep. It took him just a week's trial at the end of 1900-01, though, to convince the club he could fill William Jackson's misfiring boots at inside-left. A whole decade older, William 'Sandy' Higgins came with less potential but versatility and an enduring vitality. He had represented a host of clubs in his time, the last of which was Middlesbrough. William Smith's previous club, meanwhile, was Stockport, and so was his nickname. An inside-forward of useful qualities, one of his specialities was barren runs. He was amply able to demonstrate that in his 16 league appearances at Clayton. So, Bill Richards, William Higgins, and William Smith had been signed and the club, remember, already boasted Billy Griffiths and his namesake Morgan. If that was not enough, Mr. West topped it all by signing a Bristol Rovers inside-right called William Williams! Forget Matt Busby's vision of youth. Mr. West's obvious dream was to build a team with a Bill in every position.

With so much frantic activity taking place, Newton Heath ended up signing the same player twice! Only that reason could possibly explain Jimmy Coupar's return to Manchester. It was the same Coupar who starred in Heath's inaugural Football League season of 1892-93. He had been generously offered paid rest until his troublesome injury had cleared up. It would have been plausible that the healing process lasted eight years had he not turned up for St. Johnstone, Rotherham Town, Luton, Linfield, and Swindon Town during this time. But arguably the most successful signing of all did not have a wealth of league experience, was not called William, and did not hail from any place remotely near Birmingham. The discovery of Steve Preston would be the blueprint for all future Roy of the Rovers-type tales. A Newton Heath director named Mr. Fred Palmer had just stepped out of a pub, suitably, (it was Sunday morning, mind). The first thing that grabbed his attention was an impromptu match that was going on among the locals, and he staggered across to have a look. He would have been in his right to assume his vision was misleading him when he spotted this small fellow with the fancy footwork peppering the opponents with one arrowed blast after another. However, this was not the drink expanding his imagination. Right there on the wet grass in a Sunday morning kick-about was Newton Heath's centre-forward for the coming season. The 21-year-old from Gorton was instantly snapped up and set forth to become Heath's last ever top scorer.

A TRIP TO NORTH ROAD

There were several unfamiliar faces on the opening afternoon of 1901-02 at Bank Street. Not the handsomest of faces, though, by any stretch of the imagination. In addition to Harry Lappin and his misgivings, there was Steve Preston. It could be argued that when God made him, He broke the mould, possibly by smashing it into his face. Newton Heath's twin terrors were joined by another debutant up front, Bill Williams, while Jack Banks was making his bow at centre-back. The full line-up was: Whitehouse; Stafford, Erentz; Morgan, Banks, Cartwright; Schofield, Williams, Preston, Lappin, and Fisher. It wasn't the preferred line-up, just a suggestion. In fact, Heath seemed to field the non-preferred selection in every game bar just two unchanged elevens. Mr. West had signed more players than he knew what to do with and kept juggling them around. For instance, the inside-right berth was passed around so many men you could have changed its name to Emmanuelle. Walter 'Versatile' Cartwright, meanwhile, appeared in seven different positions in the space of three months. The multi-talented fellow was bent on covering every blade of grass one game at a time.

That opening day selection was good enough to beat Gainsborough Trinity 3-0 with Preston (2) and Lappin lapping up the goals in front of 10,000 fans. An even bigger attendance of 12,000 was present in the next game as the Heathens crumbled to a 0-5 defeat at Middlesbrough. But they won three and drew as many in their next six matches so that by the end of October, Heath sat in fourth. They could even have been joint second had a last-minute winner not been disallowed to permit Stockport to sneak out of Bank Street clutching a 3-3 draw. The top two teams were, interestingly, WBA and Preston North End. Founder members of the Football League and early giants of the game, they were now slumming it in the basement. There were other changes in the division. Bristol City and Doncaster Rovers were newly admitted while Burton Swifts and Burton Wanderers were now United but to no avail. One of the newcomers, Doncaster, exposed their naivety when they were due at Clayton on October 26th. As the Heathens warmed up with kick-off time approaching, Rovers were doing some frantic running of their own across town at North Road! They had accidentally headed to Heath's old ground. Well, it had only been eight years since Newton Heath relocated! This wasn't the first such incident but Heath did not care and used it to their advantage. Though there is no known result of their kick-about at North Road, at Bank Street, Rovers were creamed 6-0. Jimmy Coupar, whose last home Heath goal had coincidently come at North Road, made up for eight years of recuperation by banging in a hat-trick. He wasn't the leading scorer, though, for Steve Preston had made a blistering start with six goals in eight matches so far. Heath were now fourth and this life of poverty was proving to be quite easy.

The first hard challenge was up next as leaders WBA were due in town. They had collected four more points than Newton Heath but had achieved that by playing an additional two matches. This was Heath's great, and perhaps last, chance to force their way into the promotion zone, despite the deteriorating finances. All they had to do to make the dream realistic was win this match. 13,000 fans knew the enormity of the fixture. Heath's line-up was already much-changed from the opening day. Whitehouse was still in goal but both regular full-backs were missing. Billy Morgan and Walter Cartwright were kind and dropped back to fill in. Their places in the half-back line alongside Banks went to Higgins and Griffiths. As for the forward line, it sounded more like a tour of northern England: Schofield, 'Stockport' Smith, Preston, Coupar, and Fisher. It was the last named who scored his second ever league goal for the Mancunians, but that was not enough to counter the two goals that gave the away side victory. Heath were knocked out of their stride.

From then on until New Year's Day, the Heathens were able to win a couple of games to give a semblance of being in the promotion hunt, but an assortment of mishaps kept befalling them. A terrible 1-5 defeat at Preston was hardly tempered by the comedic value provided by the fact that Heath's goal was also scored by Preston – Steve, that is. Then a 1-0 victory over Burslem came at the cost of a broken ankle, that of Sandy Higgins. He tested it in two more appearances later in the season but was soon off to try retirement instead. The next home match was scheduled for Burnley's visit on Christmas Day and a bumper crowd was expected of ease the mounting debts. But Santa must have misread Heath's wish list, for the only downfall that arrived was of the very wet kind. The fixture and the promised riches were wiped out.

The last thing that Newton Heath needed was another career-ending injury on New Year's Day. Poor Joe Heathcote suffered the type of compound leg break that had grown men weeping in the stands. All 10,000 of them. Although Joe had been a fringe player for years and had to supplement his meagre wages with an additional warehouse gig, he was rather popular among the fans. As it instantly became clear his career was shattered along with his leg, a whip-round was undertaken there and then and a sizeable sum was gathered in his name.

ET TU HEALEY?

DESPITE THE PRECEDING array of problems, Newton Heath's state would soon reach even deeper levels of desperation. Rain, snow, wind, fog, rain, fog, rain and more rain always seemed to accompany home matches and bully the fair-weather fans into staying away. A couple of extended Bank Street gates might have kept the lid on the overcooked debts. Eventually things came to the boil on January 9th with the shocking news that one of the creditors had filed a petition for the winding up of the club. The creditor in question? Newton Heath's very own ex-president Mr.

William Healey. Yes, he of that lacklustre Healey tin pot. For years he had ploughed money into the club without much reward. On the contrary, he was now owed an amount Heath had been unable to repay: £242 17s 10d (about £18,000 in today's money). Not surprisingly Healey had had enough.

The rest of the directors knew he was within his rights and they didn't even oppose him in court. The judge's verdict was ruthless: Did he initiate bankruptcy proceedings? Sure. Repossess the office supplies? Certainly. Lock the Bank Street gates? Especially! Newton Heath, one of the well-known League clubs, were staring extinction in the face. They couldn't even get into their own ground to face Middlesbrough in two days. There they stood outside on a gorgeous, sunny day when a sympathetic crowd would have arrived in droves. Everyone now realized the seriousness of the matter as the newspapers relayed the daily developments and published the findings of Mr. C.J. Dibbs, the Official Receiver. His report exposed Newton Heath's private parts. Since becoming a limited company in 1892, the club had sold £766 of their £2000 worth of shares. Meanwhile, dividends paid to shareholders were kept at a maximum of zero. Now the full extent of the debts was revealed to be £2,670. Mr. Healey's portion was just the tip of the iceberg. Bank Street's owner, a William Walker, was given permission to reclaim the ground and convert it, should he wish, to a grazing field for his cattle!

Heath's plight was indeed quite dire now. This was probably the darkest moment in the club's 24 memorable years as they stared into the abyss. Long removed from the FA and Lancashire Cups, they were presently in danger of aborting their League programme as well. Already they had had the Middlesbrough fixture postponed; now lack of funds to cover travel expenses was threatening the next match at Bristol City. Should Newton Heath fail to fulfil two league obligations in a row, that would very likely bring the end of the club. And this was no wild exaggeration. Already the likes of Bootle, Darwen, and Loughborough had disappeared off the League map and were destined never to return. Would Newton Heath become another long-forgotten name that was once a Football League outfit? That was the stark reality the Heathens faced in that cold January of 1902.

It is at times like these that men are either transformed into legendary heroes or fade into the obscure past. Harry Stafford, Newton Heath Captain, stepped forward to face his destiny. Whatever could be done he was prepared to do as he rallied his players. It is not clear how much effort the rest of the Heathens put in during this crisis although it is very probable they all had an active role to play. Except for 'Cud' Fisher, that is. The little rat jumped ship with a speed previously undetected in any of his previous 44 appearances. So Stafford rallied his men, minus Fisher, and kick-started the mission to save the club. Of utmost importance was finding enough cash to go to Bristol for the Saturday match. Off he went, from house to house, targeting everyone who had donated to the club before and anyone who had never heard of Heath but was willing to help. Stafford had gone to the trouble of printing subscription lists and distributing them to every possible source in the hope they would be converted to cash.

The efforts were rewarded. Almost £100 was collected – enough for the train fare to Bristol but not the hotel bill. Manchester Reds, where were your great grandfathers? On the day of the match, eleven Heathens boarded the train, the fate of a future empire weighing on their shoulders. Stafford, deep in thought, concocted a plan for survival; Fred Erentz, the 10-year veteran, wondering whether he had ever participated in a more significant match; Walter Cartwright, restless as ever, probably sat everywhere in that carriage; and newcomer Bill Richards, questioning the wisdom of his decision to leave WBA the previous month. For five hours they travelled, arriving at Bristol City just in time for the kick-off. Not surprisingly, they lost 0-4. However, this wasn't about winning, it was about existing and making sure the club maintained a heartbeat, no matter how faint.

Newton Heath's ability to complete that trip south provided a ray of hope. They had been perhaps 24 hours away from extinction. Instead, they now realized they could possibly go on. For how long? That depended on how much money they could raise, and how quickly. At least there would be no travelling to worry about for a month: only one of the next four matches was away and that was around the corner at Stockport. But what about the home games? Was there a 'home' to play at? Relief came from an unlikely friend. Mr. Dibbs, the Official Receiver, turned out to be a top fellow. Clutching another £100 that had been raised from the directors and players like Cartwright and Stafford digging deep into their pockets, he sought Bank Street's owner, Mr. Walker, and talked him out of spending £230 on demolishing the stands. With the £100 firmly tucked in his pocket, Mr. Walker was satisfaction personified. More importantly, Heath were back home again.

At least one player had a reason to sneak a smile during this episode. Vince Hayes was the direct beneficiary of 'Cud' Fisher's treachery. He had made his debut the previous season in defence but now he was able to make the inside-left slot his own for the remainder of the season. Although he did not smoke, drink, nor cause trouble, he was a boilermaker by trade rather than a priest. However, what makes him really stick out is that he was the only Heathen to win a major trophy with the club. Hayes achieved that feat by converting to left-back, getting a spell at Brentford out of the way, and returning to Manchester United in time for the FA Cup success of 1909.

LABOUR PAINS

IN THE MEANTIME, Newton Heath were somehow staggering along week by week. It helped that the Official Receiver was taking his sweet time investigating the club's accounts and had not hurried through the liquidation orders. And the joint Football League and FA committee that was tasked with determining Heath's fate could not come to a swift conclusion either. Perhaps they could see the effort the Heathens were expending to save themselves. Or maybe they figured they would give Newton Heath more time in case something came up. Either way, they were reluctant to give this plucky club the thumbs down.

Tuesday, March 19th, brought the Newton Heath supporters the first bit of good news since the day Matthew Gillespie had been sold. They had been summoned to a meeting at the New Islington Hall in Ancoats where the directors promised to put them in the loop. And about time too. According to President Fred Palmer, it could not have been done earlier because the FA had not yet given the go-ahead to reform the club, or at least that was his excuse. Mr. James West was up next disclosing all the relevant numbers. Since the winding up order, over £400 had been collected from gate receipts, a big chunk of which was used to gag Mr. Healey. But there was still a lot of money still owed, such as the £180 in wages due to the players.

Harry Stafford had been running around tirelessly for the last couple of months, but never as productively as this day. He had been working on a survival plan for the club and now he had one question to ask: Exactly how much dough was needed to make Heath financially stable? All heads turned towards the chairman as he calculated a figure of roughly £1,000. At that moment, in what was a small bounce for man but a giant leap for Manchester United, Stafford rose and declared that there were five men who were prepared to place £200 each in the club's bank account. The hall erupted as if some thirty-something Cockney had scored a last-minute equaliser in a European Cup final. Though no one was heard offering to bear Harry's children, the raucous crowd would not be appeased until he had taken to the stand. Stafford duly obliged before commencing a historic roll of names: Mr. Davies of Old Trafford; Mr. Taylor of Sale; Mr. Bown of Denton; Mr. Jones of Manchester; and Stafford himself. The place again exploded, as if some baby-faced Norwegian had added an improbable injury time European Cup final winner. The directors, like the crowd, stunned, blew the final whistle on the meeting. They would convene again as soon as Stafford could present the gentlemen in question.

Curiosity was rife as to the identity of said gentlemen. In fact, a certain degree of mystery still exists to this day. James Bown, for instance, is sometimes mistakenly referred to as "Brown", while Charles Jones' name is replaced by a Mr. Deakin in one or two publications. James Taylor completes the list of three men who, though wealthy, were simply the associates of an even wealthier man: our old friend, John Henry Davies. With a fortune valued at around three-quarters of a million pounds, he was the oligarch behind this consortium formed to swiftly wipe off Newton Heath's astronomical debts and convert them into a superpower of the English game. Harry Stafford, at his lowest point of desperation, had sought Mr. Davies and urged him to marry himself to the labouring Newton Heath so he could oversee the birth of Manchester United and guarantee this historic event did not occur out of wedlock.

The self-made Davies cherished little more than to see the fortunes of his home town flying high. He readily responded to Stafford's pleas for he had seen the abundance of loyalty and nobility in Heath's captain. Although it had just become public knowledge, Mr. Davies had been actively confronting Heath's dilemma for over a month. The directors, in an attempt to gauge his credibility, had challenged him to sign a player for the club. Davies called their bluff and purchased inside-right James Higson from Manchester Wednesday in mid-February. During the following weeks, as the authorities gave their blessing for the restructuring of Newton Heath, Davies focused on mobilizing his squadron of rich friends. Late in the afternoon of March 19th, he informed Stafford that the takeover was on.

Of course, Newton Heath being the original prototype behind the Indiana Jones thrill-a-minute series, this was still not the end of the matter. When the directors realised that the rescue package was actually a takeover attempt that would see them ousted, they rapidly formed a defensive wall. Nobody was getting past them. To be fair, this was still a club into which they had chucked a lot of money down the years. And lest we forget, director is but an anagram of creditor. However, it could be argued that it was ultimately their inability to manage Heath's finances that now had them facing Mr. Davies' wicked free-kick. Fortunately, Mr. Davies knew how to put a bend on his kicks. The old board haggling over £110 before letting go? Pay them £210! By April 11th, they had relented and the club was Davies' at the season's end.

RE-ELECTION EVASION

BOARDROOM BATTLES AND bankruptcy perils were not enough to appease Newton Heath. The gloomy predicament had to be replicated on the pitch. Busy running around town in search of donations, the Heathens totally overlooked the opposition's penalty area. For five consecutive league matches as winter turned into spring, they did not score a single goal. When they finally did, on March 22nd, it cost them five quid. Due to play at Barnsley, Heath asked directions from a guard who, in an attempt to quash his hopes of promotion to a full-time bobby once and for all, misguided them. They arrived at Oakwell so late Barnsley complained it cost them £15 in lost revenue. It took the intervention of the president of the Football League to stir some sympathy for the bankrupt Heathens and slice the compensation fee by two-thirds. Walter Cartwright,

THE MEN WHO MADE MANCHESTER UNITED:
(Left) JH Davies, the brewing magnate who saved the club, (right) George Lawton, Davies' accountant and Heath fanatic and between the pair James Taylor (top) and James Bown (bottom), two of Davies' welathy friends co-opted on to the new board.

appearing on the left wing, and newcomer James Higson grabbed the long-awaited goals but Heath still lost 2-3.

Heath were losing too many games, as a matter of fact. The previous season, they had idled through a boring run-in to finish in mid-table. This time around the team made sure there was more excitement. As it was a bit tricky to launch a promotion drive so late in the campaign, the Heathens opted for the easier slide towards the foot of the table instead. The occupants of the bottom three places, after all, would require an application for re-election to Division Two should they wish not to drop out of the League. And by April 7th, Newton Heath had struggled enough all season to attain 16th spot and a place in the re-election zone. They had even found time to bestow upon George O'Brien the honour of becoming the last ever player signed by Newton Heath. The former Everton outside-left's solitary outing at Clayton was sufficient to grant him his claim to fame.

With three matches left, Alf Schofield instigated the revival. He picked up the ball and started dribbling until Burslem Port Vale were out of defenders. He then slotted in the equaliser to guarantee his team their first away point for three and a half months. Heath were still three points adrift of 15th place – a position occupied by Port Vale, incidentally – but hope was maintained with a 3-1 home victory over Burton United watched by the club's 500 most loyal souls.

April 23rd, 1902: at Bank Street, Clayton. Newton Heath lined up for the last league game of the season, and the last league game in their history. Chesterfield may not have been the most illustrious of opponents but, in the circumstances, they were the most appropriate. Chesterfield were two points ahead of their hosts which meant that, irrespective of results elsewhere, Newton Heath could escape re-election if they won this match by at least a two-goal margin. The Heathens' league swansong would be no dead rubber. Now, it is doubtful whether the rest of Division Two's club's directors, no matter how football-thick they were, would have turned down a re-election application by the newly-reformed Manchester United and their large travelling – and paying – support. And, indeed, all bottom three teams were ultimately re-admitted. However, there was a big chance, had the takeover not occurred and Heath had limped through bankruptcy until the season's end, that the ailing club would have been laid to rest. Especially considering Walsall were trying to whine their way back in.

Newton Heath were taking no chances. Besides, a club destined for the big time could do without the shameful aberration of having to seek re-election blemishing their future roll of honour. The noble eleven chosen to safeguard said honour were: Saunders; Stafford, Erentz; Morgan, Griffiths, Banks; Schofield, Coupar, Preston, Hayes, and Lappin. Apart from a brave 2,000 souls, Mancunians could not bear to look and stayed away. It remained goalless until shortly before half-time. Then Hayes sent in a cross and Coupar leapt into the air. He had scored in Newton Heath's very first league match against Blackburn in September 1892. Wouldn't it be fitting to score in the very last one as well? So he thought to himself and he headed the ball into the net. One-nil to Heath; halfway there. A few minutes after the break, Schofield went on a typical jinking dribble down the right before crossing. Steve Preston was lurking in the box. With ten goals so far, he was set to finish as top scorer. But to make absolutely sure, he met the centre with a header for number eleven. Though Chesterfield had a close attempt late on, the Heathens held on for the required 2-0 victory. Chesterfield joined Stockport County and Gainsborough Trinity in filling their re-election applications while Heath saved themselves the trouble with a slightly superior goal average of 0.025 of a goal, which, I'm told, is a very small number.

... AND THEY SHALL BE CALLED MANCHESTER UNITED

His Royal Majesty's judiciary system could not fold them. Neither could the Football League's lowly minnows send them down. Newton Heath had survived. One story had ended but only after scribing the outline for another. And though at the end Heath trudged off in a not too dignified manner, there was a glut of proud achievements along the way. That defeat of Chesterfield on the last day of the season was 139th victory in their ten years in the Football League. Only four other teams had won more during that span. Yet excluding the first season of 1892-93 (when the club endured a baptism of fire) and the second as well (when they were dipped in concentrated hydrochloric acid for good measure) the Heathens had won more league matches than anybody, except Aston Villa – the superpower of the era with five championships in the 1890s. This happened around the time Newton Heath boasted the proud record of just five defeats out of 94 home league matches from 1894-95 to 1899-00.

Then there were the clutch of record scores, some of which have stood the test of time: the 10-1 savaging of Wolves; the 7-0 drubbing of Grimsby Town away; that same score-line replicated in the FA Cup against West Manchester; the day the Heathens had their way with Walsall fourteen times until they could take it no more. And there was the high point in 1898, of course, when Heath were crowned the cream of Lancashire. But the good times were not restricted to the League days, for a host of memories remain from the quarter century of Heath's existence. Double figures were a common score during the Black, Powell, and Doughty era of excellence. The Manchester Cup resided at North Road for so long the purchase of Brasso became obligatory. The short-lived Football Combination of 1888-89 was unofficially declared Heath's. And who could forget that day in March 1888 when one international team fielded five Heathens in its ranks? Okay, it was only Wales, but the principality was one of the top three footballing countries at the time!

One day remained in the life of Newton Heath: April 26th, 1902. It was the day two important events occurred. One was that Newton Heath played their last ever match on that afternoon, and the reason it was their last was due to the other event: the re-naming of the club to Manchester United. For so long the club had been known as Newton Heath, and previously with the lagging LYR, but they no longer resided in that part of the city. The relocation had often created confusion for opponents. Yet the change was not done solely for the benefit of satnav-deficient visitors. The club was more cosmopolitan now and it needed to represent the whole city. Mr. Davies had a wider vision for his new acquisition, and, indeed, soon the club would be overhauled with new players, a new kit, so why not a new name? Though Newton Heath remains a cool and romantic tag, the name 'Manchester United', on the other hand, is so charismatic a title just reading it as a kid made me become a supporter for life, without being aware of past or present significance.

We should all be grateful to one Louis Rocca that the club did not become known as Manchester Celtic or Manchester Central. These were two suggestions mooted before his intervention. Luckily, the former was rejected to avoid religious connotations while the latter not only sounded like a train station, but also threatened future generations with a monstrous-sounding "There's only one Central" chant. Instead, as a young Louis modestly recounted years later, as soon as he suggested 'Manchester United' it was largely acclaimed. This streetwise character of Italian ancestry contributed so much to United's cause over the next half century it is a surprise he didn't recommend the club be called Manchester Rocca. However, at the risk of bursting Rocca's bubble, a thorough scan of newspaper articles reveals that at the close of that famous March 19th meeting when Stafford made his royal speech, an "old supporter" proposed this same name only to be swiftly shushed. And as Rocca was a mere fresh-faced tea-boy when the name change took place, he would have been even five weeks younger at the New Islington Hall meeting. In effect, he may not have dreamt the tag by himself, but Rocca retains the credit for submitting the winning proposal.

THE FINAL KICKABOUT

So, ON THIS final afternoon, the Heathens donned their white shirts for the last time. The league programme may have ended, but there remained the Manchester Cup final to contest, Heath having got there despite giving the impression all along that they did not intend to. In the first game they let Rochdale build a two-nil lead but still earned a late, late win with goals from Hayes (2) and Griffiths. Then it required two matches to get past Bolton in the semis. The final, like last year, was against Manchester City at Hyde Road. On that occasion, City flexed their First Division muscles and gave Heath a 4-0 beating, but now things were different. City had just completed the first of umpteen relegations and the majority of the 10,000-strong crowd reserved their biggest cheer to welcome the Heathens onto the arena.

James Saunders stood in goal, preferred to Jimmy Whitehouse. He would play two more matches for Manchester United the following season before eventually joining Nelson. Whitehouse also lasted one more season, then crossed town to City. At right-back, of course, was Harry Stafford. In a few months he would become United's first captain. The following summer, Harry would retire but remain influential at Bank Street as a director, scout, groundsman, and even beer overseer. There was nothing he wouldn't do for his club! Years later, having seen his efforts bear fruit with United's first period of success, he set out travelling the world a satisfied man. He headed down under to Australia but ended up in Montreal, Canada.

At left-back, as always, was Fred Erentz. He had been around in each of Newton Heath's ten Football League campaigns. His league appearances totalled 280 – more than David Beckham managed in a red shirt – while overall he was traced in 399 first-team matches. Unfortunately, the new board did not seem too eager to grant him a 400th as they were reluctant to pay him summer wages. That, and a quick look at his badly knackered knee, convinced Erentz to call time on a loyal Newton Heath career.

On the contrary, the entire half-back line and their understudies were retained for 1902-03. Morgan, Griffiths, and Cartwright would all be kitted out in red and white come September when United kicked their first ball. Cartwright even got to play in goal one more time before his retirement in 1904 after nine years of super service. Morgan left in 1903 for Watford while Griffiths lasted until 1905. Incredibly, he was joint top-scorer with 11 goals in 1903-04, but the management still gave his place to new recruit Charlie Roberts. Jack Banks, who did not make the Manchester Cup final eleven, did not make a good impression in his first United year either and moved on to Plymouth Argyle.

Patrolling the right wing was Alf Schofield, as he would go on to do for United for years. In 1906, Alf would become the only Heathen to win promotion with the new club. On Christmas Day of the same year, he played his 179th competitive match at Clayton. When a week later Billy Meredith was introduced in his position, Schofield decided to call it quits. It's a good job he did. Had he opted to wait out the Meredith mania he would have graced the reserves until 1921! Next to him stood Vince Hayes, another special Heathen. In addition to winning the FA Cup in 1909, he played in Old Trafford's opening fixture a year later. By then he had inherited Erentz's left-back place. Centre-forward Steve Preston could only wish he had inherited someone's place. Despite finishing as top scorer in 1901-02, he was only afforded a further four matches by the new regime who were still not too impressed with his three-goal return. These stats did appeal to Stockport County, though. Harry Lappin was hardly as prolific but he was treated the exact same way, only managing a handful of appearances in red before being passed on to Grimsby Town. The fifth member of the front line that day did not bother waiting around for the same severance package. Jimmy Coupar had played in Newton Heath's first Football League campaign and their last. While his initial exit was to St. Johnstone, his second was a tad more dignified. He simply retired.

These were the names that represented Newton Heath in their final kick-about. They had come a very long way since the earliest kick-about some 24 years earlier. Those original names had not made this long journey in time, but the handful of onlookers that used to huddle around the ropes which enclosed the field out of mere curiosity had grown to almost 15,000 now by the time of the farewell kick-off. All eyes were on the centre circle as the two captains, Harry Stafford and Billy Meredith, shook hands. Has there ever been a more poignant handshake on a football field? One man, whose selfless work had dragged the club to this point, passing the mantle on to another, who in time would pick them up and lead them to triumphs they could only dream about.

The Heathens were fast off the blocks, playing like a team that was running out of time. Coupar, Hayes, and Lappin took turns stinging the opposition keeper Hillman's palms. City replied with kicks of their own, aimed directly at the ankles of Schofield and Morgan. After 15 minutes, against the run of play, the will of the crowd, and the flow of happy endings, Meredith broke through on goal. Saunders rushed out to foil him, but the ball deflected kindly to Threlfall with an empty net begging to be bulged. He duly obliged to give City the lead. As was the theme all season, for Heath to overcome their adversity they would have to do it the hard way. After an even spell, the Heathens cranked the pressure. One corner was repelled but from another Schofield placed it so well he left Lappin with a tap-in. The crowd was jubilant.

The excitement was maintained into the second half. Hillman was again tested. City had a great chance when McOustra was freed, but he blazed over. As the end neared, Schofield skinned his marker and hared into the area just as Hunter hunted him down. Penalty! Newton Heath had converted the first ever spot-kick in English football back in 1891. Now such a kick could be their last meaningful act on the field. Up stepped Fred Erentz, Heath's longest-servant who had played in each of their ten Football League seasons. And, in what would remain the most fitting finale until a Danish goalie went up for a corner at the other end of the century, Erentz tucked the ball home. The Heathens were ahead and Stafford ordered everyone back. There were only a few minutes left in Newton Heath's life, but Harry thought of nothing but protecting this club till the very end.

Soon Mr. Lewis blew the final whistle to call time on our story. The cheers were deafening as Stafford approached the podium. The Manchester Cup was the first trophy Newton Heath had ever won, now lifting it would be their final act. Once more the city would provide this club with its crown, as well as, from now on, their identity.

BIBLIOGRAPHY

Back Page United – Stephen Kelly

Football Annual – Barry Hugman

Football League Player Records 1888 to 1939 – Michael Joyce

Hamlyn Illustrated History of Manchester United – Tom Tyrell and David Meek

Manchester United – Percy Young

Manchester United Pictorial History and Club Record – Charles Zahra, Joseph Muscat, Iain McCartney, and Keith Mellor

Red Devils – Richard Kurt

Tartan Reds – Iain McCartney

The Great Derby Matches – Michael Heatley and Ian Welch

The Guinness Book of Soccer Facts and Feats – Jack Rollin

The Manchester United Story – Derek Hodgson

The Rough Guide to English Football – Dan Goldstein

The Soccer Tribe – Desmond Morris

The United Alphabet – Garth Dykes

There's Only One United – Geoffrey Green

Winners and Champions – Alec Shorrocks

STATISTICS

ABBREVIATIONS:

COMPETITIONS: *Division One (D1), Division Two (D2), Football Alliance (All), Football Combination (FC), Test Matches (TM), FA Cup (FA), Lancashire Cup (LC), Manchester Cup (MC), Palatine League (PL), Friendlies (Fri), Healey Cup (HC), I=Intermediate Round, Q=Qualifying Round, QF=Quarter Final, SF=Semi Final, Fin=Final, V=Void, r=Replay*

SCORERS: *uk=Unknown Scorer, og=Own Goal*

1880-81

GAME	DATE	OPPONENTS	G	RES	ATT...	SCORERS
Fri	Nov 20	Bolton Wanderers XI	A	0-6		
Fri	Dec 4	Manchester Arcadians	A	0-0		
Fri	Jan 22	Bolton Wanderers XI	H	0-6		
Fri	Feb 5	Bootle Res	H	2-0		Cramphorn, Minchley
Fri	Feb 15	Hurst	H	0-1		

1881-82

GAME	DATE	OPPONENTS	G	RES	ATT...	SCORERS
Fri	Oct 15	Manchester Arcadians	H	3-0		Cramphorn, Rigby, Hopwood
Fri	Oct 22	Blackburn Olympic XI	A	0-4		
Fri	Nov 12	West Gorton St Marks	H	3-0	3000	E Thomas 2, J Jones
Fri	Jan 21	Haughton Green	H	4-0		uk 4
Fri	Jan 28	Haughton Green	A	1-1		uk
Fri	Mar 4	West Gorton St Marks	A	1-2		uk
Fri	Mar 11	Southport	A	2-1		uk 2
Fri	Mar 18	Manchester Arcadians	A	3-0		uk 3

1882-83

GAME	DATE	OPPONENTS	G	RES	ATT...	SCORERS
Fri	Nov 4	Manchester Arcadians	H	4-0		uk 4
Fri	Nov 18	Crewe Alexandra	A	2-7		uk 2
Fri	Nov 25	Bentfield	H	3-1		uk 3
Fri	Dec 2	Middleton	H	4-3		uk 4
Fri	Jan 13	Astley Bridge Res	H	1-1		uk
Fri	Jan 20	Bentfield	A	2-4		uk 2
Fri	Feb 10	Manchester Arcadians	A	0-0		
Fri	Feb 17	Crewe Alexandra	H	0-3		

1883-84

Game	Date	Opponents	G	Res	Att'd	Scorers
Fri	Oct 6	Astley Bridge A	H	0-1		
Fri	Oct 13	Haughton Dale	H	2-2		uk 2
Fri	Oct 20	St Helen's	A	3-2		uk 3
LC1	Oct 27	Blackburn Olympic Res	H	2-7		uk 2
Fri	Dec 1	Manchester Arcadians	H	4-0		uk 4
Fri	Dec 8	Earlestown	A	0-8		
Fri	Jan 5	Bootle Wanderers	H	6-0		uk 6
Fri	Jan 12	Bentfield	A	1-1		uk
Fri	Jan 19	St Helen's	H	3-1		uk 3
Fri	Jan 26	Haughton Dale	A	1-0		uk
Fri	Jan 30	St Helen's	H	3-1		Latham, Morris, uk
Fri	Feb 2	Greenheys	H	1-0		uk
Fri	Feb 9	Bootle Wanderers	A	1-1		uk
Fri	Feb 23	Blackburn Olympic XI	H	0-0		
Fri	Mar 1	Hurst Brook Olympic	A	1-3		(og)
Fri	Mar 8	Manchester Arcadians	A	4-0		uk 4
Fri	Mar 15	Astley Bridge Res	A	0-0		
Fri	Mar 29	Greenheys	A	1-5		Black

1884-85

Game	Date	Opponents	G	Res	Att'd	Scorers
LC1	Sep 20	Haydock Temperence	H	4-0		uk 4
Fri	Oct 4	Earlestown Res	H	2-1		uk 2
Fri	Oct 11	Haughton Dale Res	A	2-1		Siddons, uk
LC2	Oct 25	Baxenden	A	1-4		uk
Fri	Nov 8	Greenheys	H	3-1	2000	Jordan, Blears, Gotheridge
Fri	Nov 15	Pendleton Olympic	H	3-1		Jordan, Prow, (og)
Fri	Nov 22	Oughtrington Park	A	4-2		Jordan, Beach, Rigby, T Davies
Fri	Nov 29	Heywood	H	5-1		Beach 4, T Davies
Fri	Dec 6	Manchester Res	H	5-1		uk 5
Fri	Dec 13	Dalton Hall	H	4-1		Gotheridge, T Davies, Beach, Blears
Fri	Dec 20	Levenshume	A	4-0		Gotheridge, Prow, uk 2
Fri	Dec 27	Heywood	A	1-1		uk
Fri	Jan 3	Eccles	H	0-0		
Fri	Jan 10	Oughtrington Park	H	3-2		Gotheridge 2, uk
Fri	Jan 17	Gorton	A	3-1		Jordan 2, Gotheridge
Fri	Jan 24	Stretford	H	12-0		Jordan 3, Gotheridge, Lomax 2, Blears 2, Morris, T Davies, uk 2
MC1	Jan 31	Eccles	H	3-2	400	uk 3
Fri	Feb 7	Doncaster Rovers	A	2-2		uk 2
MC1r	Feb 14	Eccles	N	3-0		Gotheridge, T Davies, Blears
Fri	Feb 21	Gorton	H	6-0		Blears 2, Siddons, Mitchell, Black, (og)
MC2	Mar 7	Manchester	A	3-0		Blears, Jordan, T Davies
Fri	Mar 14	Greenheys	H	3-1		Morris, Jordan, Gotheridge
Fri	Mar 21	West Manchester	H	5-4		Siddons 2, Earp, Gotheridge, McGregor
Fri	Mar 28	Earlestown	A	0-2	1000	
Fri	Apr 4	Blackburn Olympic XI	H	0-1		
Fri	Apr 11	Stretford	A	0-0		
MCSF	Apr 18	Dalton Hall	N	4-3	3000	T Davies 2, Earp, Howles
MCFin	Apr 25	Hurst	N	0-3	3500	

1885-86

Game	Date	Opponents	G	Res	Att'd	Scorers
Fri	Aug 29	Crewe Alexandra	H	1-3		Gotheridge
Fri	Sep 12	Kearsley	A	11-2		uk 11
Fri	Sep 19	Blackburn Olympic XI	H	3-4		uk 3
Fri	Sep 26	Bolton W Swifts	H	0-3		
Fri	Oct 10	Macclesfield	A	4-3		W Mitchell 2, Stanton, Dixon
Fri	Oct 17	Baxenden	A	2-2		uk 2
Fri	Oct 24	Blackpool St John	A	2-0		uk 2
Fri	Oct 31	Crewe Britannia	H	3-1		Gotheridge, Stanton, Beach
Fri	Nov 7	Darwen & District	H	1-1	750	uk 1
Fri	Nov 14	Crewe Britannia	A	3-0		Gotheridge, Beach 2
Fri	Nov 21	Darwen Hibernian	A	2-1		Watkins, uk
Fri	Nov 28	Furness Vale Rovers	H	2-0		Watkins, H Davies
Fri	Dec 5	Greenheys	H	4-1		Watkins 2, W Mitchell, (og)
Fri	Dec 12	West Manchester	H	1-0	500	W Mitchell
MC1	Dec 19	Eccles	H	2-0	500	Gotheridge, Watkins
Fri	Jan 2	Pendleton Olympic	H	5-0	800	Watkins, uk 4
Fri	Jan 16	Macclesfield	H	3-3	1200	Gotheridge, Moran, H Davies
MC2	Jan 23	Gorton Villa	H	5-0		uk 5
Fri	Jan 30	Southport Central	H	4-0	1000	Earp 2, Stanton, H Davies
Fri	Feb 6	Lower Hurst	H	2-3		uk 2
MC3	Feb 13	Thornham	H	10-0	1800	uk 10
Fri	Feb 20	Blackburn Olympic XI	H	3-1	3000	Earp, Watkins, H Davies
Fri	Feb 27	Irwell Springs	H	2-0	2000	Longton, uk
Fri	Mar 6	West Manchester	A	1-2		uk
MCSF	Mar 13	Hurst	N	3-1	6000	Gotheridge, Watkins 2
Fri	Mar 20	Baxenden	H	4-3	1000	Earp, uk 3
Fri	Mar 27	Pendleton Olympic	A	2-2		uk 2
Fri	Mar 29	Blackburn Olympic	A	0-3		
MCFin	Apr 3	Manchester	N	2-1	6000	Black, Watkins
Fri	Apr 10	Furness Vale Rovers	A	2-1		Earp, Longton
Fri	Apr 17	Accrington Res	H	2-1	1500	Earp, Blears
Fri	Apr 23	Bell's Temperence	A	1-1		Longton
Fri	Apr 24	Darwen & District	H	2-1	2000	Longton, uk
Fri	Apr 26	WBA Res	H	1-0	2000	uk
Fri	May 8	Manchester	H	2-3		Earp 2
Fri	May 15	Salford & District	A	2-0		Gotheridge, Watkins
Fri	May 22	South Shore	A	1-1	800	uk

1886-87

Game	Date	Opponents	G	Res	Att'd	Scorers
Fri	Sep 4	Northwich Victoria	A	0-5		
Fri	Sep 11	Oswaldtwistle Rov	H	2-4	1000	Gotheridge, uk
Fri	Sep 18	Stanley	A	2-0		J Davies, Longton
Fri	Sep 25	Hurst	A	1-3	4500	uk
Fri	Oct 2	Manchester	H	8-1		J Doughty 2, Gotheridge 2, J Davies, Burke, Longton, H Davies
Fri	Oct 9	Oswaldtwistle Rov	A	2-1	2000	uk 2
Fri	Oct 16	Rawtenstall	A	3-3		uk 3
Fri	Oct 23	Burslem Port Vale	H	4-0	3500	uk 4
FA1	Oct 30	Fleetwood Rangers	A	2-2	2000	J Doughty 2
Fri	Nov 6	Blackburn Olymp	H	4-2	3000	J Doughty, Gotheridge, Burke, Mitchell
Fri	Nov 13	Irwell Springs	A	0-3		
Fri	Nov 20	Rawtenstall	H	0-0	3000	
Fri	Nov 27	Macclesfield	H	1-0	1500	J Doughty
Fri	Dec 4	Manchester	A	3-2		H Davies, Blears, Foster
Fri	Dec 11	Hurst	H	5-0	7000	J Doughty 3, Gotheridge, H Davies
Fri	Dec 18	Bury	A	0-0		
Fri	Dec 25	Burton Wanderers	H	0-0	5000	
Fri	Dec 27	Notts Rangers	H	0-1		
Fri	Jan 1	Crewe Alexandra	A	0-2		
Fri	Jan 15	Irwell Springs	H	1-0		Bates
Fri	Jan 22	Witton	H	0-0	3000	
Fri	Jan 29	Stanley	H	2-0		Foster, H Davies
Fri	Feb 5	Macclesfield	A	4-1	1000	J Doughty, J Davies, Gotheridge, Reed
MC1	Feb 12	Hooley Hill	H	7-0	2000	Whatmough, Burke, Gotheridge 2, H Davies, Bates, uk
MC2	Feb 19	Gorton Association	H	11-1		J Doughty, J Davies 2, H Davies 2, Gotheridge, Bates, Wright, Burke, Whatmough, (og)
Fri	Feb 26	Hurst	A	3-1	4000	J Doughty, H Davies 2
Fri	Mar 5	Derby Midland	H	3-1		Gotheridge, Bates, Tait
Fri	Mar 12	Nottm Jardines	H	2-2	4000	Gotheridge, Bates
MC3	Mar 19	Gorton Villa	H	8-0	6000	J Doughty 3, Bates, Gotheridge 2, H Davies, Wright
Fri	Mar 26	Blackburn Olymp	A	0-3		
MCSF	Apr 2	Ten Acres	N	1-0	7000	R Doughty
Fri	Apr 8	Halliwell	H	0-0	6000	
Fri	Apr 9	Gainsborough Tr	H	1-0		Bates
Fri	Apr 11	Accrington	H	0-3	4000	
Fri	Apr 16	Crewe Alexandra	H	2-3		Gotheridge, H Davies
MCFin	Apr 23	West Manchester	N	1-2	4000	Gotheridge
Fri	Apr 30	Bolton Wanderers	H	0-5	8000	
Fri	May 14	Blackburn Rovers	H	1-0	5000	Tait

STATISTICS

1887-88

Game	Date	Opponents	G	Res	Att'd	Scorers
Fri	Sep 3	Accrington	H	2-1	4000	R Doughty, J Owen
Fri	Sep 10	Bell's Temperence	A	1-2	3000	R Doughty
Fri	Sep 17	Earlstown	H	7-0		R Doughty 2, Tait 3, Wright, O'Donnell
Fri	Sep 24	West Manchester	H	6-0	6000	R Doughty 2, Tait, Wright, Gotheridge, (og)
Fri	Sep 28	Bolton Wanderers	A	2-1		J Doughty, Tait
Fri	Oct 1	Derby Midland	A	3-0		J Doughty, J Owen, O'Donnell
Fri	Oct 8	Hurst	H	3-1	2000	Gotheridge, Tait, J Davies
Fri	Oct 15	Padiham	H	3-0	4000	J Doughty 2, J Davies
Fri	Oct 22	Accrington	A	1-2	2000	R Doughty
Fri	Oct 29	Burnley	H	0-0	8000	
Fri	Nov 5	Ten Acres	H	9-0	5000	J Doughty, R Doughty 3, Gotheridge 2, Tait 2, Wright
Fri	Nov 12	Hurst	A	2-1	5000	R Doughty 2
Fri	Nov 19	Nottm Jardines	H	8-0		J Doughty 3, R Doughty, H Davies 2, Gotheridge, Powell
Fri	Nov 26	Crewe Alexandra	H	1-0	5000	R Doughty
Fri	Dec 3	Ten Acres	A	1-0	3000	R Doughty
Fri	Dec 10	West Manchester	A	2-2	3000	J Doughty, R Doughty
Fri	Dec 17	Astley Bridge	A	0-1		
Fri	Dec 24	Leek	H	3-0	3000	J Doughty, Tait 2
Fri	Dec 26	Burslem Port Vale	H	0-0	5000	
Fri	Dec 31	London Casuals	H	2-1		Gotheridge, uk
Fri	Jan 2	Burton Wanderers	H	2-1	2000	Haughton, (og)
Fri	Jan 7	Bolton Wanderers	H	0-1	7000	
Fri	Jan 14	Astley Bridge	H	3-0	4000	J Doughty 2, R Doughty
Fri	Jan 21	Gorton Villa	H	8-1	2000	J Doughty, R Doughty, Tait 3, Gotheridge 2, J Davies
Fri	Jan 28	Oswaldtwistle Rov	H	1-0	3000	J Doughty
Fri	Feb 4	Bell's Temperence	H	4-2	4000	Gotheridge 2, Tait 2
Fri	Feb 11	Crewe Alexandra	A	0-0		
Fri	Feb 18	Oswaldtwistle Rov	A	0-6		
Fri	Feb 25	Bootle	A	0-1		
Fri	Mar 3	Blackburn Olymp	H	1-2	4000	Gotheridge
MC2	Mar 17	Hooley Hill	A	7-0		J Doughty, R Doughty 2, Burke, uk 3
Fri	Mar 24	Rawtenstall	H	7-0		J Doughty 2, R Doughty 2, J Davies 2, Wright
Fri	Mar 30	Halliwell	H	0-1	5000	
Fri	Mar 31	Mitchell's St Geo	H	2-2	6000	Wright, Gotheridge
Fri	Apr 2	Accrington	H	0-1	7000	
Fri	Apr 7	Burnley	A	1-7	2000	Wright
MCSF	Apr 14	Hurst	N	2-0	3000	J Doughty, R Doughty
Fri	Apr 21	Derby Midland	H	6-1	2500	J Doughty 2, R Doughty 2, Wright, Gotheridge
Fri	Apr 23	Bolton Wanderers	H	3-3	2500	J Doughty, J Davies, Wright
MCFin	Apr 28	Denton	N	7-1	8000	J Doughty 3, R Doughty 2, Burke, J Davies
Fri	Apr 30	Hyde	A	1-1	3000	J Doughty
Fri	May 5	Preston North End	H	1-1	10000	J Davies
Fri	May 12	Denton	A	4-1		J Doughty, R Doughty, Poland, uk
Fri	May 19	Wolverhampton	H	2-1		R Doughty, uk
Fri	May 21	Aston Villa	H	1-0	2000	Poland

1888-89

Game	Date	Opponents	G	Res	Att'd	Scorers
Fri	Sep 01	Bolton	H	1-0	7000	Gotheridge
Fri	Sep 08	Blackburn	H	2-1	6000	J Owen 2
FC 01	Sep 15	Walsall Town Swifts	H	2-1	3000	Gale 2
FC 02	Sep 22	Darwen	H	4-3	4000	J Doughty 3, Gale
FC 03	Sep 29	Gainsborough Trinity	A	5-1	2000	J Doughty 2, Walton, Gotheridge, (og)
Fri	Oct 6	Canadians XI	H	0-2	7000	
FC 04	Oct 13	Derby Midland	A	1-1	1800	Walton
FC 05	Oct 20	Leek	H	4-1	3000	J Doughty, R Doughty, Gotheridge 2
Fri	Oct 27	Witton	H	2-2	4000	J Doughty, Tait
FC 06	Nov 3	Leek	A	5-0		J Doughty 3, R Doughty, Tait
FC 07	Nov 10	Burslem Port Vale	A	1-1		Davies
Fri	Nov 17	West Manchester	H	5-0	4000	J Doughty 3, R Doughty, J Owen
FC 08	Nov 24	Halliwell	H	2-0	3000	Tait, R Doughty
FC 09	Dec 1	Bootle	A	1-0		Powell
Fri	Dec 8	West Manchester	A	1-2	4000	Tait
MC1	Dec 15	West Manchester	A	2-1	5000	J Doughty, R Doughty
Fri	Dec 22	Darwen Old Wandrs	H	4-0		J Doughty 3, uk
Fri	Dec 24	Davenham	H	13-1		J Doughty 2, R Doughty 2, Gale 2, Tait, Davies, Gotheridge, uk 4
Fri	Dec 25	West Manchester	H	4-0		J Doughty 2, Gale 2
Fri	Dec 26	Wolverhampton	A	1-6		Tait
Fri	Dec 29	Corinthians	H	0-4	4000	
Fri	Dec 31	3rd Lanark Rifle Vol.	H	1-0	2500	R Doughty
Fri	Jan 1	Hearts	H	1-2		Haughton
Fri	Jan 2	Casuals	H	1-0		Tait
FC 10	Jan 5	Darwen	A	0-6		
Fri	Jan 12	Sheffield Wednesday	A	1-2	1500	G Owen
FC 11	Jan 19	Burslem Port Vale	H	3-0	3000	G Owen, Gale, Burke
FC 12	Jan 26	Bootle	H	4-0	4000	J Doughty, Gale, R Doughty, Davies
Fri	Feb 2	Bolton	A	1-3	2000	R Doughty
Fri	Feb 16	Rotherham Town	H	7-2	2000	J Doughty, Tait 2, Davies, G Owen, Gotheridge 2
Fri	Feb 21	Walsall Town Swifts	A	3-0	1000	J Doughty 2, Farman
Fri	Feb 23	Preston	H	1-0	8000	J Doughty
Fri	Feb 26	Ardwick & District	N	3-2	12000	J Doughty, Burke, uk
FC 13	Mar 2	Derby Midland	H	2-0	3000	Gotheridge, Tait
Fri	Mar 9	Nottingham Forest	A	2-2	4000	Davies, R Doughty
MC2	Mar 16	Ardwick	H	4-1	2000	J Doughty, Gotheridge 2, J Owen
Fri	Mar 18	Bootle	A	1-2	2000	J Doughty
Fri	Mar 23	Nottingham Forest	H	3-1	2000	J Doughty, Gotheridge, Tait
FC 14	Mar 30	South Shore	H	0-1	3000	
MCSF	Apr 6	Manchester Welsh	N	2-1	1500	J Doughty, J Owen
Fri	Apr 13	South Shore	A	2-2	4000	J Doughty, Tait
Fri	Apr 15	Everton	A	1-3	1500	Jarrett
Fri	Apr 19	Small Heath	H	1-0	4000	R Doughty
Fri	Apr 20	Sheffield Wednesday	H	1-2	5000	J Doughty
Fri	Apr 22	WBA	H	1-3	8000	Tait
MCFin	Apr 27	Hooley Hill	N	7-0	4000	J Doughty 3, Gale 2, R Doughty, Gotheridge
Fri	Apr 29	Manchester Welsh	H	5-0		J Doughty 3, Burke, (og)
Fri	May 4	Grimsby Town	A	0-3		
Fri	May 11	Preston	H	1-1	3000	J Doughty
Fri	May 18	Derby St Luke's	H	2-1	3000	Farman, G Owen
Fri	May 20	Ardwick	A	1-2	3000	Stewart
Fri	May 25	Darwen	H	3-2	2000	J Doughty 2, Farman

1889-90

Game	Date	Opponents	G	Res	Att'd	Scorers
Fri	Sep 2	Stoke	A	1-2		R Doughty
Fri	Sep 5	Gorton Villa	A	2-0	15000	Gotheridge, (og)
Fri	Sep 7	Bolton	H	1-1	7000	J Doughty
Fri	Sep 14	Witton	H	2-1		Tait, Mitchell
Fri	Sep 16	Burslem Port Vale	A	1-0		J Doughty
All 01	Sep 21	Sunderland Albion	H	4-1	3000	J Doughty, Wilson 2, Stewart
All 02	Sep 23	Bootle	A	1-4	3000	Tait
All 03	Sep 28	Crewe Alexandra	A	2-2	2000	Stewart, (og)
Fri	Oct 5	Newton Heath Central	H	5-0	2500	J Doughty 2, Davies, (og) 2
Fri	Oct 12	Gainsborough Trinity	H	3-0	2000	G Owen, Davies, (og)
All 04	Oct 19	Walsall Town Swifts	A	0-4	600	
All 05	Oct 26	Birmingham St Geo	A	1-5	500	J Doughty
LC1	Nov 2	Halliwell	A	1-2	2000	Stewart
All 06	Nov 9	Long Eaton Rangers	H	3-0	2500	J Doughty 2, Farman
Fri	Nov 16	Sheffield United	H	7-1	2000	J Doughty 3, Farman, Wilson, Davies, (og)
Fri	Nov 23	West Manchester	A	2-3		G Owen, uk
Fri	Nov 24	Stoke	H	6-2		J Doughty 2, Farman, Wilson, Stewart, G Owen
All 07	Nov 30	Sheffield Wednesday	A	1-3	5000	J Doughty
All 08	Dec 7	Bootle	H	3-0	4000	J Doughty, Farman, Stewart
All V	Dec 21	Walsall Town Swifts	H	3-0	1000	J Doughty, Farman, (og)
Fri	Dec 25	Belfast District	H	2-1	5000	Wilson, uk
Fri	Dec 26	West Manchester	A	7-0	7000	J Doughty, Farman 2, Wilson, Craig, G Owen, uk
Fri	Dec 27	Rotherham Town	A	1-1	2000	Farman
All 09	Dec 28	Darwen	A	1-4	5000	G Owen
Fri	Jan 1	Hearts	H	4-2	7000	J Doughty 2, Farman 2
Fri	Jan 2	Cambuslang	H	2-1		G Owen, Craig
All V	Jan 4	Grimsby Town	H	4-1	4000	J Doughty, Craig 2, Wilson
Fri	Jan 13	West Manchester	A	1-0	4000	R Doughty
FA1	Jan 18	Preston	A	1-6	7000	Craig
All 10	Jan 25	Sunderland Albion	A	0-2	4000	
Fri	Feb 1	Ardwick	A	3-0	10000	J Doughty, Farman, Wilson
All 11	Feb 8	Grimsby Town	A	0-7	2400	
All 12	Feb 15	Nottingham Forest	A	3-1	800	Stewart 2, Wilson
Fri	Feb 22	Halliwell	H	0-1	3000	
All 13	Mar 1	Crewe Alexandra	H	1-2	2000	G Owen
Fri	Mar 3	Sheffield United	A	1-2	1000	Craig
Fri	Mar 8	Derby Junction	H	3-1		J Doughty, G Owen, uk
All 14	Mar 15	Small Heath Alliance	A	1-1	2000	Farman
All 15	Mar 22	Long Eaton Rangers	A	3-1	2000	Farman, Wilson 2
All 16	Mar 29	Darwen	H	2-1	5000	Stewart, Davies
Fri	Apr 4	Clapton	H	2-1	6000	J Doughty, Stewart
All 17	Apr 5	Nottingham Forest	H	0-1	4000	
All 18	Apr 7	Small Heath Alliance	H	9-1	4000	J Doughty 2, Farman, Wilson, Stewart 3, R Doughty, Craig
MCSF	Apr 12	Denton	N	4-1	4000	Stewart, Farman 2, G Owen
All 19	Apr 14	Grimsby Town	H	0-1	3000	
All 20	Apr 19	Birmingham St Geo	H	2-1	2500	J Doughty, Craig
All 21	Apr 21	Walsall Town Swifts	H	2-1	1000	Davies, Stewart
All 22	Apr 26	Sheffield Wednesday	H	1-2	4000	Craig
MCFin	May 3	Royton	N	5-2	4000	Craig 3, Farman, G Owen
Fri	May 10	Preston	H	0-4	6000	
Fri	May 12	Heywood	A	0-4		
Fri	May 17	Bolton	A	1-1	6000	Stewart

1890-91

Game	Date	Opponents	G	Res	Att'd	Scorers
Fri	Sep 1	Burslem Port Vale	H	5-1	4000	Milarvie 2, Farman 2, Evans
Fri	Sep 2	Hyde	A	2-1	1500	Milarvie 2
All 01	Sep 6	Darwen	H	4-2	6000	J Doughty, Farman, Evans, Owen
Fri	Sep 8	Burslem Port Vale	A	4-4	1500	
All 02	Sep 13	Grimsby Town	A	1-3	3000	Stewart
All 03	Sep 20	Nottingham Forest	H	1-1	5000	J Doughty
Fri	Sep 22	Burnley	A	4-3		J Doughty, Evans, Sharpe, Farman
All 04	Sep 27	Stoke	A	1-2	2000	Milarvie
FAQ1	Oct 4	Higher Walton	H	2-0	3000	Farman, Evans
All 05	Oct 11	Bootle	A	0-5	4000	
All 06	Oct 18	Grimsby Town	H	3-1	4000	Evans, Ramsay, Sharpe
FAQ2	Oct 25	Bootle	A	0-1	3000	
Fri	Oct 25	Darwen	H	1-6	3000	Evans
All 07	Nov 1	Crewe Alexandra	H	6-3	4000	Evans, Farman, Ramsay, Stewart 2, Craig
All 08	Nov 8	Walsall Town Swifts	A	1-2	3000	Sharpe
Fri	Nov 15	Ardwick	H	4-1	10000	Sharpe, Farman, Ramsay, Stewart
All 09	Nov 22	Nottingham Forest	A	2-8	2000	Evans, Farman
All 10	Nov 29	Sunderland Albion	H	1-5	2000	Ramsay
Fri	Dec 6	South Shore	H	3-1	2000	Ramsay, Milarvie, Sharpe
All 11	Dec 13	Small Heath Alliance	H	3-1	1000	Sharpe, Milarvie, (og)
Fri	Dec 25	Belfast Distillery	H	8-4	2500	Stewart 5, R Doughty, Owen, Sharpe
All 12	Dec 27	Bootle	H	2-1	5000	Stewart, Milarvie
Fri	Jan 1	Cambridge Trinity	H	6-1	3000	Stewart 2, Craig 3, Farman
Fri	Jan 2	Ardwick	A	1-1		Farman
All V	Jan 3	Walsall Town Swifts	H	5-2	1000	Stewart 2, Sharpe, uk 2
All 13	Jan 5	Stoke	H	0-1	3000	
All 14	Jan 10	Birmingham St Geo	A	1-6	1000	Farman
All 15	Jan 17	Walsall Town Swifts	H	3-3	1500	Owen, Ramsay, Milarvie
All 16	Jan 24	Sheffield Wednesday	A	2-1	3000	Stewart, Sharpe
Fri	Jan 31	Preston North End	H	3-1	10000	Stewart, Milarvie, Farman
LC1	Feb 7	Witton	A	4-3		Craig, Milarvie, uk 2
Fri	Feb 7	Derby Midland	H	1-5		Phasey
All 17	Feb 14	Crewe Alexandra	A	1-0	3000	Farman
LC2	Feb 19	Preston North End	A	1-3	2000	Farman
All 18	Feb 21	Sheffield Wednesday	H	1-1	4000	Craig
Fri	Feb 28	Ardwick	A	3-1	11000	Farman, Ramsay, Stewart
All 19	Mar 7	Small Heath Alliance	A	1-2	2000	Sharpe
Fri	Mar 9	Burslem Port Vale	A	1-2	1000	(og)
All 20	Mar 14	Birmingham St Geo	H	1-3	2000	Sharpe
MCSF	Mar 21	Stockport	N	3-1	6000	Milarvie 2, Stewart
Fri	Mar 27	Clapton	H	4-1	3000	Sharpe 2, Farman, Craig
All 21	Mar 28	Darwen	A	1-2	2000	Ramsay
Fri	Mar 30	Accrington	H	2-5	4000	Milarvie, R Doughty
Fri	Apr 4	South Shore	A	2-1		Ramsay, Sharpe
Fri	Apr 8	Bury	H	2-1		Ramsay, J Doughty
All 22	Apr 11	Sunderland Albion	A	1-2	3500	Ramsay
Fri	Apr 13	Burnley	H	1-2	2000	Milarvie
MCFin	Apr 18	Ardwick	N	0-1	10000	
Fri	Apr 20	West Manchester	A	0-4	1000	
Fri	Apr 25	Bootle	H	1-1		J Doughty
Fri	Apr 27	Preston North End	H	1-1	3000	Milarvie

STATISTICS

1891-92

Game	Date	Opponents	G	Res	Att'd	Scorers
Fri	Sep 1	Burslem Port Vale	H	2-1	1500	Farman, Edge
Fri	Sep 5	Blackpool	H	1-1	4000	Farman
Fri	Sep 7	Bolton Wanderers	H	0-2	2500	
All 01	Sep 12	Burton Swifts	A	2-3	2000	Donaldson, Farman
Fri	Sep 14	Preston	H	1-1	3000	Edge
All 02	Sep 19	Bootle	H	4-0	5000	Edge 3, Farman
Fri	Sep 21	Stockport County	A	1-2	1000	Donaldson
All 03	Sep 26	Birmingham St Geo	A	3-1	300	Donaldson 2, Stewart
FAQ1	Oct 3	Ardwick	H	5-1	11000	R Doughty, Farman 2, Edge, Sneddon
All 04	Oct 10	Ardwick	H	3-1	4000	Donaldson, Farman 2
Fri	Oct 12	Burslem Port Vale	A	3-1	1000	uk 3
All 05	Oct 17	Grimsby Town	A	2-2	3000	Donaldson 2
Fri	Oct 24	Heywood	H	3-2		Farman, Henrys, Owen
All 06	Oct 31	Burton Swifts	H	3-1	4000	Farman, Edge, J Doughty
All 07	Nov 7	Crewe Alexandra	A	2-0	3000	Donaldson, (og)
FAQ3	Nov 14	South Shore	A	2-0	2000	Farman, J Doughty
All 08	Nov 21	Lincoln City	H	10-1	6000	Donaldson 3, Hood 2, Stewart 2, Farman, Sneddon, (og)
Fri	Nov 23	Sheffield United	A	2-3	3000	Donaldson 2
Fri	Nov 24	Darwen	A	2-2	500	Donaldson, Sneddon
All 09	Nov 28	Walsall Town Swifts	A	4-1	2500	Donaldson 3, Farman
FAQ4	Dec 5	Blackpool	H	3-4	4000	Farman, Edge 2
All 10	Dec 12	Sheffield Wednesday	A	4-2	4000	Farman 2, Sneddon, Owen
All 11	Dec 19	Ardwick	A	2-2	13000	Farman 2
Fri	Dec 25	Bolton Wanderers	A	3-6		Hood, Sneddon, uk
All 12	Dec 26	Small Heath	H	3-3	7000	Edge 2, Farman
All 13	Jan 1	Nottingham Forest	H	1-1	16000	Edge
Fri	Jan 2	Canadians XI	H	5-1	2000	Edge, Farman 2, Hood 2
All 14	Jan 9	Bootle	A	1-1	2000	Hood
Fri	Jan 16	Bury	H	2-1	3000	Donaldson 2
Fri	Jan 23	Small Heath	H	7-2		Donaldson 3, Hood 2, Farman, Sneddon
All 15	Jan 30	Crewe Alexandra	H	5-3	3000	Donaldson 3, Sneddon, R Doughty
LC1	Feb 6	Bury	H	2-3	6000	Farman, Sneddon
MC3	Feb 13	West Manchester	H	3-1		Donaldson, Sneddon, Stewart
All 16	Feb 20	Sheffield Wednesday	H	1-1	7000	Hood
All 17	Feb 27	Small Heath	A	2-3	3000	Farman , Sneddon
All 18	Mar 5	Walsall Town Swifts	H	5-0	4000	Farman 2, Sneddon 2, McFarlane
MCSF	Mar 12	Bolton Wanderers	N	1-3		Edge
Fri	Mar 15	Everton	A	1-3		Sneddon
All 19	Mar 19	Nottingham Forest	A	0-3	9000	
All 20	Mar 26	Grimsby Town	H	3-3	6000	Donaldson 2, Farman
All 21	Apr 2	Lincoln City	A	6-1	2000	Sneddon, Mathieson, uk 4
Fri	Apr 4	Sheffield United	H	2-1	3000	Donaldson, Farman
All 22	Apr 9	Birmingham St Geo	H	3-0	6000	Donaldson 2, Hood
Fri	Apr 11	Welsh Ints XI	H	0-1	4000	
Fri	Apr 15	Renton	H	3-3		Donaldson, Mathieson 2
Fri	Apr 16	Accrington	H	0-2		
Fri	Apr 18	Blackpool	A	0-3		
Fri	Apr 23	West Manchester	A	2-1	3000	Stewart, Edge
Fri	Apr 25	Darwen	H	2-1	2000	Donaldson, Edge
Fri	Apr 26	Aston Villa	H	2-5	2000	Donaldson, Mathieson
Fri	Apr 30	Notts County	H	0-0	3000	

291

1892-93

GAME	DATE	OPPONENTS	G	RES	ATT'D	SCORERS
Fri	Sep 1	Fairfield	H	3-0		Donaldson, Farman 2
D1 01	Sep 3	Blackburn	A	3-4	8000	Donaldson, Farman, Coupar
Fri	Sep 5	Darwen	H	3-1		Donaldson 2, Farman
D1 02	Sep 10	Burnley	H	1-1	10000	Donaldson
Fri	Sep 13	Darwen	A	1-3	2000	Coupar
D1 03	Sep 17	Burnley	A	1-4	7000	Donaldson
D1 04	Sep 24	Everton	A	0-6	10000	
D1 V	Sep 26	Everton	H	1-1		uk
D1 05	Oct 1	WBA	A	0-0	4000	
Fri	Oct 3	Burslem Port Vale	A	3-1		Carson, uk 2
D1 06	Oct 8	WBA	H	2-4	9000	Donaldson, Hood
D1 07	Oct 15	Wolverhampton	H	10-1	4000	Donaldson 3, Stewart 3, Farman, Carson, Hendry, Hood
D1 08	Oct 19	Everton	H	3-4	4000	Donaldson, Farman, Hood
D1 09	Oct 22	Sheffield Wed	A	0-1	6000	
D1 10	Oct 29	Nottingham Forest	A	1-1	6000	Farman
D1 11	Nov 5	Blackburn	H	4-4	12000	Farman 2, Carson, Hood
Fri	Nov 8	Darwen	A	1-1	2000	Perrins
D1 12	Nov 12	Notts County	H	1-3	8000	Carson
D1 13	Nov 19	Aston Villa	H	2-0	7000	Fitzsimmons, Coupar
D1 14	Nov 26	Accrington	A	2-2	3000	Fitzsimmons, Colville
D1 15	Dec 3	Bolton Wanderers	A	1-4	3000	Coupar
D1 16	Dec 10	Bolton Wanderers	H	1-0	4000	Donaldson
D1 17	Dec 17	Wolverhampton	A	0-2	5000	
D1 18	Dec 24	Sheffield Wed	H	1-5	7000	Hood
D1 19	Dec 26	Preston	A	1-2	4000	Coupar
D1 20	Dec 31	Derby County	H	7-1	3000	Donaldson 3, Farman 3, Fitzsimmons
Fri	Jan 2	Ardwick	A	5-3	12000	Donaldson, Farman, Fitzsimmons 2, Stewart
Fri	Jan 3	Fairfield	A	5-4	2000	Stewart, Farman, Fitzsimmons, uk 2
D1 21	Jan 7	Stoke City	A	1-7	1000	Coupar
D1 22	Jan 14	Nottingham Forest	H	1-3	8000	Donaldson
FA1	Jan 21	Blackburn	A	0-4	7000	
D1 23	Jan 26	Notts County	A	0-4	1000	
LC1	Jan 28	Bury	A	0-4	6000	
Fri	Feb 4	Linfield	A	0-2		
D1 24	Feb 11	Derby County	A	1-5	5000	Fitzsimmons
Fri	Feb 18	Burnley	H	2-1	2000	Donaldson 2
MC3	Feb 25	West Manchester	A	2-1	10000	Fitzsimmons 2
D1 25	Mar 4	Sunderland	H	0-5	15000	
D1 26	Mar 6	Aston Villa	A	0-2	4000	
Fri	Mar 11	Burnley	A	0-3		
Fri	Mar 13	Bootle	A	4-1		Donaldson 2, Peden, McNaught
MCSF	Mar 18	Bury	N	3-1	10000	Donaldson, Fitzsimmons 2
Fri	Mar 20	Grimsby Town	H	3-3	1000	Cassidy, Hood, uk
Fri	Mar 27	Ardwick	H	3-2	2000	Coupar, Fitzsimmons, Stewart
D1 27	Mar 31	Stoke City	H	1-0	10000	Farman
D1 28	Apr 1	Preston	H	2-1	9000	Donaldson 2
Fri	Apr 3	Scottish Junior Int	H	2-0	4000	Donaldson, Hood
D1 29	Apr 4	Sunderland	A	0-6	3500	
D1 30	Apr 8	Accrington	H	3-3	3000	Donaldson, Fitzsimmons, Stewart
Fri	Apr 10	Ardwick	A	2-1	3000	Farman, R Doughty
Fri	Apr 13	Grimsby Town	H	2-2		Cassidy, uk
MCFin	Apr 15	Bolton Wanderers	N	2-1	10000	Cassidy, (og)
TM	Apr 22	Small Heath	N	1-1	4000	Farman
TMr	Apr 27	Small Heath	N	5-2	6000	Farman 3, Cassidy, Coupar
Fri	Apr 29	Ardwick	A	0-3		

STATISTICS

1893-94

Game	Date	Opponents	G	Res	Att'd	Scorers
D1 01	Sep 2	Burnley	H	3-2	10000	Farman 3
Fri	Sep 6	Liverpool	A	0-1		
D1 02	Sep 9	WBA	A	1-3	4500	Donaldson
D1 03	Sep 16	Sheffield Wednesday	A	1-0	7000	Farman
Fri	Sep 20	Liverpool	H	0-3	1000	
D1 04	Sep 23	Nottingham Forest	H	1-1	10000	Donaldson
D1 05	Sep 30	Darwen	A	0-1	4000	
D1 06	Oct 7	Derby County	A	0-2	7000	
D1 07	Oct 14	WBA	H	4-1	8000	Donaldson, Peden 2, Erentz
D1 08	Oct 21	Burnley	A	1-4	7000	Hood
D1 09	Oct 28	Wolverhampton	A	0-2	4000	
D1 10	Nov 4	Darwen	H	0-1	8000	
D1 11	Nov 11	Wolverhampton	H	1-0	5000	Davidson
D1 12	Nov 25	Sheffield United	A	1-3	2000	Fitzsimmons
D1 13	Dec 2	Everton	H	0-3	6000	
D1 14	Dec 6	Sunderland	A	1-4	5000	Campbell
D1 15	Dec 9	Bolton Wanderers	A	0-2	5000	
D1 16	Dec 16	Aston Villa	H	1-3	8000	Peden
D1 17	Dec 23	Preston North End	A	0-2	5000	
Fri	Dec 25	Ardwick	H	2-1	8000	Hood, Fitzsimmons
Fri	Dec 26	West Manchester	A	2-3	7000	Donaldson, Farman
Fri	Dec 30	Queen's Park	A	2-3	4000	McNaught, Farman
Fri	Jan 1	Dundee	A	1-2	4000	Hood
Fri	Jan 2	King's Park	A	3-1		McNaught, Farman, uk
D1 18	Jan 6	Everton	A	0-2	8000	
D1 19	Jan 13	Sheffield Wednesday	H	1-2	9000	Peden
LC1	Jan 20	Everton	A	1-7	10000	Peden
FA1	Jan 27	Middlesbrough	H	4-0	5000	Donaldson 2, Farman, Peden
D1 20	Feb 3	Aston Villa	A	1-5	5000	Mathieson
MC1	Feb 3	Bolton Wanderers	A	2-3	2000	Farman, Graham
PL 1	Feb 6	Accrington	H	1-3	2000	Parker
FA2	Feb 10	Blackburn Rovers	H	0-0	18000	
FA2r	Feb 17	Blackburn Rovers	A	1-5	5000	Donaldson
PL 2	Feb 17	Bury	A	0-3	1000	
PL 3	Feb 22	Darwen	H	6-1		Donaldson 5, McNaught
Fri	Mar 1	Liverpool	A	0-3		
D1 21	Mar 3	Sunderland	H	2-4	10000	Peden, McNaught
D1 22	Mar 10	Sheffield United	H	0-2	5000	
D1 23	Mar 12	Blackburn Rovers	H	5-1	5000	Donaldson 3, Farman, Clarkin
D1 24	Mar 17	Derby County	H	2-6	7000	Clarkin 2
D1 25	Mar 23	Stoke City	H	6-2	8000	Clarkin, Farman 2, Peden 2, Erentz
D1 26	Mar 24	Bolton Wanderers	H	2-2	10000	Donaldson, Farman
D1 27	Mar 26	Blackburn Rovers	A	0-4	5000	
Fri	Mar 27	West Manchester	H	5-1	400	Farman 2, McNaught, Clarkin, (og)
D1 28	Mar 31	Stoke City	A	1-3	4000	Clarkin
Fri	Apr 2	Liverpool	H	2-0		Donaldson, Clarkin
D1 29	Apr 7	Nottingham Forest	A	0-2	4000	
Fri	Apr 9	Ardwick	A	2-1		Donaldson, Rothwell
PL 4	Apr 10	Accrington	A	2-1	300	uk 2
D1 30	Apr 14	Preston North End	H	1-3	4000	Mathieson
PL 5	Apr 16	Bury	H	2-2		Mathieson, Prince
PL 6	Apr 16	Everton	A	1-7		uk
PL 7	Apr 18	Bolton Wanderers	H	1-4		Prince
PL 8	Apr 21	Everton	H	2-2		Mathieson, Rothwell
TM	Apr 28	Liverpool	N	0-2	3000	

1894-95

Game	Date	Opponents	G	Res	Att'd	Scorers
Fri	Sep 1	St Bernard's	H	2-5	3000	Donaldson 2
D2 01	Sep 8	Burton Wanderers	A	0-1	3000	
D2 02	Sep 15	Crewe Alexandra	H	6-1	6000	Smith 2, Dow 2, Clarkin, McCartney
D2 03	Sep 22	Leicester Fosse	A	3-2	6000	Smith, Dow 2
Fri	Sep 24	Stockport County	A	3-0	4000	Clarkin, Coupar, Davidson
Fri	Sep 27	Queen's Park	H	3-3	2000	Clarkin 2, Dow
Fri	Sep 29	Hibernians	H	2-1	3000	Smith, Dow
D2 04	Oct 6	Darwen	A	1-1	6000	Donaldson
D2 05	Oct 13	Woolwich Arsenal	H	3-3	4000	Donaldson 2, Clarkin
D2 06	Oct 20	Burton Swifts	A	2-1	5000	Donaldson 2
D2 07	Oct 27	Leicester Fosse	H	2-2	3000	Smith, McNaught
D2 08	Nov 3	Manchester City	A	5-2	14000	Smith 4, Clarkin
D2 09	Nov 10	Rotherham Town	H	3-2	4000	Donaldson, Peters, Davidson
D2 10	Nov 17	Grimsby Town	A	1-2	3000	Clarkin
D2 11	Nov 24	Darwen	H	1-1	5000	Donaldson
D2 12	Dec 1	Crewe Alexandra	A	2-0	600	Smith, Clarkin
D2 13	Dec 8	Burton Swifts	H	5-1	4000	Smith 2, Peters 2, Dow
D2 14	Dec 15	Notts County	A	1-1	3000	Donaldson
D2 15	Dec 22	Lincoln City	H	3-0	2000	Donaldson, Millar, Smith
D2 16	Dec 24	Burslem Port Vale	A	5-2	1000	Donaldson, Millar, Smith, Clarkin, McNaught
Fri	Dec 25	Sunderland	H	1-3	7000	Smith
D2 17	Dec 26	Walsall Town Swifts	A	2-1	1000	Stewart, Millar
D2 18	Dec 29	Lincoln City	A	0-3	3000	
D2 19	Jan 1	Burslem Port Vale	H	3-0	5000	Millar 2, Rothwell
D2 20	Jan 5	Manchester City	H	4-1	12000	Donaldson, Smith, Clarkin 2
D2 21	Jan 12	Rotherham Town	A	1-2	2000	Erentz
LC1	Jan 19	Bolton Wanderers	A	1-2		McNaught
MC1	Jan 26	Bolton Wanderers	A	0-4		
PL 1	Jan 26	Liverpool	H	3-0	4000	Smith, Millar, McNaught
FA1	Feb 2	Stoke City	H	2-3	7000	Smith, Peters
PL 2	Feb 9	Bury	A	0-1	3000	
Fri	Feb 16	West Manchester	A	2-0	6000	Smith, Peters
Fri	Feb 23	Derby County	H	1-1	3000	Smith
PL 3	Feb 27	Bury	H	2-3	3000	McNaught, Rothwell
D2 22	Mar 2	Burton Wanderers	H	1-1	6000	Peters
D2 V	Mar 9	Walsall Town Swifts	H	14-0	5000	Smith 6, Cassidy 4, Donaldson, Clarkin, Peters, McCartney
PL 4	Mar 16	Liverpool	A	1-1	5000	uk
D2 23	Mar 23	Grimsby Town	H	2-0	9000	Cassidy 2
D2 24	Mar 30	Woolwich Arsenal	A	2-3	6000	Donaldson, Clarkin
D2 25	Apr 3	Walsall Town Swifts	H	9-0	6000	Cassidy 2, Smith 2, Donaldson 2, Peters 2, Clarkin
D2 26	Apr 6	Newcastle United	H	5-1	5000	Cassidy 2, Smith 2, (og)
D2 27	Apr 12	Bury	H	2-2	15000	Cassidy, Donaldson
D2 28	Apr 13	Newcastle United	A	0-3	4000	
D2 29	Apr 15	Bury	A	1-2	10000	Peters
D2 30	Apr 20	Notts County	H	3-3	12000	Cassidy, Smith, Clarkin
TM	Apr 27	Stoke City	N	0-3	10000	
Fri	Apr 29	Blackburn Rovers	H	2-2		uk 2

STATISTICS

1895-96

Game	Date	Opponents	G	Res	Att'd	Scorers
Fri	Sep 2	Fairfield	H	2-1	2500	Kennedy 2
D2 01	Sep 7	Crewe Alexandra	H	5-0	6000	Cassidy 2, Smith, Kennedy, Aitken
D2 02	Sep 14	Loughborough	A	3-3	3000	Cassidy 2, McNaught
D2 03	Sep 21	Burton Swifts	H	5-0	9000	Cassidy 2, Donaldson 2, Kennedy
D2 04	Sep 28	Crewe Alexandra	A	2-0	2000	Smith 2
D2 05	Oct 5	Manchester City	H	1-1	12000	Clarkin
D2 06	Oct 12	Liverpool	A	1-7	7000	Cassidy
D2 07	Oct 19	Newcastle United	H	2-1	8000	Cassidy, Peters
D2 08	Oct 26	Newcastle United	A	1-2	8000	Kennedy
D2 09	Nov 2	Liverpool	H	5-2	10000	Peters 3, Smith, Clarkin
D2 10	Nov 9	Woolwich Arsenal	A	1-2	9000	Cassidy
Fri	Nov 11	Luton Town	A	1-4		Kennedy
D2 11	Nov 16	Lincoln City	H	5-5	8000	Cassidy, Clarkin 2, Collinson, Peters
D2 12	Nov 23	Notts County	A	2-0	3000	Cassidy, Kennedy
D2 13	Nov 30	Woolwich Arsenal	H	5-1	6000	Cartwright 2, Clarkin, Kennedy, Peters
D2 14	Dec 7	Manchester City	A	1-2	18000	Cassidy
D2 15	Dec 14	Notts County	H	3-0	3000	Cassidy, Donaldson, Clarkin
D2 16	Dec 21	Darwen	A	0-3	3000	
Fri	Dec 25	Manchester City	A	1-3	10000	Clarkin
Fri	Dec 26	Dundee	H	0-0		
D2 V	Dec 28	Leicester Fosse	H	2-0		Donaldson, Kennedy
D2 17	Jan 1	Grimsby Town	H	3-2	8000	Cassidy 3
D2 18	Jan 4	Leicester Fosse	A	0-3	7000	
D2 19	Jan 11	Rotherham Town	H	3-0	3000	Donaldson 2, Stephenson
LC1	Jan 18	Bury	H	1-2		Fitzsimmons
MC3	Jan 25	Fairfield	H	2-5		Fitzsimmons, Kennedy
FA1	Feb 1	Kettering Town	H	2-1	6000	Donaldson, Smith
D2 20	Feb 3	Leicester Fosse	H	2-0	1000	Smith, Kennedy
D2 21	Feb 8	Burton Swifts	A	1-4	2000	Vance
FA2	Feb 15	Derby County	H	1-1	20000	Kennedy
FA2R	Feb 19	Derby County	A	1-5	6000	Donaldson
Fri	Feb 22	Reading	A	2-2		Smith, Clarkin
Fri	Feb 24	Woolwich Arsenal	A	1-6	1000	Vance
D2 22	Feb 29	Burton Wanderers	H	1-2	1000	McNaught
D2 23	Mar 7	Rotherham Town	A	3-2	1500	Smith, Kennedy, Donaldson
D2 24	Mar 14	Grimsby Town	A	2-4	2000	Smith, Kennedy
D2 25	Mar 18	Burton Wanderers	A	1-5	2000	Dow
Fri	Mar 21	Sunderland	H	0-1	6000	
D2 26	Mar 23	Burslem Port Vale	A	0-3	3000	
D2 27	Apr 3	Darwen	H	4-0	1000	Kennedy 3, McNaught
D2 28	Apr 4	Loughborough	H	2-0	4000	Smith, Donaldson
D2 29	Apr 6	Burslem Port Vale	H	2-1	5000	Smith, Clarkin
D2 30	Apr 11	Lincoln City	A	0-2	2000	
Fri	Apr 18	Ashton North End	A	1-1		uk
Fri	Apr 20	Oldham County	A	3-0		Smith, Kennedy, Rothwell
Fri	Apr 22	Crewe Alexandra	H	1-2		Vance

1896-97

Game	Date	Opponents	G	Res	Att'd	Scorers
D2 01	Sep 1	Gainsborough Trinity	H	2-0	4000	McNaught 2
D2 02	Sep 5	Burton Swifts	A	5-3	3000	Cassidy, Brown, Bryant, Draycott, McNaught
D2 03	Sep 7	Walsall	H	2-0	7000	Cassidy, Donaldson
D2 04	Sep 12	Lincoln City	H	3-1	7000	Cassidy 2, Donaldson
D2 05	Sep 19	Grimsby Town	A	0-2	3000	
D2 06	Sep 21	Walsall	A	3-2	7000	Brown, Draycott, McNaught
D2 07	Sep 26	Newcastle United	H	4-0	7000	Cassidy 3, Donaldson
D2 08	Oct 3	Manchester City	A	0-0	20000	
D2 09	Oct 10	Small Heath	H	1-1	7000	Draycott
D2 10	Oct 17	Blackpool	A	2-4	5000	Draycott, Bryant
D2 11	Oct 21	Gainsborough Trinity	A	0-2	4000	
D2 12	Oct 24	Burton Wanderers	H	3-0	4000	Cassidy 3
Fri	Oct 31	Fairfield	A	2-2		Donaldson, uk
D2 13	Nov 7	Grimsby Town	H	4-2	5000	Cassidy 2, Donaldson, Jenkyns
Fri	Nov 14	Luton Town	A	1-0		Bryant
Fri	Nov 21	Fairfield	H	5-0		Cassidy, Gillespie 3, McNaught
D2 14	Nov 28	Small Heath	A	0-1	4000	
LC1	Dec 5	West Manchester	H	4-1	10000	Cassidy, Donaldson, Bryant 2
FAQ1	Dec 12	West Manchester	H	7-0	6000	Cassidy 2, Gillespie 2, Rothwell 2, Bryant
D2 15	Dec 19	Notts County	A	0-3	5000	
D2 16	Dec 25	Manchester City	H	2-1	18000	Donaldson, Smith
D2 17	Dec 26	Blackpool	H	2-0	9000	Cassidy 2
D2 18	Dec 28	Leicester Fosse	A	0-1	8000	
D2 19	Jan 1	Newcastle United	A	0-2	17000	
FAQ2	Jan 2	Nelson	H	3-0	5000	Cassidy, Donaldson, Gillespie
D2 20	Jan 9	Burton Swifts	H	1-1	3000	Donaldson
FAQ3	Jan 15	Blackpool	H	2-2	1500	Donaldson, Gillespie
MC3	Jan 16	Manchester City	A	1-0	18000	Smith
FAQ3r	Jan 20	Blackpool	A	2-1	1500	Cassidy, Boyd
LC2	Jan 23	Burnley	A	1-2	5000	(og)
FA1	Jan 30	Kettering Town	H	5-1	5000	Cassidy 3, Donaldson 2
D2 21	Feb 6	Loughborough	H	6-0	5000	Boyd, Donaldson, Smith 2, Draycott, Jenkyns
FA2	Feb 13	Southampton St M's	A	1-1	8000	Donaldson
FA2r	Feb 17	Southampton St M's	H	3-1	7000	Cassidy, Bryant 2
D2 22	Feb 20	Leicester Fosse	H	2-1	8000	Donaldson, Boyd
FA3	Feb 27	Derby County	A	0-2	12000	
D2 23	Mar 2	Darwen	H	3-1	3000	Cassidy 2, Boyd
MCSF	Mar 10	Bury	N	0-2		
D2 24	Mar 13	Darwen	A	2-0	2000	Cassidy, Gillespie
D2 25	Mar 20	Burton Wanderers	A	2-1	3000	Gillespie, (og)
D2 26	Mar 22	Woolwich Arsenal	H	1-1	3000	Boyd
D2 27	Mar 27	Notts County	H	1-1	10000	Bryant
D2 28	Apr 1	Lincoln City	A	3-1	1000	Jenkyns 3
D2 29	Apr 3	Woolwich Arsenal	A	2-0	6000	Boyd, Donaldson
D2 30	Apr 10	Loughborough	A	0-2	3000	
HC SF	Apr 12	Fairfield	H	4-0		Cassidy, Boyd, Donaldson, Gillespie
TM 1	Apr 19	Burnley	A	0-2	10000	
TM 2	Apr 21	Burnley	H	2-0	7000	Boyd, Jenkyns
TM 3	Apr 24	Sunderland	H	1-1	18000	Boyd
TM 4	Apr 26	Sunderland	A	0-2	8000	
HC Fin	Apr 30	Manchester City	A	5-2	6000	Cassidy 2, Donaldson 2, Bryant

STATISTICS

1897-98

Game	Date	Opponents	G	Res	Att'd	Scorers
Fri	Sep 1	Blackpool	H	0-0		
D2 01	Sep 4	Lincoln City	H	5-0	5000	Boyd 3, Cassidy, Bryant
Fri	Sep 7	Bury	A	2-2	2000	Boyd 2
D2 02	Sep 11	Burton Swifts	A	4-0	2000	Boyd 3, Cassidy
D2 03	Sep 18	Luton Town	H	1-2	8000	Cassidy
D2 04	Sep 25	Blackpool	A	1-0	2000	Smith
D2 05	Oct 2	Leicester Fosse	H	2-0	6000	Boyd 2
Fri	Oct 6	Bury	H	1-3	1500	Cassidy
D2 06	Oct 9	Newcastle United	A	0-2	12000	
D2 07	Oct 16	Manchester City	H	1-1	20000	Gillespie
D2 08	Oct 23	Small Heath	A	1-2	6000	Bryant
Fri	Oct 26	Grimsby Town	A	1-3	1500	Gillespie
D2 09	Oct 30	Walsall	H	6-0	6000	Cassidy 2, Donaldson 2, Bryant, Gillespie
D2 10	Nov 6	Lincoln City	A	0-1	2000	
D2 11	Nov 13	Newcastle United	H	0-1	7000	
D2 12	Nov 20	Leicester Fosse	A	1-1	6000	Wedge
D2 13	Nov 27	Grimsby Town	H	2-1	5000	Wedge, Bryant
LC1	Dec 4	Wigan County	H	6-0	1000	Morgan 3, Cassidy 2, Boyd
D2 14	Dec 11	Walsall	A	1-1	2000	Boyd
D2 15	Dec 25	Manchester City	A	1-0	16000	Cassidy
D2 16	Dec 27	Gainsborough Trinity	A	1-2	3000	Boyd
D2 17	Jan 1	Burton Swifts	H	4-0	6000	Carman, Boyd, McNaught, Bryant
D2 18	Jan 8	Woolwich Arsenal	A	1-5	8000	F Erentz
D2 19	Jan 12	Burnley	H	0-0	7000	
D2 20	Jan 15	Blackpool	H	4-0	4000	Boyd 2, Cassidy, Cartwright
LC2	Jan 22	Manchester City	H	1-0	15000	Collinson
FA1	Jan 29	Walsall	H	1-0	6000	(og)
MC3	Feb 5	Bury	H	2-2	10000	Cassidy, Boyd
FA2	Feb 12	Liverpool	H	0-0	12000	
FA2r	Feb 16	Liverpool	A	1-2	6000	Collinson
LCSF	Feb 19	Bolton Wanderers	N	4-1	13000	Collinson 2, Boyd, Gillespie
MC3r	Feb 22	Bury	A	3-2	4000	Boyd 3
D2 21	Feb 26	Woolwich Arsenal	H	5-1	6000	Cassidy, Collinson, Bryant 2, Boyd
MCSF	Mar 5	Manchester City	A	1-1	18000	Collinson
D2 22	Mar 7	Burnley	A	3-6	3000	Collinson, Bryant 2
MCSFr	Mar 12	Manchester City	A	1-2	14000	Cassidy
Fri	Mar 18	Grimsby Town	H	3-0		Owen 2, uk
D2 23	Mar 19	Darwen	A	3-2	2000	Boyd 2, McNaught
D2 24	Mar 21	Luton Town	A	2-2	2000	Boyd, Cassidy
LCFin	Mar 26	Blackburn Rovers	N	2-1	10000	Collinson 2
D2 25	Mar 29	Loughborough	H	5-1	2000	Cassidy 2, Boyd 3
D2 26	Apr 2	Grimsby Town	A	3-1	2000	Cassidy 2, Boyd
D2 27	Apr 8	Gainsborough Trinity	H	1-0	5000	Cassidy
D2 28	Apr 9	Small Heath	H	3-1	4000	Gillespie, Boyd, Morgan
Fri	Apr 12	Sheffield United	A	4-1	3000	Gillespie, Cassidy, Bryant 2
D2 29	Apr 16	Loughborough	A	0-0	1200	
D2 30	Apr 23	Darwen	H	3-2	4000	Collinson 2, Bryant
HCFin	Apr 27	Manchester City	H	2-4	3000	Collinson, Gillespie
Fri	Apr 30	Gainsborough Trinity	H	2-1	200	Collinson 2

1898-99

GAME	DATE	OPPONENTS	G	RES	ATT'D	SCORERS
Fri	Sep 1	Chorley	H	1-0		Jones
D2 01	Sep 3	Gainsborough Trinity	A	2-0	2000	Cassidy, Bryant
D2 02	Sep 10	Manchester City	H	3-0	20000	Cassidy, Boyd, Collinson
D2 03	Sep 17	Glossop	A	2-1	6000	Cassidy, Bryant
D2 04	Sep 24	Walsall	H	1-0	8000	Gillespie
D2 05	Oct 1	Burton Swifts	A	1-5	2000	Boyd
D2 06	Oct 8	Burslem Port Vale	H	2-1	10000	Cassidy, Bryant
D2 07	Oct 15	Small Heath	A	1-4	5000	Cassidy
D2 08	Oct 22	Loughborough	H	6-1	2000	Cassidy 2, Collinson 2, Brooks 2
Fri	Oct 29	Manchester City	A	1-2	14000	Turner
D2 09	Nov 5	Grimsby Town	H	3-2	5000	Cassidy, Gillespie, Brooks
D2 10	Nov 12	Barnsley	H	0-0	6000	
D2 11	Nov 19	New Brighton Tower	A	3-0	5000	Cassidy, Collinson 2
D2 12	Nov 26	Lincoln City	H	1-0	4000	Bryant
D2 13	Dec 3	Woolwich Arsenal	A	1-5	6000	Collinson
D2 14	Dec 10	Blackpool	H	3-1	5000	Cassidy, Collinson, Cunningham
D2 15	Dec 17	Leicester Fosse	A	0-1	8000	
LC1	Dec 19	Darwen	H	5-0	500	Cassidy 2, Bryant 2, Boyd
D2 16	Dec 24	Darwen	H	9-0	2000	Cassidy 3, Bryant 3, Gillespie 2, (og)
D2 17	Dec 26	Manchester City	A	0-4	25000	
D2 18	Dec 31	Gainsborough Trinity	H	6-1	2000	Collinson 2, Boyd, Bryant, Cartwright, Draycott
D2 19	Jan 2	Burton Swifts	H	2-2	6000	Cassidy, Boyd
Fri	Jan 7	Manchester City	H	2-0	4000	Ratcliffe, Boyd
D2 20	Jan 14	Glossop	H	3-0	12000	Gillespie, Erentz, Cunningham
LC2	Jan 16	Blackburn Rovers	A	1-6	3000	Gillespie
D2 21	Jan 21	Walsall	A	0-2	3000	
FA1	Jan 28	Tottenham Hotspur	A	1-1	15000	Cassidy
FA1r	Feb 1	Tottenham Hotspur	H	3-5	6000	Bryant 3
D2 22	Feb 4	Burslem Port Vale	A	0-1	6000	
MC3	Feb 6	Bury	H	1-4	300	Collinson
Fri	Feb 14	Aston Villa	H	1-1	4000	Boyd
D2 23	Feb 18	Loughborough	A	1-0	1500	Bryant
D2 24	Feb 25	Small Heath	H	2-0	12000	Boyd, Roberts
D2 25	Mar 4	Grimsby Town	A	0-3	4000	
Fri	Mar 11	WBA	H	2-0	4000	Bryant 2
D2 26	Mar 18	New Brighton Tower	H	1-2	20000	Cassidy
D2 27	Mar 25	Lincoln City	A	0-2	3000	
D2 28	Apr 1	Woolwich Arsenal	H	2-2	5000	Cassidy, Bryant
D2 29	Apr 3	Blackpool	A	1-0	3000	Cassidy
D2 30	Apr 4	Barnsley	A	2-0	4000	Lee 2
D2 31	Apr 8	Luton Town	A	1-0	1500	Lee
D2 32	Apr 12	Luton Town	H	5-0	3000	Cassidy, Gillespie, Cartwright, Morgan, Lee
D2 33	Apr 15	Leicester Fosse	H	2-2	7000	Cassidy, Gillespie
D2 34	Apr 22	Darwen	A	1-1	1000	Morgan
HCFin	Apr 24	Manchester City	H	1-2	1500	Lee

1899-00

GAME	DATE	OPPONENTS	G	RES	ATT'D	SCORERS
D2 01	Sep 2	Gainsborough Trinity	H	2-2	8000	Cassidy, Lee
D2 02	Sep 9	Bolton Wanderers	A	1-2	5000	Ambler
D2 03	Sep 16	Loughborough	H	4-0	6000	Cassidy, Bain, Griffiths, (og)
D2 04	Sep 23	Burton Swifts	A	0-0	2000	
D2 05	Sep 30	Sheffield Wednesday	A	1-2	8000	Bryant
Fri	Oct 2	Renton	H	2-1		Cassidy, (og)
D2 06	Oct 7	Lincoln City	H	1-0	5000	Cassidy
D2 07	Oct 14	Small Heath	A	0-1	10000	
D2 08	Oct 21	New Brighton Tower	H	2-1	5000	Cassidy 2
FA1	Oct 28	South Shore	A	1-3	3000	Jackson
D2 09	Nov 4	Woolwich Arsenal	H	2-0	5000	Jackson, Roberts
D2 10	Nov 11	Barnsley	A	0-0	3000	
Fri	Nov 18	Blackpool	H	0-0		
D2 11	Nov 25	Luton Town	A	1-0	3000	Jackson
Fri	Nov 29	Manchester City	H	0-1		
D2 12	Dec 2	Burslem Port Vale	H	3-0	5000	Cassidy 2, Jackson
LC1	Dec 9	Bolton Wanderers	A	3-2		Cassidy 2, Parkinson
D2 13	Dec 16	Middlesbrough	H	2-1	5000	Erentz, Parkinson
D2 14	Dec 23	Chesterfield	A	1-2	2000	Griffiths
D2 15	Dec 26	Grimsby Town	H	7-0	2000	Cassidy 2, Bryant 2, Jackson, Parkinson, (og)
D2 16	Dec 30	Gainsborough Trinity	A	1-0	2000	Parkinson
Fri	Jan 1	Manchester City	A	1-2	6000	Fitzsimmons
D2 17	Jan 6	Bolton Wanderers	H	1-2	5000	Parkinson
D2 18	Jan 13	Loughborough	A	2-0	800	Parkinson, Jackson
D2 19	Jan 20	Burton Swifts	H	4-0	5000	Parkinson, Gillespie 3
LC2	Jan 27	Southport Central	A	0-1	3000	
D2 20	Feb 3	Sheffield Wednesday	H	1-0	10000	Bryant
D2 21	Feb 10	Lincoln City	A	0-1	3000	
D2 22	Feb 17	Small Heath	H	3-2	12000	Cassidy, Godsmark, Parkinson
MC3	Feb 21	Bury	A	0-5	1500	
D2 23	Feb 24	New Brighton Tower	A	4-1	8000	Collinson 2, Godsmark, Smith
Fri	Feb 27	Manchester City	H	1-0		(og)
D2 24	Mar 3	Grimsby Town	H	1-0	12000	Smith
D2 25	Mar 10	Woolwich Arsenal	A	1-2	3000	Cassidy
D2 26	Mar 17	Barnsley	H	3-0	6000	Cassidy 2, Leigh
D2 27	Mar 24	Leicester Fosse	A	0-2	8000	
D2 28	Mar 31	Luton Town	H	5-0	6000	Cassidy 3, Godsmark 2
D2 29	Apr 7	Burslem Port Vale	A	0-1	3000	
D2 30	Apr 13	Leicester Fosse	H	3-2	10000	Jackson, Gillespie, Griffiths
D2 31	Apr 14	Walsall	H	5-0	5000	Jackson 2, Gillespie, Erentz, Foley
D2 32	Apr 17	Walsall	A	0-0	3000	
D2 33	Apr 21	Middlesbrough	A	0-2	8000	
D2 34	Apr 28	Chesterfield	H	2-1	6000	Holt, Grundy

1900-01

Game	Date	Opponents	G	Res	Att'd	Scorers
D2 01	Sep 1	Glossop	A	0-1	2000	
D2 02	Sep 8	Middlesbrough	H	4-0	8000	Leigh, Grundy, Jackson, Griffiths
D2 03	Sep 15	Burnley	A	0-1	2000	
D2 04	Sep 22	Burslem Port Vale	H	4-0	6000	Leigh, Grundy, Schofield, Smith
Fri	Sep 26	Manchester City	A	0-0		
D2 05	Sep 29	Leicester Fosse	A	0-1	6000	
LC1	Oct 1	Southport Central	A	1-0		Schofield
D2 06	Oct 6	New Brighton Tower	H	1-0	5000	Jackson
D2 07	Oct 13	Gainsborough Trinity	A	1-0	2000	Leigh
D2 08	Oct 20	Walsall	H	1-1	8000	Schofield
LC2	Oct 22	Manchester City	A	0-2	4000	
D2 09	Oct 27	Burton Swifts	A	1-3	2000	Leigh
Fri	Nov 3	Bristol Rovers	H	1-2		Fisher
D2 10	Nov 10	Woolwich Arsenal	A	1-2	8000	Jackson
MC3	Nov 17	Rochdale	H	4-0		Collinson 2, Lawson, Jackson
D2 11	Nov 24	Stockport County	A	0-1	5000	
D2 12	Dec 1	Small Heath	H	0-1	5000	
D2 13	Dec 8	Grimsby Town	A	0-2	4000	
D2 14	Dec 15	Lincoln City	H	4-1	4000	Leigh 2, Schofield, H Morgan
Fri	Dec 18	Grimsby Town	A	1-2		H Morgan
D2 15	Dec 22	Chesterfield	A	1-2	4000	(og)
D2 16	Dec 26	Blackpool	H	4-0	10000	Leigh, W Morgan, Schofield, Griffiths
D2 17	Dec 29	Glossop	H	3-0	8000	Leigh 2, H Morgan
D2 18	Jan 1	Middlesbrough	A	2-1	12000	Schofield 2
FAI	Jan 5	Portsmouth	H	3-0	5000	Jackson, Stafford, Griffiths
D2 19	Jan 12	Burnley	H	0-1	10000	
D2 20	Jan 19	Burslem Port Vale	A	0-2	1000	
FA1	Feb 9	Burnley	H	0-0	10000	
FA1r	Feb 13	Burnley	A	1-7	4000	Schofield
D2 21	Feb 16	Gainsborough Trinity	H	0-0	3000	
D2 22	Feb 19	New Brighton Tower	A	0-2	2000	
D2 23	Feb 25	Walsall	A	1-1	2000	W Morgan
D2 24	Mar 2	Burton Swifts	H	1-1	5000	Leigh
D2 25	Mar 13	Barnsley	H	1-0	6000	Leigh
D2 26	Mar 16	Woolwich Arsenal	H	1-0	5000	Leigh
D2 27	Mar 20	Leicester Fosse	H	2-3	2000	Fisher, Jackson
D2 28	Mar 23	Blackpool	A	2-1	2000	Griffiths 2
MCSF	Mar 25	Glossop	N	0-0	1500	
D2 29	Mar 30	Stockport County	H	3-1	4000	Leigh, Schofield, H Morgan
MCSFr	Apr 1	Glossop	N	1-0		Leigh
D2 30	Apr 5	Lincoln City	A	0-2	5000	
D2 31	Apr 6	Small Heath	A	0-1	6000	
D2 32	Apr 9	Barnsley	A	2-6	3000	W Morgan, Jackson
D2 33	Apr 13	Grimsby Town	H	1-0	3000	H Morgan
D2 34	Apr 27	Chesterfield	H	1-0	1000	Leigh
MCFin	Apr 29	Manchester City	A	0-4	5000	

STATISTICS

1901-02

Game	Date	Opponents	G	Res	Att'd	Scorers
D2 01	Sep 7	Gainsborough Trinity	H	3-0	10000	Preston 2, Lappin
D2 02	Sep 14	Middlesbrough	A	0-5	12000	
D2 03	Sep 21	Bristol City	H	1-0	6000	Griffiths
D2 04	Sep 28	Blackpool	A	4-2	4000	Schofield, Preston 2, (og)
LC1	Oct 1	Nelson	A	0-0		
D2 05	Oct 5	Stockport County	H	3-3	5000	Schofield 2, Preston
LC1r	Oct 9	Nelson	H	2-0	2000	Schofield, Fisher
D2 06	Oct 12	Burton United	A	0-0	3000	
D2 07	Oct 19	Glossop	A	0-0	5000	
LC2	Oct 21	Southport Central	A	0-5		
D2 08	Oct 26	Doncaster Rovers	H	6-0	7000	Coupar 3, Preston, Griffiths, (og)
D2 09	Nov 9	WBA	H	1-2	13000	Fisher
D2 10	Nov 16	Woolwich Arsenal	A	0-2	3000	
D2 11	Nov 23	Barnsley	H	1-0	4000	Griffiths
D2 12	Nov 30	Leicester Fosse	A	2-3	4000	Preston, Cartwright
D2 13	Dec 7	Preston North End	A	1-5	3000	Preston
FA1	Dec 14	Lincoln City	H	1-2	4000	Fisher
D2 14	Dec 21	Burslem Port Vale	H	1-0	3000	Richards
D2 15	Dec 26	Lincoln City	A	0-2	4000	
D2 16	Jan 1	Preston North End	H	0-2	10000	
D2 17	Jan 4	Gainsborough Trinity	A	1-1	2000	Lappin
D2 18	Jan 18	Bristol City	A	0-4	6000	
D2 19	Jan 25	Blackpool	H	0-1	3000	
D2 20	Feb 1	Stockport County	A	0-1	3000	
D2 21	Feb 11	Burnley	H	2-0	1000	Preston, Lappin
D2 22	Feb 15	Glossop	H	1-0	4000	Erentz
MC3	Feb 18	Rochdale Town	A	3-2	1000	Hayes 2, Griffiths
D2 23	Feb 22	Doncaster Rovers	A	0-4	3000	
D2 24	Mar 1	Lincoln City	H	0-0	6000	
D2 25	Mar 8	WBA	A	0-4	8000	
D2 26	Mar 15	Woolwich Arsenal	H	0-1	3000	
D2 27	Mar 17	Chesterfield	A	0-3	2000	
D2 28	Mar 22	Barnsley	A	2-3	2500	Cartwright, Higson
D2 29	Mar 28	Burnley	A	0-1	3000	
D2 30	Mar 29	Leicester Fosse	H	2-0	2000	Griffiths, Hayes
D2 31	Apr 7	Middlesbrough	H	1-2	2000	Erentz
MCSF	Apr 9	Bolton Wanderers	N	1-1	3000	Preston
MCSFr	Apr 14	Bolton Wanderers	N	1-0	3000	Preston
D2 32	Apr 19	Burslem Port Vale	A	1-1	2000	Schofield
D2 33	Apr 21	Burton United	H	3-1	500	Preston, Cartwright, Griffiths
D2 34	Apr 23	Chesterfield	H	2-0	2000	Preston, Coupar
MCFin	Apr 26	Manchester City	A	2-1	15000	Erentz, Lappin

Printed in Great Britain
by Amazon

28237034R00178